Everybody's Fly

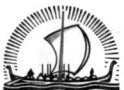

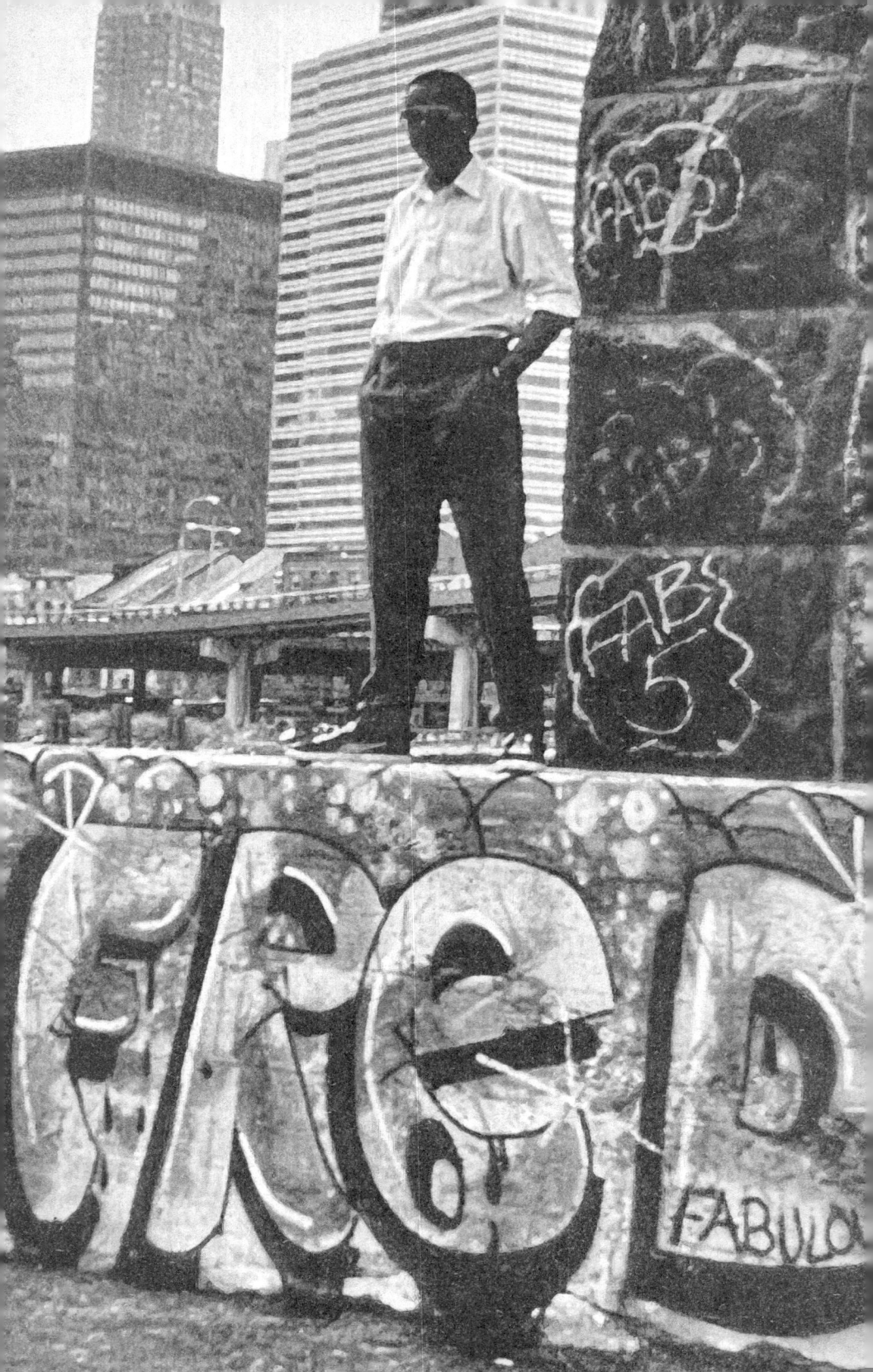

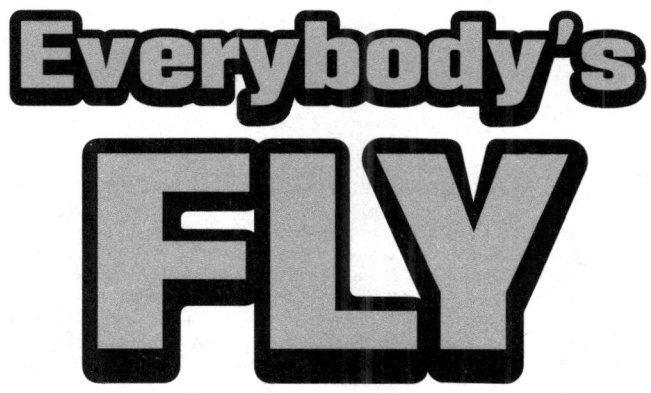

Everybody's FLY

A Life of Art, Music, and Changing the Culture

**FRED BRATHWAITE
aka FAB 5 FREDDY**

with Mark Rozzo

VIKING

VIKING
An imprint of Penguin Random House LLC
1745 Broadway, New York, NY 10019
penguinrandomhouse.com

Copyright © 2026 by Fred Brathwaite, Inc.

Penguin Random House values and supports copyright. Copyright fuels creativity, encourages diverse voices, promotes free speech, and creates a vibrant culture. Thank you for buying an authorized edition of this book and for complying with copyright laws by not reproducing, scanning, or distributing any part of it in any form without permission. You are supporting writers and allowing Penguin Random House to continue to publish books for every reader. Please note that no part of this book may be used or reproduced in any manner for the purpose of training artificial intelligence technologies or systems.

VIKING and VIKING ship colophon are registered trademarks of
Penguin Random House LLC.

Image credits may be found on pages 325–26.

DESIGNED BY MEIGHAN CAVANAUGH

LIBRARY OF CONGRESS CATALOGING-IN-PUBLICATION DATA
Names: Fab 5 Freddy, 1959– author | Rozzo, Mark author
Title: Everybody's fly : a life of art, music, and changing the culture /
Fab 5 Freddy with Mark Rozzo.
Description: New York, NY : Viking, [2026]
Identifiers: LCCN 2025037043 (print) | LCCN 2025037044 (ebook) |
ISBN 9780593834909 hardcover | ISBN 9780593834916 ebook
Subjects: LCSH: Fab 5 Freddy, 1959– | Artists—United States—Biography |
LCGFT: Biographies | Autobiographies
Classification: LCC NX512.F33 A2 2026 (print) | LCC NX512.F33 (ebook) |
DDC 700.92 [B]—dc23/eng/20251203
LC record available at https://lccn.loc.gov/2025037043
LC ebook record available at https://lccn.loc.gov/2025037044

Printed in the United States of America
1st Printing

The authorized representative in the EU for product safety and compliance is
Penguin Random House Ireland, Morrison Chambers, 32 Nassau Street,
Dublin D02 YH68, Ireland, https://eu-contact.penguin.ie.

Dedicated to my parents,
Fred and Theresa Brathwaite

CONTENTS

Prologue: December 1979   1

Phase 1
THE COME UP

1. May I please speak with Thelonious Monk?   9
2. Where they jammin' at?   33
3. Many will come, but few will be chosen   53
4. Fuck it, let's move this to galleries   73

Phase 2
UPTOWN/DOWNTOWN

5. Be resolute, fear no sacrifice, and surmount every difficulty   91
6. This is what's popping *now*   107
7. Yo, Fred, I just saw your train!   125
8. I was born and raised on planet Mars   137

9. Man, I thought you two were the po-po! 157

10. A whole new art world ready to replace the old one ... 177

11. It's about time we got some publicity for this goddam rap shit ... 195

Phase 3
ANY MEANS NECESSARY

12. This stuff is really fresh! 219
13. Who the hell is on this plane? 239
14. His wig will glow and then people will know it's a wig ... 259
15. I met Gene Kelly! I hung out with him! 281
16. Let his soul run wild 299

Afterword 319

Acknowledgments 321
Image Credits 325

Everybody's Fly

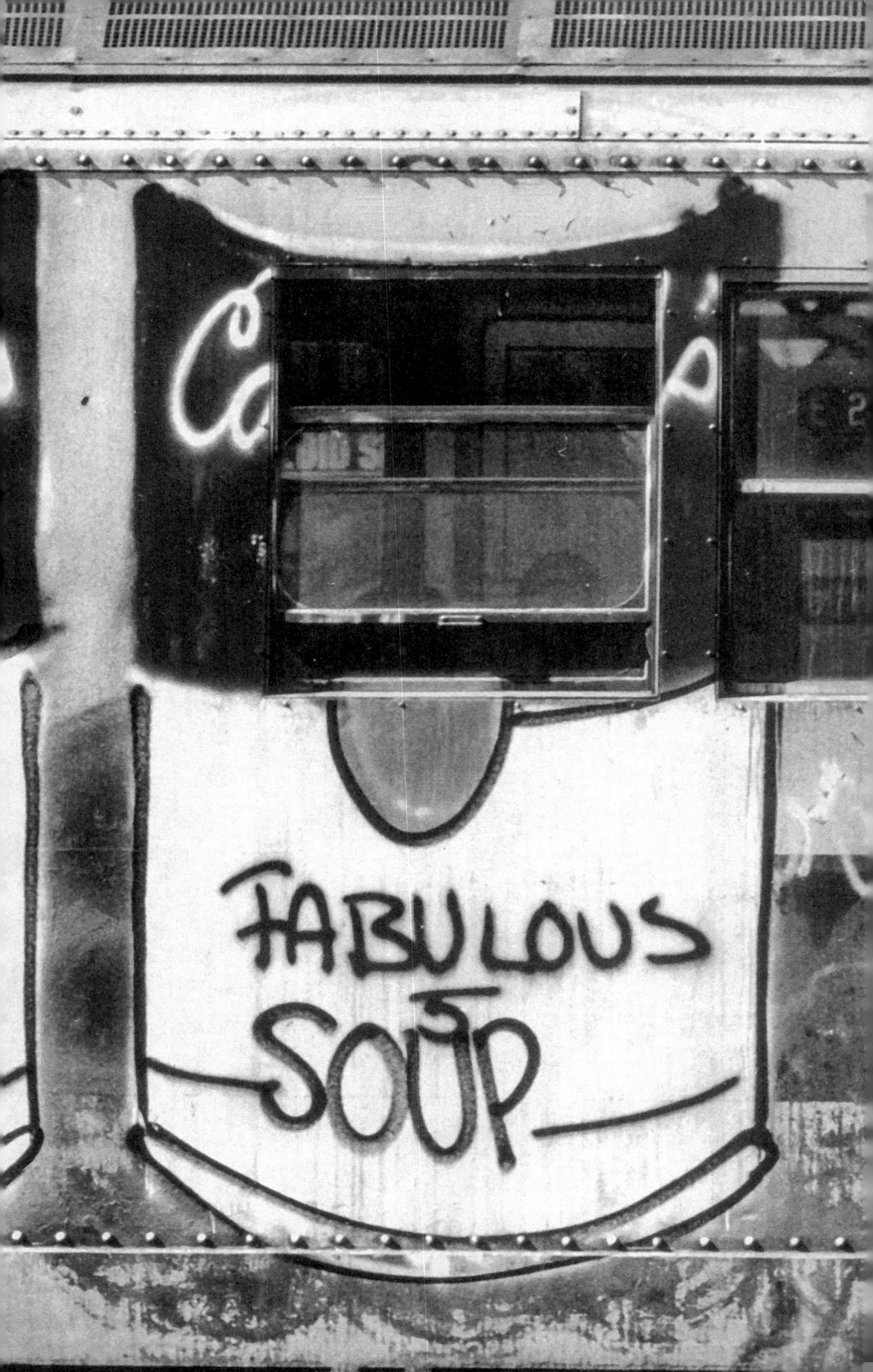

Prologue

December 1979

I had a head on my shoulders. I was always thinking. From the beginning.

Whenever I played hooky from school, I didn't just hang around and party—I went on adventures. I'd hit the subway and head into Manhattan, usually to the museums—the Met, the Frick, the Whitney, the Guggenheim, MoMA. Or I'd ride the A train all the way to the end—up to Washington Heights, where the Cloisters sat perched above the Hudson, or out to Far Rockaway, where the city gave way to the ocean.

On a freezing night at the end of 1979, I set out on another subway adventure. I rode an uptown 5 with my friend Lee Quiñones to the train yard—what we called a layup—at Baychester Avenue in the Bronx. I was from Bed-Stuy, Lee from the Lower East Side. Up there, it felt like another world—practically suburban.

I'd met Lee about a year earlier, after being blown away by his graffiti skills—he was simply the best in the game. I tracked him down at his high school and pitched him on the idea of teaming up. Not long after, we were showing our work in Rome, in the first international gallery show dedicated to this wild new art form born on the streets of New York.

Now that we had taken graffiti to the art world, I wanted to bring the art world to graffiti. I envisioned a statement piece, something bold that connected the dots between graffiti and Pop Art. I'd been thinking a lot about the parallels, how both movements subverted everyday imagery, how both challenged what could be considered art.

I believed deeply that among the thousands of graffiti writers were many true artists—people with talent, skill, and a point of view. These so-called public menaces? They knew about art. They weren't delinquents, or savages, or some kind of naive folk artists. And it was time to show that graffiti could go beyond just the words, the letters—it could take on new subjects, new forms, new ideas.

So Lee and I set out to execute the whole-car piece I'd been dreaming up for months: a rolling homage to Andy Warhol, in the form of a Campbell's soup can train.

Now, unlike Lee—the maestro of whole cars and handball-court murals—I wasn't the kind of guy with a piece book full of elaborate sketches. So I kept it simple. I first mapped out the design in ballpoint pen in a little spiral-bound notebook; eventually I settled on the idea of four Campbell's soup cans, lined up in two vertical pairs, stretching the full height of a car. In the center: FRED. Running through it all: a blue arrow motif, clean and sharp, signifying motion.

Lee and I had a key to the cars, and he knew how to use it. We cranked up the heat inside and stashed our paint near a vent under the seats, so it wouldn't coagulate while we got to work.

We went at it hard, spraying the lineup of four Campbell's soup cans. That meant a ton of white and red paint. I had never done anything this massive or time-consuming before, and Lee schooled me—

PROLOGUE

on the planning, the dos and don'ts, and most of all, how to keep my ears and eyes open in case the cops showed up.

And they *did* show up sometimes. New York was in a panic over Krylon and Rust-Oleum back then, and Lee was the city's most-wanted graffiti outlaw. And even if the cops didn't get you, the third rail might. One misstep and you were done.

That freezing night was like whole-car boot camp. We worked our asses off on the gold medallions at the center of each can, and the little fleur-de-lis ring that circled the bottom. The Campbell's name—in that classic white script on red—was actually easy to emulate. The calligraphic style had a natural graffiti feel. But instead of flavors like cream of mushroom or split pea, we wrote "POP," "DADA," "ART," "TOMATO." In the center, the name FRED, sprayed in a fade from red to yellow, with "POP POP POP POP POP ART!" floating above it. Inside the head of the blue arrow at the far right, I wrote: "SUB URBAN REALISM ©79." And as a shoutout to Lee's legendary old crew—whose mantle we were now carrying—we tagged the right-hand corner with "FABULOUS 5IVE."

Before we knew it, the sun was coming up. We hauled ass out of there. That morning, when the Campbell's soup can train started rolling down the 5 line, jaws dropped every time it pulled into a station.

There would be other statements. Other pieces. Other collaborations. Other adventures.

I kept honing my craft, determined to bring graffiti-inspired art into the art world for real. I hooked up with the downtown post-punk scene, where everything was avant-garde: art, music, film, fashion. I connected that scene to the new underground sound coming from uptown: rap. Together, we helped evolve it into the global force we call hip-hop. Later, I would become the face of hip-hop on MTV, back when that network had the cultural zeitgeist in a headlock.

Through it all, I stayed focused on living creatively, making connections, catalyzing culture, and pushing back against any boundary that dared to block my path.

When I hopped the A train as a kid, I always knew where I wanted to go. My father and his friends used to talk about how, as Black men of their generation, they were always running into barriers. Where I wanted to go was *beyond*. And nothing was going to stop me.

The glory of the Campbell's soup can train was short-lived. Almost immediately, the city sent it through the buffing machine.

Erased forever. But not the memory.

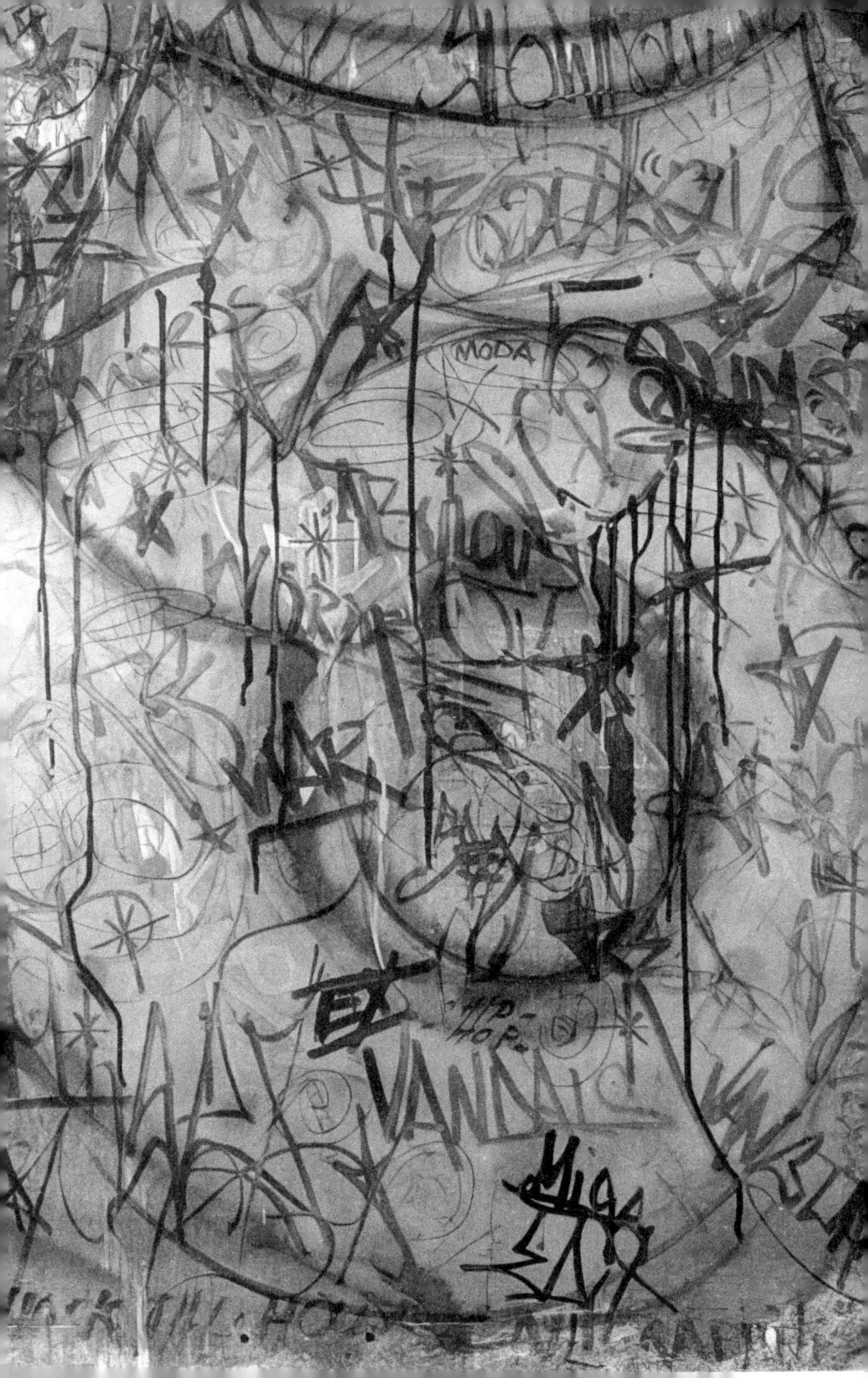

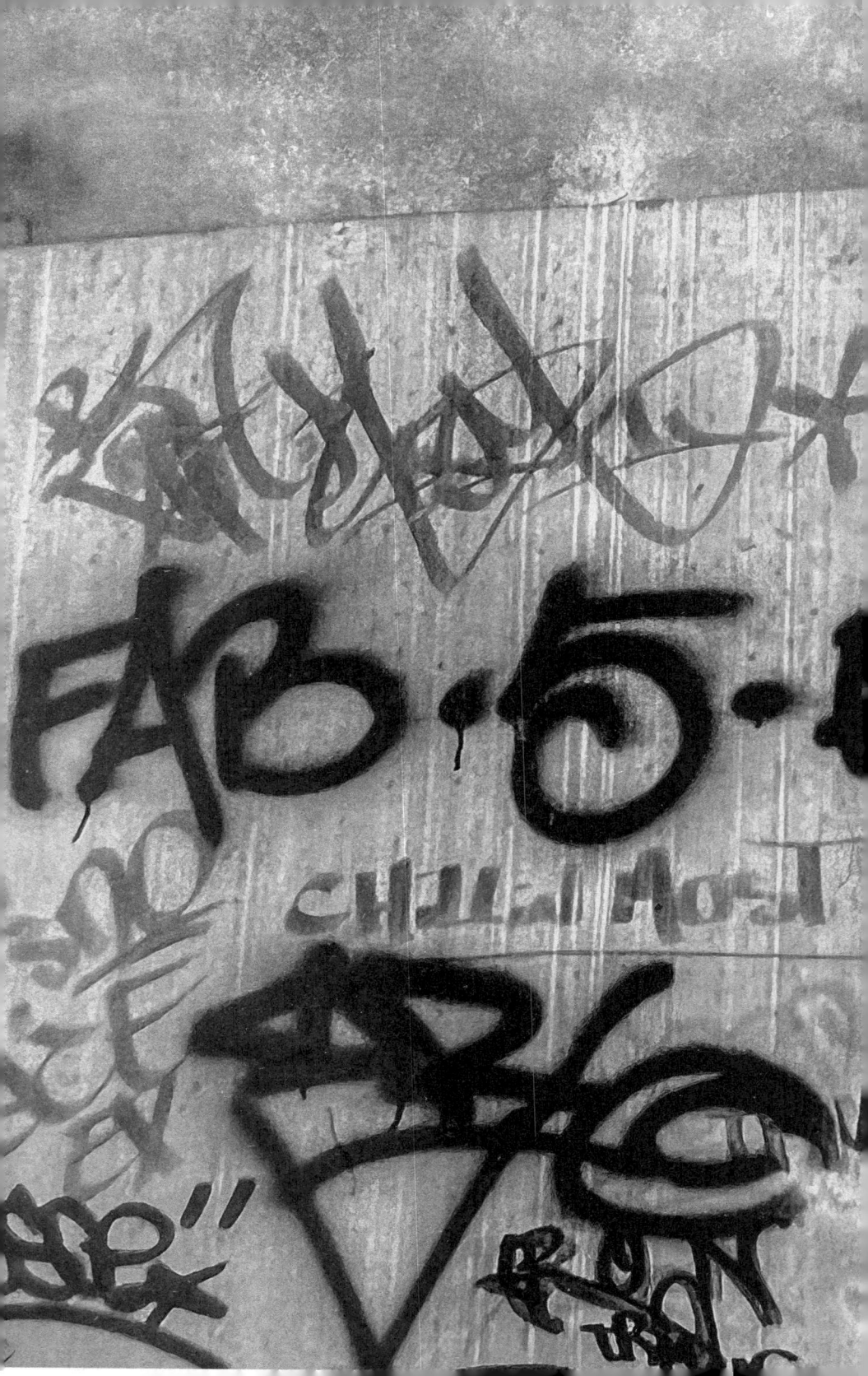

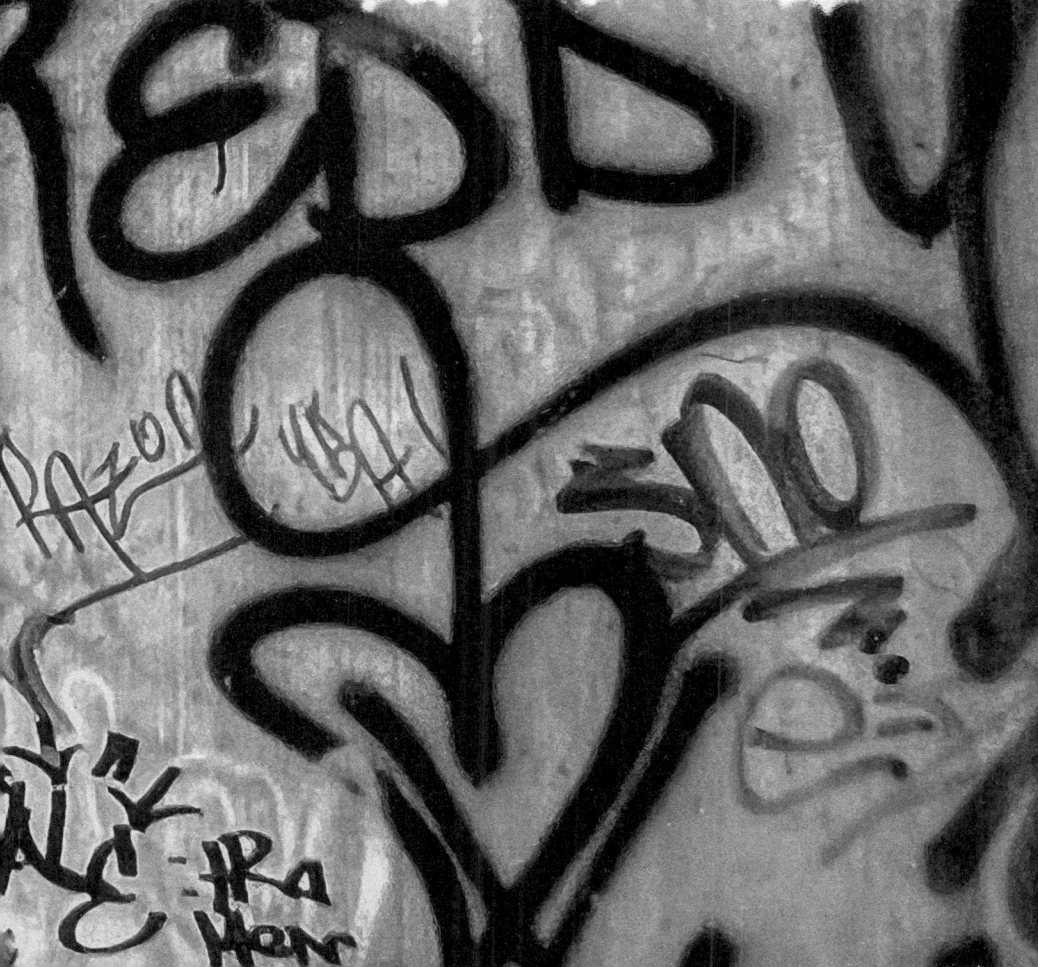

Phase 1
THE COME UP

1

May I please speak with Thelonious Monk?

The house on Hancock Street is four stories tall, including the ground floor—a classic brownstone, smack in the middle of the block, with Lewis Avenue at one end and Sumner (now Marcus Garvey) at the other. The street is lined with linden trees, and most of the houses looked like ours—one brownstone after another with a few midsize apartment buildings interspersed.

They say Bed-Stuy is the largest brownstone neighborhood in all of Brooklyn, and Brooklyn's got more brownstones than anywhere. My father's family had owned the house on Hancock Street for at least a generation by the time I came along, in the late fifties. My parents, Fred and Theresa, were proud to own a whole house, even if they were always renting out rooms and floors to boarders or putting up relatives. My own bedroom moved around from one spot to another, depending on who was staying where and what needed to be done.

There was a hierarchy in the hood. You either owned a house or rented a room or an apartment. People on Hancock Street—and all over Bed-Stuy—could get real snobbish about it. I had friends whose families owned homes, and those kids were told to play in front of their own houses. Their parents didn't want them running with what they saw as the wilder, more "urban" kids—the ones who grew up in apartments. Bad influences.

I was lucky. My parents never said it outright, but I knew they couldn't stand that attitude. Plenty of parents didn't want their kids hanging with the ghetto kids I ran with—and I ran with the best of the worst. As long as I got myself home by curfew, everything was cool. But if I came in late, I'd be in seriously deep shit.

So my parents gave me a leash, but they kept it long. That gave me an explorer's mindset. It kept me out of a ton of trouble too. I wasn't the kind of kid who stayed out all night getting into crazy stuff, but I wasn't sitting on my stoop all day either, bored out of my mind bouncing a pink Spaldeen against the steps.

When I go back and walk around Bed-Stuy now, I can still see what it was in the 1960s and '70s. The hood was so alive back then, and kids were everywhere. There were endless games in the streets: Johnny on the pony, skelly, Ringolevio, punchball, stickball. If there was ever a dispute, it got settled with a fair fight. Being "nice with your hands" was a serious reputation builder.

Some kids kept pigeons in coops on their rooftops. We'd go up there and hang out, surveying the entire neighborhood like it was our kingdom. I made friends with the old sign painter on Reid Avenue (now Malcolm X Boulevard) who let me watch him hand-paint his lettering and graphics. On the corners, there'd be guys passing a pint of cheap wine while four-part harmonizing soul ballads. Older folks congregated around bars and lounges like the White Swan or the Charlo. Some of these establishments sponsored bus rides—to Bear Mountain, or up to Peg-Leg Bates, the "Interracial

Country Club" in Kerhonkson, for a day away. Trips into Manhattan were rare.

On weekends, some folks sold home-cooked soul food to help make the rent, the menus handwritten on index cards. My mom would jot down our order and send me to pick it up. A big night out was dinner at McDonald's—not the fast-food joint but the most popular upscale restaurant in the hood, at Stuyvesant and Macon. The waiters wore uniforms, families dined out in style, and I was taught how to properly deal with a napkin. The best thing about McDonald's Dining Room was that each table had its own little jukebox loaded with Motown and Stax singles. Local politicians and church brass ate there on the regular. For my parents and me, it was reserved for big occasions—kindergarten graduation, my confirmation, or Easter Sunday after church.

There were characters popping all over the place. Uncle Joe was the cook at Charlo's, the bar on the corner of our block. They'd let me in, which was exciting, but I'd skip the bar and head straight to the back, to the little kitchen. That's where I'd place my order with Uncle Joe, while he told stories about his days as a chef on Pullman cars. The man had been everywhere—and knew his way around a chicken. He could cook his ass off, and his fried chicken and crackling cornbread were the best around.

Then there was Gold Coast—the smooth operator who ran the numbers game known as "policy" out of a garage at Lewis and Halsey. He was always dressed in golf clothes. Moe was the barber on Lewis Avenue around the corner, the first to cut my hair when I was a toddler and the guy who cut it throughout my childhood.

At the firehouse on Hancock, when the firemen were out fighting fires—or responding to false alarms—we'd sneak inside, run up the stairs, and slide down the pole a few times before they came back. I can't remember who ran the Snowball, the little shop where we got snow cones and penny candy on Lewis Avenue. But that was the spot on those sticky-hot summer days when somebody, maybe the firemen, would jack open a hydrant to cool us down.

Down toward the Sumner end of Hancock, across the street from our house, you could slip between two buildings and into an open, rubble-strewn lot. It was part of the long-abandoned Rand Rubber Company factory complex. Empty lots and the few abandoned buildings adjacent to them became our personal playground and clubhouse. We did all the classic ghetto shit back there. Sometimes we'd find dirty-ass mattresses lying around—left behind after people moved out, piss stains and all. We'd stack them up in a pile and jump out a second-floor window onto them. Ghetto gymnastics! The place was our own amusement park.

We were obsessed with *The Little Rascals*—watched it religiously, broke down every episode, tried to reenact it all. We put on fake revues, built go-karts out of wooden milk crates, two-by-fours, and baby-carriage wheels. We had some good play days.

While we were having the time of our young lives, an older crowd of dope fiends were busy ripping the copper wiring out of the factory—burning the insulation off, selling the metal for drug money.

It was the Great Migration that created the Bed-Stuy I knew coming up. Millions of Black folks had poured in from the South, escaping the brutality of Jim Crow and sharecropping—which was basically slavery by another name. Northern cities like New York, Philadelphia, and Boston needed factory labor, and that's how a lot of the parents and grandparents of my friends ended up in Brooklyn.

There was a Southern Black feeling all over the neighborhood. You could hear it in the accents and taste it in the food. There was even a house on our block that looked like it had been lifted straight out of a small Southern town. One story, wooden, country style, with a porch out front. In the yard stood a big pear tree. When the pears dropped, we'd run in, gather a bunch, and put them in a paper bag, and in a few days they'd be ready to eat.

The family next door to that house was Guyanese—and that was the other huge influence in Bed-Stuy. It felt like every other family in the hood was from the West Indies: Barbados, Grenada, Haiti, Trinidad, Jamaica—you name it. My grandparents on both sides went back to Barbados and Guyana.

As a kid, I spent a few summers in Barbados with my mother's family. It was heaven on earth. Only when I went back as an adult did I realize how poor they were. But when you're a kid, you don't *know* poor—you're just running around having fun. My father's family down there weren't as much fun: super religious. Church three or four times a week. Everything was about God. My father had become a nonbeliever, but even so, during my single-digit years, we still observed Sundays in our house. Church in the morning at John Wesley Methodist. Then home, and sticking close to it for the rest of day. Honestly, the only thing I really remember about church was falling asleep in the middle of it.

The West Indians brought a lot to the table, including their own ways of dealing with hard times and straight-up racism, especially when it came to owning property. I remember grown-ups talking about the "susu," a kind of informal loan system between family and friends. It was a way around the banks, who wouldn't lend to Black folks in redlined neighborhoods. Families would chip in over time, and when someone really needed money—whether it was for an emergency or a down payment—they would take their turn getting a share from the susu. It was like Bed-Stuy had its own underground economy.

The reason we owned the house on Hancock Street was because my dad's family was, for lack of a better word, entrepreneurial. One uncle owned a livery business and had a whole fleet of limousines for funerals and weddings. I always heard talk about a family-run employment agency back during the Great Depression, helping lift up other Black folks when times were tight. It made sense, since my grandfather, Frederick Theophilus Brathwaite, had been prominent in Marcus Garvey's movement. He even headed one of the Brooklyn chapters of Garvey's United Negro Improvement Association. Garvey laid it all out in 1918: U.N.I.A. formed as an organization that would "work for the general uplift of the Negro peoples of the world. And the members pledge themselves to do all in their power to conserve the rights of their noble race and to respect the rights of all mankind, believing always in the Brotherhood of Man and the Fatherhood of God. The motto of the organization is: One God! One Aim! One Destiny!" I don't think that Garveyite spirit—Black empowerment, achievement, justice, and solidarity—has ever left our family.

That first Fred Brathwaite—Guyanese with Bajan heritage—came to America with his first wife and settled in Harlem. One of his businesses involved stenography. The Brathwaites were important enough to sit for James Van Der Zee, the great Harlem Renaissance portrait photographer, in 1907. His wife died young, but they had a daughter I was lucky enough to know. Her first name was Frederica, and she lived to be a hundred. My own father—another Frederick Brathwaite, middle name DeLacy—was from my grandfather's second marriage. That second marriage prompted a move to Brooklyn, where the family settled on Cumberland Street. (My grandfather died before I was born, and my grandmother died when I was still very young.)

Eventually, I came along as the third consecutive Frederick Brathwaite, but I'm not a III or a Jr., because the middle names changed with each generation. I was given the middle name Leroy, after one of my father's friends—a well-known Brooklyn basketball player, Leroy "Lefty" Morris. Originally, my dad wanted my middle name to be Lumumba, after Patrice Lumumba, the first prime minister of the Democratic Republic of the Congo. My mother said, "No way."

Over on her side, it was a similar story of Black diaspora—coming from the islands, with a stop in Harlem before landing in Brooklyn. The only grandparents I really got to know were on my mother's side: her mom, Irene Graeves, and *her* mom, my great-grandmother, Maude Gibbs. My grandmother was one of the first Black people to move into the Sheepshead Bay projects, out near Coney Island. To me, as a kid, the projects were *the ultimate*. To be able to run around free in a park-like setting—no cars, no streets, just monkey bars, slides, swings, and seesaws—that was pure nirvana. Going out to Sheepshead Bay for the weekend to see my grandmother was like a weekend in the Hamptons. I had no idea the projects had a "bad" reputation. It was all fun to me. (Back then, kids even bragged about having relatives in the projects—some parents actually wanted to move there.)

My grandmother's apartment was just a couple of stops from Coney Island. I could see the lights of the Wonder Wheel and the old Parachute Jump from her bathroom window. It was a dream.

Sheepshead Bay was a mostly Jewish neighborhood, and I always felt like my mom and grandmother were deeply connected to that Jewish sensibility. It was another influence in our house. It also meant that we had easy access to bagels, lox, cream cheese, whitefish—the whole shebang. My mother loved noshing on those treats, which she had grown up eating thanks to her Jewish friends. Her family had lived in Sheepshead Bay too, back when she was a girl. I grew up with all that good stuff—back in the days before bagels were available everywhere.

T he kitchen at Hancock Street was in the back, on the first floor. That was my mother's domain. She was a killer cook—and she would throw down some amazing meals back there. She worked as a nurse in hospitals all over Brooklyn, often pulling late shifts. It amazed me how she could care for the sick and dying and still take such good care of me and my father.

The kitchen opened onto a nice-size backyard, fenced in, with a patch of lawn that never stood a chance—our dogs ran it down to bare dirt. We always had a couple of large dogs. I remember my dad going out there and feeding them boiled chicken backs. I'm sure those dogs got on the nerves of our cranky next-door neighbor, Mr. St. Hill. He was always telling us kids what *not* to do. Every Halloween, his house got hit with eggs.

My mother often shared her kitchen with her best friend, Doris Henderson, who I think of as my other mother. They met when they were about sixteen, back when both families were living in the Kingsborough Houses in Crown Heights. (My mom's family, like my dad's, had moved from Harlem to Brooklyn.) Doris was a Southern gal, from New Bern, North Carolina—part of the great Black migration north. When my parents moved into the house on Hancock, Doris and her son, Reggie, who was several years older than me, moved in too. They took a small apartment upstairs.

My mom and Doris were as close as two friends could be—like sisters. I would hang out in the kitchen and watch them chitchat, every day, nonstop. Doris taught my mom the finer points of Southern cooking, and my mom taught Doris all the best Barbadian recipes. I remember my mom telling me how when I was a baby with a nasty cold, Doris was babysitting me—like she often did. She saw I could barely breathe from the congestion. I was crying uncontrollably, from frustration and discomfort. Doris didn't hesitate. She sucked the thick slime out of my nose and spat it out—just like that. I could breathe again.

That's the kind of woman she was. Doris wasn't just my other mother—she became like a big sister too. Her family became my family: a bunch of aunts, uncles, and cousins. I would go down to North Carolina to visit them, and they'd come up to Brooklyn to visit us. That was my extended family.

My father was an accountant—a math whiz who worked with numbers all day, but he was curious about *everything*. His domain was the cellar. He'd tricked out our basement with a reel-to-reel tape deck, a shortwave radio, and tons of books. Our house was stuffed with analog everything—magazines, vinyl records, newspapers. We had subscriptions to *Time*, *Life*, *Look*, *Newsweek*, *The New Yorker*, *Popular Science*, and *Esquire*—plus *Ebony* and *Jet*, of course.

But my dad's basement wasn't like some suburban man cave with wood paneling and carpet. You could see the old tree-trunk posts and heavy beams holding the house up. If you jumped, you'd conk your head on the low ceiling. The floor was cracked cement. It felt like the kind of place where spies might gather.

And that's pretty much what went on down there. The cellar was where my dad gathered his posse, like a secret cabal. On many nights, they'd talk for hours about everything from music to radical politics. Names like Malcolm X, Che Guevara, Huey Newton, and Chairman Mao came up constantly, their pictures lining the walls. My dad's friends were smart, articulate men. But they were also hip, slick, totally street. That made a lasting impression on me. They would drink wine. They would smoke—cigarettes and cannabis both. There was a little compartment in the cellar ceiling where my dad kept his stash. It wasn't quite discreet enough. When I got a little older, I started tapping into it. In the meantime, I'd just roll up a piece of toilet paper and pretend I was huffing on a joint.

When my dad had his friends over, I would put my ear to the closed door at the top of the cellar stairs, trying to catch audio snapshots of what they were talking about as they debated, argued, laughed, and yelled.

"Man, they're really getting into it now!" my mother would say from the kitchen, laughing.

At least four nights a week, four or five guys would come by to see my dad. He was a compelling talker. A deep thinker. He used his voice like Sonny Rollins blowing his horn. And he was *informed*. He was tuned in to shortwave radio, picking up news from around the world. He read everything he could get his hands on—books by and about Marx, Lenin, Mao, and other radical, progressive, anti-colonialist, or African-nationalist thinkers: Frantz Fanon, C. L. R. James, Kwame Nkrumah.

The basement was where my dad held court. It was the place his friends came to sort through what was going down in the world. The civil rights movement was on. Fists were being raised in protest. African nations were rising up, throwing off colonialism. Change was in the air.

My dad was primed for it, having grown up in a Garveyite household and come up through the New York jazz scene. His best friend at Boys' High in Brooklyn was Max Roach, the incredible bebop drummer. They stayed friends for life.

Max was my godfather—one of the biggest influences on who I would become. He was the best-dressed person I'd ever seen, a kind of brown-skinned Clark Gable who was always wearing the coolest, flyest gear. Casual, but decked out, the way bebop guys always were. To this day, I love that look.

I remember telling other kids, "Yo, I know Max Roach!" And they'd be like, "Aw, you don't know him." But he was practically family.

Jazz consciousness was everywhere in our house. You'd hear *Jazz at Massey Hall* on the turntable—Charlie Parker and Dizzy Gillespie having an epic cutting contest on "Salt Peanuts." You'd see jazz on the bookshelves, on the coffee table. Sometimes when my father's jazz friends came over, he would dig out his treasured copy of *Harlem on*

THE COME UP

My Mind, the catalogue from a major photography exhibit at the Met. They would pore over those vintage photos of Black folks in historic Harlem. One image always lit them up: *A Great Day in Harlem*—that incredible black-and-white photo Art Kane shot for *Esquire* in the 1950s. Dozens of jazz musicians standing in front of a Harlem townhouse. It became a kind of game for them, calling out names: "That's Lester Young! There's Monk! Look at Diz and Sonny Rollins!"

I would watch them, bug-eyed. And pretty soon I started to know the faces too, along with the sounds each of those musicians made. Seeing how into it I was, Max gave me a practice drum kit. But playing an instrument just wasn't in the cards for me.

Some of the jazz guys my dad knew were part of an extended friend group from way back in the early 1950s. They called themselves the Chessmen. They were all from Brooklyn, and the group included the sculptor Jimmy Gittens, who ran the government-funded New Sculpture Workshop and was like a big brother to me; Willie Jones, a jazz drummer turned activist; and the photographer Jimmy Morton, who shot inside the jazz clubs. And, of course, Max Roach and Lefty Morris.

In their younger days, jazz and chess were what they lived for. They taught me to play chess when I was eight years old and filled my head with jazz lore. I heard endless tales about old Brooklyn clubs like the Putnam Central and Tony's Club Grandean. They told me about how the Chessmen pooled their money to rent a huge Victorian house at 212 Gates Avenue. It became their own jazz clubhouse, with musicians dropping in to jam.

There were stories about Miles, Bird, and Monk. Stories about my dad hitting the road with the Clifford Brown–Max Roach Quintet, playing gigs at the Beehive in Chicago. And there were many mentions of the Baroness Kathleen Annie Pannonica de Koenigswarter, known as Nica. She was a legendary jazz patron, a Rothschild heiress, and, for a while, part of their world. They talked about her pulling up in a Rolls or a Bentley—in the hood. They said this rich white lady left her whole life behind after hearing Monk's "'Round Midnight" and gave herself to the cause of jazz. That blew my mind. She literally helped feed Monk's family when his cabaret card was taken away and he couldn't perform.

From an early age, I gravitated toward the music and aura of Thelonious Monk—still my favorite musician. Maybe it was that deceptively simple way he played piano—*boom, bing, blang*. I just thought, "Wow, I really like this guy." One day—I can't remember how old I was, but I was definitely in single digits—I picked up my dad's phone book. And there it was: Monk's number.

I dialed it.

His wife, Nellie, picked up.

"May I please speak with Thelonious Monk?" I asked.

Nellie kindly explained that her husband was resting and couldn't come to the phone. I can't imagine what she thought about getting a call from a little boy in Brooklyn, but she patiently answered all my questions.

"Jazz is like a conversation, Freddy," she told me in her sweet voice. "You know, one musician starts off by stating a point. The rest of the song is the other musicians sharing their own interpretations, their elaborations on that point."

That jewel Nellie dropped on me helped me realize later that my father's melodious, conversational cadence was inspired by the jazz musicians he loved so much.

Some of the first imagery that really hit me came from the jazz album covers in my parents' record collection. They were often illustrated with moody photographs or abstract paintings, always paired with sleek typography and sharp graphics. The art directors at labels like Blue Note and Verve were clearly tuned in to the contemporary art of the time.

One of the records I played so much I nearly wore it out was Max's

THE COME UP

We Insist!, featuring his "Freedom Now Suite." Every time I listened to that record, I would stare at the cover. It was a stark black-and-white photo—three Black men sitting at a lunch counter, solemn, looking over their shoulders at the camera. Behind them, a white guy works the counter. The image didn't look like any other album cover I'd seen. The vibe felt serious and unusual.

I asked my parents: "What's happening here? What's this about?"

They told me that Black people weren't allowed to sit and be served at lunch counters in the South. That this image—and the record itself—was a form of protest.

We're standing up for ourselves now. We're not putting up with this shit anymore.

One thing I remember asking my dad and his friends was why everything used to look black-and-white back in the old days.

My dad stopped in his tracks.

"What do you mean, Frederick?"

I had a hard time explaining what I meant, but I tried.

"When you watch old movies, everything's black-and-white."

I figured that's how it used to be. A grayscale world, devoid of color.

Thanks to *Million Dollar Movie*, *The Late Show*, and *The Late Late Show*, I was fully locked into the black-and-white world of old movies. Whenever I woke up in the middle of the night, I would sneak over to the TV and switch it on. I would drift along with those movies—sometimes half asleep—until the screen faded into a test pattern, signaling the end of the broadcast day.

My connection with TV and cinema was incredibly strong—like it was for a lot of kids in my generation. I'm glad those late-night shows played the classics. And I'm even more glad my father and his friends appreciated them. (Otherwise, my dad usually called TV the "boob tube" or the "idiot box.") They had their favorites, and I would hear them talk about movies like *The Treasure of the Sierra Madre*, starring Humphrey Bogart.

"Oh man, that was *dynamite*," they'd say.

I'd be listening, thinking, "Okay, gotta see that."

This was long before VHS or Roku, so if a great movie came on, you had to catch it. I absorbed *The Grapes of Wrath*, the Sherlock Holmes movies with Basil Rathbone, all the Charlie Chan films. And anything with Mae West, whose sassiness reminded me of some of my mother's friends. Her tough, sexy vibe lit up my young imagination.

Over on PBS, Channel 13, I stumbled into a whole world by just flipping through the dial. It might be a Kurasawa movie, a Fellini movie, or Shirley Clarke's *The Cool World*, about gangs in Harlem. That one was totally pivotal.

And if something came on like *Carmen Jones* (with a cameo from Max Roach) or *Nothing but a Man* (starring Max's wife, Abbey Lincoln), the phone would start ringing. My dad's friends would call to give us the heads-up, and my parents would be excited to tune in. (Incidentally, my folks refused to get a color TV for the longest time. But Doris had one upstairs, so that's where I first saw the colors of the NBC peacock.)

Movies had a visceral effect on me. Later, the experience of seeing *Shaft*—in an actual movie theater—was transformative. Not just for me, but for everyone I knew. Black heroes like that simply didn't exist in the movies. But here was this badass—played by Richard Roundtree—moving through the world with power, attitude, and style. And that soundtrack by the genius Isaac Hayes, who remarkably won an Oscar for the theme song. *"I'm talkin' 'bout Shaft (Then we can dig it)."* Later, I'd learn more about Gordon Parks, the director. His elegant swagger. His photography. His music. His writing. Everything he did put a frame around the Black American experience—and elevated it. He was a contemporary Renaissance man.

When it came to TV shows, I watched all the usual suspects: *The Beverly Hillbillies, Green Acres, Perry Mason, The Wild Wild West, Leave It to Beaver, Batman, The Green Hornet*—you know, the good shit. Mornings and afternoons were for cartoons: *Bugs Bunny, Courageous Cat and Minute Mouse, The Flintstones, The Jetsons, Captain America*, and, of course, *Popeye*.

I was so into the fantasy world of TV, I often felt like I was *inside* the television. Once, I even tried to get the characters out. I remember this one episode of *Popeye* where the electrical shape of his fist traveled down a telephone line, came out the other end, and punched his nemesis, Brutus, in the face. That blew my mind. I was about five years old, and I figured that had to be how it worked—*that's* how the characters got on the screen. They were traveling through the wire! So I thought: If I can scratch the wire and get a spark, the cartoons should come out, like genies from a bottle. So I grabbed a knife and scraped the wire connecting the TV to the wall—the power cord. I got a few sparks to come out, maybe some smoke. But no cartoon characters. And thankfully, no flames.

My parents didn't understand.

"What were you trying to do, Frederick?!"

I tried to explain, but they were not at all happy when they saw that exposed wire.

"You could have burned the whole house down!"

Two major events stand out from those years. My father and his friends were always talking about civil rights. He had gone to the March on Washington in 1963 and followed every twist and turn of Martin Luther King's career. He also followed Malcolm X, attending several of his Harlem rallies. One of the guys in the regular cellar crew, Willie Jones, knew Malcolm and used to record his speeches on a portable reel-to-reel machine—so Malcolm could listen back and study them. I remember hearing those tapes in our house.

On a Sunday afternoon in February 1965, my dad and Willie went up to the Audubon Ballroom in Harlem to hear Malcolm speak. Willie brought his tape machine. He set it up. The wheels started to turn. And then—gunshots.

Malcolm was killed.

For the rest of their lives, my father and Willie talked about witnessing Malcolm's assassination, trying to process that tragedy. Every once in a while, they would load that same tape onto a machine and play it back. I remember it well.

First, you heard Malcolm greet the crowd: "As-Salaam Alaikum."

The crowd answered back.

Then a disturbance: "Hey man, get your hands out of my pocket!"

My father and Willie must've told the story a hundred times.

That shout caused people to turn around—toward the back of the ballroom. And that's when the shooters up front opened fire. One of the first bullets damaged Willie's microphone. You can hear it on the tape.

The mic drops in volume. Then, faintly, more gunshots. By then, Malcolm was on the floor.

It was chaos in the room. People were scrambling.

My father was among the first to rush the stage—to see what had happened to Malcolm.

Then, not knowing if there were more shooters, he and Willie panicked and ran backstage, ducking behind a curtain or scrim.

As my dad told it, Willie found a small hole to peek through.

"That's a bullet hole, Willie!" my dad said. "Get away from that!"

THE COME UP

I heard this story told so many times, I felt like I had been at the Audubon Ballroom that awful day.

Three years later, Martin Luther King was assassinated.

My father always kept the radio in our kitchen tuned to 1010 WINS or WBAI if it wasn't a station playing jazz. That's how we heard the news.

I remember him crying out—his voice full of anguish: "This is unbelievable! They killed Martin! Martin is gone!"

It was the heaviest mood I can ever remember settling over our house. The phone started ringing off the hook—his cellar crew, checking in.

Soon enough, we were hearing reports of unrest on Fulton Street. The radio was saying Harlem was on fire. Brooklyn too.

My dad said, "Come on, let's go up on the roof."

From up there, we could see several fires glowing in the distance, all around us.

Then Paul Chandler, one of my dad's closest friends—a young, charismatic community activist—showed up at the house. He brought along this young cat named Carlos, but everyone called him Sun.

My dad said, "Come on, let's go to Brownsville to check on what's happening out there."

Paul was respected all over the borough. He believed he could calm things down if shit got too serious. So we all piled into my dad's black, four-door '57 Chevy. I don't remember exactly what my mom was doing just then—but I highly doubt she thought this was a good idea. (For all I know, she might have been on one of her night shifts.)

I was in the front seat, next to my dad. Paul and Carlos were in the back. It was already dark. We drove down Troy Avenue to Atlantic and stopped at the light, wanting to make the left toward Brownsville. As we sat there, I looked out the window to my right—and saw an older white man in a suit, running full speed straight at our car.

In my memory, it plays in slow motion.

He ran right up, yanked open the door—and dived in on top of me.

The second he got in, there was a loud *bang!* on the roof. Two Black guys had been chasing him. One of them had a thick, baseball bat–size piece of cable, and he smacked it across the roof of my dad's Chevy.

If the car door had been locked, it would have been just awful.

I slid out from under this man, who kept apologizing, almost in tears.

My dad jumped out of the car.

"What the *fuck* are you guys doing?" he shouted.

It might have been the angriest I'd ever seen him.

"I said, *What are you doing?*"

The guy with the thick-ass cable said, "Man, bro, they just killed King. *Bro, they just killed King!*"

My dad pointed to the terrified man in the passenger seat.

"He's not the enemy!" he yelled. "This man is NOT our enemy!" Then, with almost equal fury: "And did you just put a dent in my fuckin' car?!" The two guys snapped out of it, backed down, apologizing. The light turned green. My dad got back in the car and started driving.

I was sitting there between my dad and this terrified white man, and my young heart was racing. He kept saying, over and over, "Thank you, oh my God, thank you… oh my God…"

It was like a record stuck in a groove.

My dad, Paul, and Carlos were all trying to calm him down. Turned out he'd been working nearby and was walking to the Long Island Rail Road stop several blocks away—heading home to the suburbs.

My dad said, "Listen. King was killed, and it's not safe for you out here. I'm gonna take you to the precinct nearby. You'll be all right."

So we drove him to the police station, the Seventy-Seventh Precinct on Utica Avenue. Before letting him out, my dad gave him a final warning: "Listen to me. Don't you let them send you out alone. Make sure they escort you to the train! It is not safe out here."

No question—if we had not been sitting at that stoplight, door unlocked, in that exact moment, that man would have been killed.

We made it out to Brownsville. It wasn't burning. But people were milling around—like something could pop off at any minute. Paul talked to them, cooling them off a little. But in the days and nights that followed, Molotov cocktails would be thrown. Shops looted. Everywhere, the anger was palpable. Riots and fires broke out in over a hundred cities across the country. It felt like we had entered a new age.

That time burned itself into my consciousness. Between the political awareness in my household and the events unfolding around the world, there was no doubt that I would be shaped by the ideals of equality and racial justice that my father and his friends upheld. The deaths of Malcolm and King were galvanizing for millions of people—including me. The grown-ups around me were paying attention. They were listening, questioning, looking for alternatives to oppression and racism—everything they saw as the dark side of the American narrative. Those ideals were embedded in me.

They stayed with me as I came of age, chose a life of art, and started looking for the threads that connect people and movements. Always trying to search for positivity in all things—but never backing down from a fight, if it came to that.

One of the guys my dad was really into was Robert F. Williams, who had a shortwave radio program called *Radio Free Dixie*, broadcast out of Cuba—and later, China. Williams had been an NAACP leader *and* an NRA chapter head in North Carolina during Jim Crow, from the 1950s into the early '60s. He chose to stand up to the Klan—arming himself to the teeth and preaching a civil rights gospel of "armed self-reliance."

He and his people fought fire with fire. These were folks who were not afraid to chuck a Molotov cocktail when the situation called for it. Williams was controversial—no question. A proto-Panther. He eventually became a fugitive for standing up to racist hate, fleeing to Cuba and then, at Mao's invitation, to China. While in exile, he got Mao to issue a statement in support of Black Americans following King's assassination. A poster was made of that statement: "The evil system of colonialism and imperialism arose and throve with the enslavement of negroes and the trade in negroes, and it will surely come to its end with the complete emancipation of the Black people."

My dad hung that poster on the wall of our basement to inspire him and his friends. The imagery was intense. So were the graphics in a lot of the radical publications my dad kept around, like the Black Panther Party newspapers, featuring powerful work by Emory Douglas—the Panthers' Minister of Culture. Douglas was the in-house artist and designer for the movement. His style was bold, dramatic, and direct. So along with the ideas, I was also absorbing an aesthetic.

I remember a few times, late at night, around my bedtime, sitting in the cellar with my dad as he listened to *Radio Free Dixie*. It played a mix of blues, R&B, and the wildest, most out-there jazz, all interspersed with intense, unforgettable Black-power messages: "In the cause of freedom and justice, let our battle cry be heard around the world. Freedom! Freedom! Freedom now, or death!"

My dad often walked me to my elementary school in the morning—Holy Rosary, a big Gothic building on Bainbridge Street—on his way to catch the A train to his office in the Wall Street area. Every day, he wore a crisp suit and bow tie. He was very much a bow-tie guy.

I wore my Catholic school uniform: gray pants, white shirt, dark-blue tie, dark-blue blazer with the Holy Rosary crest stitched on the chest. I would take off as much of that uniform as possible on my walk home after school.

I throw with my left hand. But thanks to the nuns at Holy Rosary, I hold a pen in my right. They insisted I write with my right hand—by "insisted," I mean they whipped my ass if I didn't. The nuns were generous with corporal punishment, and I got my share.

I also got a stutter. Years later, I read a study that said stuttering can be triggered when you force a child to switch handedness. My stutter was mild, but it caused me embarrassment. Sometimes, when a teacher called on me in class, I'd just lock up. Other times, the stutter got me picked on. That's when my dad's friend Jimmy Gittens stepped in. He taught me how to use my fists—how to be nice with my knuckles—if things ever got too real.

Even so, I mostly believed all the shit the nuns and priests told us—like how your guardian angel is always hovering nearby, looking after you. Any time I tried to talk about spiritual matters with my father, he'd be like, "That's garbage!"

At which my mother would jump in: "Stop, Freddy! You're confusing him!"

My folks didn't argue much, but when they did, it reminded me of Alice and Ralph Kramden in *The Honeymooners*, but with cursing.

My dad appreciated the quality of a Catholic education—at least compared to the public-school options in Bed-Stuy. But he was not feeling the religious part of it. So at school, I would hear about the Immaculate Conception; at the dinner table, I would hear about dialectical materialism. My dad was always looking for alternatives—spiritually, economically—to the way things were in our country. After all, what we were living under was pretty horrible.

Those walks with my dad to school were like extensions of the think-tank atmosphere he created in the cellar. I remember one morning when a guy in a flashy new Cadillac pulled over to say hello. After he drove off, my father said, "He's a poverty pimp."

A what?

That's when I learned about local "activists" who weren't doing anything for the community with the anti-poverty funds they got from the government—just setting themselves up.

I also remember noticing something strange as we walked down Stuyvesant Avenue toward Holy Rosary, through well-to-do Stuyvesant Heights. It was a beautiful area, full of big, elegant townhouses. Most of the Black folks coming in and out of them had lighter skin. That perplexed me. I asked my father what was up. It was a hard lesson to absorb—about racism, colorism, and socioeconomics.

We often walked past the Macon branch of the New York Public Library, a place that became an obsession, a haven. I got deep into art books, architecture books. At some point, it hit me: *Somebody* had to design every room, every hallway. Somebody decided how high the ceilings should be, what the moldings looked like, how the electrical and plumbing would run. The realization that an actual person had drawn all that blew my mind. I decided I wanted to be an architect.

I started checking out stacks of architecture books—getting lost in the work of Frank Lloyd Wright and tripping out on the Greco-Roman influence on so many buildings. I accumulated a ton of books—and some of them I never bothered to bring back. I probably still owe money to the Macon branch for unpaid fines.

One Christmas, during the height of my architecture obsession, all I wanted was a Rapidograph pen. It was a technical drawing pen with a precise point that architects used for mechanical drawings. That thing must have cost thirty bucks—which felt like all the money in the world.

I begged my mother for it. She got me one: a Christmas miracle.

Naturally, I ended up destroying it, but it was fun while it lasted. And it unleashed my obsession with pens and paint—creating images, leaving marks. I think there was also something in the iconography of Holy Rosary that sparked my fascination with visual representation in all its many forms—from Renaissance paintings to comic books.

As much as the spiritual stuff confused me—and some of the nuns were cruel—I actually thought it might be cool to be an altar boy. My dad must have thought I was nuts, but I signed up to be one. During altar boy training, you got to see where everything was stored in the chapel: the wine, the chalices, the vestments. It felt like secret knowledge—access to some kind of weird force.

One day, I snuck into the chapel, cracked open a box of communion wafers, and ate fifty of them. The nuns had taught us it was the body of Christ. So I figured the more I ate, the more spirit power—*superpower*, really—I'd have. I waited for something to kick in, but nothing happened. I sat there, stunned and disappointed.

I shared my discovery with another kid who was also training to be an altar boy. He snitched, and that ended my would-be altar boy career. That's when I stopped believing in the Catholic mythology the nuns were selling us.

These days, Holy Rosary is a luxury apartment building. Whenever I walk past it now, it feels like I'm having an out-of-body experience.

2

Where they jammin' at?

The first record I ever bought was a 45 of "The Name Game" by Shirley Ellis.

"Shirley, Shirley, bo-birley, banana fanna fo-firley..."

She is practically rapping on that tongue-twister of a song. I played it over and over, memorizing every fun word. The sleeve came with instructions for singing along—everyone seemed to know how.

My mother loved that record, and the first copy we had was actually hers. It got scratched when a ball I was playing with bounced onto the turntable. So she gave me a dollar and sent me around the corner to the record store on Sumner Avenue to get a new one.

Mom loved everything from Billie Holiday to Johnny Hartman to Nancy Wilson to Sarah Vaughan. My dad was into horn and piano players, but she was into the singers. It was amazing to hear her sing along with Dinah Washington or Etta Jones—two of her favorites, and two women she'd hung out with now and then. She could really hold a note, and one of my great regrets is that I never recorded her.

On the more contemporary side, whenever the hottest stuff from

Motown or Stax came on the radio, my mother would give me a quarter to perform the newest dances—the monkey, the hitch hike, the wobble—for her and Doris.

"Come on, Frederick! Do that dance for us!"

I was happy to oblige.

My dad, being so plugged into jazz, never cared for that stuff. But that changed when James Brown started wearing an Afro and released "Say It Loud—I'm Black and I'm Proud." At that moment, for my dad, James Brown became a leader, a voice for Black people. He was no longer the guy with the slick suits and processed hair; he was the guy Who Stood Up.

It didn't hurt that the accounting firm my dad worked for also represented James Brown. When he told me that, I couldn't believe it.

"Wait—really? You *know* James Brown?"

"Yeah," he said. "I met him at the office a couple of times. He spends about a hundred dollars a day."

"What?! *A hundred dollars?!* For real?!" It was the most money ever.

Some of the older teenage Black guys in the community were Five Percenters—a Muslim offshoot—and for whatever reason, the ones we knew were big into rock. That's how I first got exposed to Jimi Hendrix and Janis Joplin. The Beatles were inescapable. And just like I did with Thelonious Monk, I actually tried to get them on the phone. I dialed zero and took it from there. I got switched all the way to some friendly international operators with British accents who were probably getting fifty calls like that a day. I never managed to get through, but the operators were nice to me.

At home, if the radio wasn't on WBAI—where every conversation, like the nightly news, was about the Vietnam War, civil rights, and the rise of activism—it was often tuned to WRVR, the jazz station affiliated with Riverside Church in Upper Manhattan. I have vivid memories of hearing Ed Beach and his show *Just Jazz* on WRVR. He was a total hipster with a massive collection of music and an unreal delivery: "*Just Jazz.* Ed Beach here." He possessed the coolest voice on radio, suave, hip, and intelligent—almost like he was mumbling. My dad listened religiously and recorded a lot of his shows on his reel-to-reel machine, which was how a lot of aficionados collected music back then.

Also big on the radio in our house was Phil Schaap on WKCR, the Columbia University station, where he'd started out as a student DJ. For the birthdays of pivotal jazz figures, Schaap would put on marathon sessions—hours and hours of music celebrating the likes of Louis Armstrong, Count Basie, Charles Mingus, John Coltrane, and, above all, Max Roach and Charlie Parker. Schaap was an awe-inspiring scholar of Bird's career—meticulous, microscopic—and that level of deep, obsessive knowledge earned him my father's lasting respect.

Another DJ who was a major voice in our household was Jocko Henderson, my mom's favorite. Jocko swung between Philly and NYC, where we listened to him on WWRL—"The Big RL," 1600 on the AM dial. He was like an early rapper, long before rap was a thing: "*Eee-tiddly-ock, this is Jock, and I'm back on the scene with the record machine....*" Jocko was the king of rapid-fire jive.

Jocko's on-air partner in crime at WWRL was Frankie "Hollywood" Crocker, a young DJ who then became a star in his own right when he brought Black music to FM radio in a major way as the program director of WBLS. Frankie Crocker rewrote the whole game. Aside from my father, he probably had the biggest influence on me musically growing up. He had the smoothest voice of all time, and he played all the freshest, cutting-edge Black music—soul and funk—from Barry White to Parliament to Stevie Wonder to Earth, Wind & Fire, often interviewing the biggest artists on air. Every day between four and eight p.m., those in the know tuned their radios to Frankie Crocker on BLS.

He didn't follow a Top 40-style playlist like other commercial jocks did. He played what he wanted—and that could mean a David

Bowie cut like "Fame" or Elton John's "Bennie and the Jets," which he helped break in the Black market. He spun the Rolling Stones. Sometimes, out of nowhere, he'd drop Frank Sinatra's "New York, New York" or "My Way." I remember when he played "I Shot the Sheriff" by Eric Clapton—that was a huge record, one I loved instantly. A few months later, he started playing a different version. Same song, but now the guy singing it had a West Indian accent. My friend Frank across the street was Guyanese, so I asked him, "Yo, what's up with that new version of 'I Shot the Sheriff'?" Frank said, "That's the original! It's by Bob Marley. *Rastafari!*"

I was like, "Oh. Who is that?"

Frank told me that Marley had dreadlocks and was a Jamaican Rasta. So I went down to Chin Randy's Caribbean record store on St. Johns Place and bought the Wailers' album *Burnin'*—that's how I got into Bob Marley.

It turned out Marley had been struggling to connect with Black audiences in the United States, even as his international profile was growing. His manager told him, "We gotta get you with Frankie Crocker." And sure enough, Crocker helped break Bob Marley—and the entire genre of reggae—for a whole generation of Black listeners. I would later see Marley perform at Madison Square Garden, opening for the Commodores, in a show hosted by none other than Frankie Crocker.

Other Black stations and DJs would run rapid-fire commercials for "No Money Down!" ghetto furniture or cheap, street-corner wine brands like Thunderbird and Wild Irish Rose. (The streets were littered with the dark-green broken glass from those bottles.) Frankie didn't allow that kind of advertising. He wanted WBLS—"World's Best-Looking Sound!"—to be classier, more cosmopolitan. He brought a new level of sophistication and coolness to the presentation of Black music on the radio. He was a major pioneer, helping to position WBLS as a station not just for Bed-Stuy, Harlem, or the South Bronx, but for the suburbs too.

THE COME UP

Frankie knew that style mattered. Voice mattered. He gave people a sound they could identify with and aspire to. And he was one of the first to popularize the term "rap." "They call me Candy," he'd say in that silky voice of his, "cause my rap is so sweet."

My first concert was Sly and the Family Stone at Madison Square Garden. I was maybe fourteen years old. I went on my own and sat way, way up in the cheap seats, loving every minute of it. But most of my early experiences with live musical phenomena weren't in big arenas; they came from mobile DJs—the guys who first brought us disco.

Before anyone ever thought of Studio 54 or *Saturday Night Fever*, disco was a street thing, a Black and Latin thing. The name came from the discotheques of the 1960s, but the energy was something new. Disco inspired pioneering DJs like Kool Herc and helped lay the foundation for what eventually became hip-hop.

This is how it would go down: On certain warm summer nights in Bed-Stuy, during a quiet moment, you might hear a low rumble in the distance. Your ears would tune in. You'd stop whatever you were doing. "Yo, *did you hear that bass*?" You'd wait, listening for it again. "Yo, *it's a jam!*"

Then you'd round up some other homies—everyone bored with nothing else to do—and follow that trail of sound. Others would be following it too. A chorus would go up: "*Yo, where they jammin' at? Where they jammin' at?*"

The sound might lead you all the way down to St. John's Park, across Atlantic Avenue, more than ten blocks away, where you'd find four hundred people dancing their asses off to a massive sound system tapped into the base of a streetlight for power.

The phenomenon of mobile DJs was a classic example of teenagers creating something to entertain themselves—just like rock 'n' roll had been a generation earlier. I first heard about it from my Aunt Pearl, my mom's younger sister, who lived out in Sheepshead Bay. She was plugged into the world of popular disco DJs who were spinning in hip clubs well before I was ever on the scene. She'd bring me flyers for parties she'd gone to—the same ones I'd later hear promoted on WBLS.

In the summer, some of these big-name DJs would come to the hood for park jams and block parties. Sometimes posters would go up at major intersections or subway stations, and you'd see their names in bold letters: DJ Grandmaster Flowers, Pete DJ Jones, DJ Plummer, Maboya. They were legends, icons—practically gods in the community.

On the appointed day, they would appear out of nowhere. A crew would roll in, set up turntables and sound systems in a neighborhood park, and brand-new sounds would flood the streets. These mobile DJs would entertain eager ghetto kids who didn't have much going on, keeping the party going late into the night. And then, as quickly as they came, they'd be gone.

I went to so many of those jams. I was young, trying to look older, dressing up and practicing being confident and cool, like a proto B-boy, which was all about sending a message: *I'm not to be fucked with*. You had to know how to carry yourself. How to hold a stance that was cool yet tough, ready for whatever. There were always dangerous guys around, and you had to be prepared in case someone stepped to you to take what was yours—your money, your sneakers, your gear, your pride.

At the jams, when I wasn't chasing girls for a dance, I'd stand right up near the front and absorb everything the mobile DJs were doing. That's when I realized that a lot of the kids standing up close weren't just there to dance. They wanted to be DJs themselves. And what those DJs were doing was mesmerizing.

This was before cutting or scratching came into the mix. That came later. What they were doing was mixing—two turntables, a mixer, a killer sound system, and music that never stopped. "Fly, Robin, Fly" by Silver Convention. "Rock Your Baby" by George McCrae. And the biggest of them all: "Love Is the Message" by MFSB. That one—imported from Philly—was *the* Brooklyn party anthem. It spread like wildfire across the borough, then the city. The orchestral breakdown was funky and euphoric, building to a mind-blowing release. Pure joy. Pure ecstasy.

The mobile DJs would take those records—many of which you'd never even hear on the radio—and create extended versions of them on the fly. Seamlessly switching back and forth between the turntables, they kept the party raging for hours.

Flowers was the original Grandmaster. He'd earned the title. He grew up in the Farragut Houses in Brooklyn and was among the first DJs to mix two records, creating long, uninterrupted grooves and overlaying sounds that had never been blended before. Flowers could rock the joint. He made total rhythmic magic—choosing the perfect sequence of records, building tension and energy, and pulling everyone together in a giant hug of agreement and good times.

His system was kicking, with that deep, essential bass. One of the things people always talked about was how many watts a DJ had: "Oh, he got a thousand watts!" "Yo, my man got two thousand!" People would marvel at the quality of the sound just as much as they admired the DJ himself. A lot of folks still had all-in-one hi-fi units at home—those big furniture-like consoles with a TV, radio, and turntable, all pushing out sound through one solitary speaker. Stereo systems were next level, the new kid on the scene. So when Grandmaster Flowers showed up with a rig that had more speakers than you could count—and seven thousand watts of pure, blasting power—minds (and eardrums) were blown.

Brooklyn DJs were famous for their sound—booming, loud, and

crystal clear. The Queens guys had decent sound too. But many of the Bronx guys I heard had the worst-sounding shit. I remember hearing how some Bronx DJs ripped public-address speakers out of the subway—basically using whatever they could get their hands on to cobble systems together, as the Bronx was the city's poorest borough. But here's the thing: To make up for their busted gear, the Bronx DJs would, in time, bring forth radical innovations that would eventually change the entire game. (I later heard that during the blackout of '77, a whole lot of sound equipment was liberated from electronics stores in the Bronx and pressed into service for the cause.)

Because local mobile DJs were becoming popular, everybody wanted to be one. In Bed-Stuy, our neighborhood heroes were Master D (aka DJ Lance) and Frankie D. A friend of mine from Hancock Street named Jeffrey Morrison eventually styled himself DJ Spy. For a while, it seemed like every block had its own wannabe DJ building a rig, chasing sound.

Sometimes there were DJ battles, much like the old battle-of-the-bands competitions my father and his jazz friends used to talk about. I remember one especially wild battle at the 13th Regiment Armory, the giant brick castle at Sumner and Jefferson, around the corner from our house. Four DJs, four ill sound systems: Master D, Frankie D, Maboya, and the Disco Twins—identical twins named Reggie and Robert from Queens who had a mad system that filled the Armory's huge, echoing space.

In the early days, the DJs rarely, if ever, played established clubs. But in the early '70s, as Manhattan's economy struggled, a new wave of disco-party promoters began striking deals with restaurant owners in the city. The idea was simple: Rent out the restaurant after hours, take out the tables and chairs to create a dance floor, and let the promoters keep the door money while sometimes getting a slice of the bar.

Those makeshift discos drew a young, stylish crowd of Black and Latin partygoers from the outer boroughs. Spots like Nemo's, the

THE COME UP

Riverboat Cafe, Super Star Cafeteria, and Nell Gwynn's Tavern—where I went once or twice—were part of that first wave. They all tried to be posh. That meant no sneakers allowed. So if you were a street cat who only had sneakers in your closet—which was true for a lot of us—you stayed home.

The younger, sneaker-wearing crowd stuck with the house parties and outdoor jams. And sartorially speaking, that's where it was really happening: a crazy, ever-changing mix of colors, fabrics, silhouettes, and attitude. It was a visual feast as much as a sonic one. So much swagger on display.

Frankie Crocker would show up at these parties and jams too. The hot underground records that the mobile DJs used to rock the house and shake up the crowd—Frankie would take note and spin them on WBLS. The top DJs were always on the hunt for rare, obscure tracks—cutting-edge stuff that got tested live in the parks, well before it reached the radio, if it ever did. Some of those tracks came from our local Brooklyn hero bands: Crown Heights Affair, B.T. Express, Brass Construction. They were part of what came to be known as the Brooklyn Funk Sound.

Frankie started promoting those very parties and jams on the air: *"Four dollars at the door!"* And with that, the influence of the mobile DJs—and the disco music they spun—began to expand beyond the park jams and the pop-up clubs. Week by week, throughout the '70s, disco kept getting bigger. And Frankie Crocker was right there with it, helping turn this street thing into a full-blown craze.

O ver time, the mobile DJs started slipping a new kind of music into their sets. It was *different*. Real intense tunes with killer breakdowns and a lot of attitude—stuff you'd never heard before.

And when they dropped, you could feel it in the crowd. There was a ripple, a surge of energy.

They'd spin "Apache" by the Incredible Bongo Band, "Seven Minutes of Funk" by the Whole Darn Family, "Take Me to the Mardi Gras" by Bob James, or "Super Sporm" by Captain Sky. All of them had funky, hard-hitting drums and a different, insatiable vibe. The DJs would loop them, smoothly mixing back and forth between records, and the crowd would go crazy. I'd been to enough jams to know that this was some new shit.

I remember going up to a DJ at a park jam and asking, "Yo, what *is* that? What do you call it?"

"Oh, that's the Uptown Sound," he said.

Uptown. Maybe Upper Manhattan, maybe the Bronx. I wasn't sure—I was a Brooklyn kid. But I told one of my homies that we needed to find more of this Uptown Sound, trace it to its source. "Yo, money, let's go up to the Bronx!"

We didn't make it that far. We hopped off the A train at 125th Street, wandered around Harlem asking, "Where they jammin' at?" But most people had no idea what we were talking about. We didn't find the Uptown Sound that day. But something different had arrived. Something new. Something powerful. I couldn't figure out how to connect with it yet. That would happen later.

Graffiti was starting to get heavy—on the trains, on the streets—and by the early 1970s I was seeing mysterious names and numbers all over the A train: Frank 207, Turok 161, SJK 171. In those early days, when I was still dealing with the nuns at Holy Rosary, graffiti was pretty straightforward. A name, or a name and a number. That was it, that was the tag. Magic markers, maybe spray paint. Nothing elaborate.

It felt like a New York adolescent game—the next step up after skelly and Ringolevio. I wanted to play.

As usual, I wanted to know *everything*. Who were these people? Why were they were doing it? How were they were doing it? What did they write with? Who was the best? Those questions led me all the way up to Washington Heights, to Dyckman Street, a good hour on the A train. I'd walk around that hood, snooping for clues, recognizing the same names I'd seen on the train scrawled on walls and subway stations.

The biggest legend of them all was Taki 183, a Greek-American kid who became known as New York's graffiti godfather. What I later learned was that Taki worked as a messenger—he'd get jobs all over the city, and he'd write his name everywhere until "Taki 183" was ubiquitous. Everyone seemed to have heard of Taki 183—*The New York Times* even wrote about him. The "183" turned out to be the street he lived on.

I started putting stuff up here and there, on corners around my own hood. My earliest tags were Bull 99, which I did with my Brooklyn buddy Herb 99, and Showdown 177. I guess I didn't think I could just go with Fred Hancock.

The graffiti wave had started in the '60s, but there's always been graffiti—going all the way back to the ancient world. In the twentieth century, there was Kilroy, the cartoon face with the long nose hanging over a wall, drawn by GIs wherever they went during the Second World War: *Kilroy Was Here*. My dad fought with the 827th Tank Destroyer Battalion, and I like to imagine he spotted a Kilroy or two during his time in Uncle Sam's segregated army in Europe.

After Charlie Parker died in 1955, beatniks and cool cats in New York started writing "Bird Lives" all over town—tiny acts of reverence on walls, lampposts, and subway seats. Then, while Taki was doing his thing in New York, there was Cornbread in Philadelphia—a legendary writer who became the star of early Philly graff. Philly was always close to New York in terms of flavor and culture, and Cornbread and other writers from down there would sometimes come up to New York and tag. Their lettering style was different: long, narrow, slick. We called it Broadway Style, but we probably should have called it Broad Street Style.

Cornbread, it was said, once even tagged a *plane*. Just an amazing character.

Guys like Taki and Cornbread were driven by something more than whatever made the average kid write his name on a wall, or carve it into a tree, or scratch it onto a school desk. There was something deeper—maybe ultimately indefinable—behind what pushed graffiti to become a major form of expression in the '70s, especially in New York City and especially among young people of color.

But I think a lot of it came out of the spirit of rebellion and protest that we'd grown up around as little kids in the '60s. On TV, we saw the endless demonstrations filling streets coast to coast: antiwar protests, civil rights marches, women's rights rallies. That countercultural attitude was still in the air when graffiti blew up—doing your thing, disrespecting authority, shaking up the hierarchy, expressing yourself, pushing back against the Man, the system, all the bullshit that created oppression and ghettoes and tried to keep people down.

In Brooklyn, taggers had their own unique style—flamboyant, dramatic, a kind of John Hancock flair. You'd see tags all along Fulton Street, at Albee Square Mall, on Flatbush Avenue, and at major intersections across the borough. Some tags seemed like they belonged to gangs: Ex-Vandals, Last Survivors, Magic Inc. But these weren't street gangs in the violent-criminal sense. They were crews, united by Krylon and Magic Markers, bonded by creativity and competition. I got into the act and would often tag the name of a clique I ran with, the 113 Hell Cats.

I noticed a couple of the mobile DJs' names showing up on walls too—so there was clearly some kind of connection between this new musical phenomenon in the hood and this new visual eruption. One of those names was Flowers. That overlap between sound and sight became even more obvious one day when I was in the downtown Brooklyn shopping district, checking out a record store on Fulton Street—one of those spots that would play music out front to pull people in.

There were always cool guys hanging out there, sort of dancing to the hottest tunes. I noticed one of them had painted the side of his jeans—something that was a thing for a minute in the '70s. And what was painted down the length of one leg, in bold yellow letters with a red drop shadow, was the word *FLOWERS*. That's when I realized that the Grandmaster and the tagger were one and the same. That moment hit me—an early sign that these cultures were linked, the music and the graffiti.

After Holy Rosary, I got into John Dewey High School, on Avenue X in Gravesend, next to Coney Island. It was a long-ass train ride to get there, well over an hour with a couple of connections—and I always made sure to bring comic books and magazines for the trip. Sometimes it was superhero stuff, sometimes *Mad*, or *Horror Tales*, or *Hot Rod*.

The school was still new then, modern, experimental, and super progressive. It was one of the most desired high schools in New York City—like Brooklyn Tech or Bronx Science—damn near Ivy League level. You had to be smart to get in.

Thing is, my grades at Rosary weren't bad, but I didn't get in. Not at first. I applied and was rejected—though I didn't know that at the time. A few years into my high school career, my mother told me that she had lobbied to get me admitted. She met with the assistant principal and made an impassioned plea on my behalf. And it worked.

Dewey was known for being diverse. In truth, it was mostly white. But my mother wanted me to have the experience of moving through different spaces, meeting and mixing with all kinds of kids. And that's exactly what happened.

It was an interesting experience for me—like it is for most high school kids—navigating among all the different types: the jocks, the party people, the nerds. There were Black kids, Latin kids, Asian kids. There were these kids I always thought of as the sons and daughters of the mob. Real outer-Brooklyn types. Always like, "Fuckin' A!" "Hey, Tony!" "Fuhgeddaboudit!" "The fuck you lookin' at?" Seriously tough, ready-to-rumble guys.

Somehow, I ended up tight with one of them, a kid nicknamed Tomato Face. So I'd kick it with that crew from time to time. I also hung out with the Black party folks who were into the same mobile-DJ disco stuff I was into.

And then there was another group: kids who'd apparently cycled through six hundred schools across the city. Wild, difficult-to-manage hardheads who were apparently smart enough to get into Dewey. They reminded me of some of my more questionable pals in Bed-Stuy. There was some grimy shit going down with that crowd, and at a certain point I thought, *This is not cool.* Some of them were clearly on a path to prison.

By then, I was pretty into smoking weed, and that helped bridge some gaps between the various groups at Dewey. I got cool with all kinds of people, and under the bleachers was where we'd go to light up—usually smoking my dad's weed. One day, my mom found a roach, or maybe some Bambú rolling papers, in my pocket and freaked out.

THE COME UP

My father pulled me aside, talked it through, and the resolution was, "Well, Frederick, if you're going to smoke, do it at *home*."

Black folks had been getting put away for this stuff. Even though my parents thought weed was relatively harmless, they knew there could be a heavy price to pay. I learned to be careful.

I got my nerd on too. Like I had at Holy Rosary, I spent a lot of time in the library, poking around and looking at whatever caught my interest. One of my favorite teachers—social studies—was in charge of one of the school publications, *The Gadfly*, so I started doing illustrations and hanging around that crew. (My father had written funny columns for his unit's newspaper during the war, so maybe it was in the blood.) The white kids who ran *The Gadfly* were super into *National Lampoon*, the off-the-wall humor magazine, so I started picking it up too. I got into writers like Michael O'Donoghue, who went on to help create *Saturday Night Live*. They also turned me on to Robert Crumb's underground comics, which I loved. It was a dynamic mix of kids and interests at Dewey—and looking back, it reflects the person I ultimately became.

I was still very much into anything visual, spending a lot of time with art books and absorbing the different art movements and periods. I would use the student MTA pass they gave us and just go—sometimes cutting school. Free transportation to the Metropolitan Museum of Art! Places like the Met, the Brooklyn Museum, the Guggenheim, and MoMA were wonderlands to me. Like art Disneylands. So I gorged myself in those grand spaces where art lived. Flipping through books and then seeing the real thing in person—that was an intense feeling. I remember being blown away seeing Mondrian's *Broadway Boogie Woogie* at MoMA. It was so modest in size for such a hugely important work of art.

Needing to be around art and wanting to make it. Thinking about artists and their worlds. It was all pivotal. Maybe New York City itself could be an art gallery. A museum of my own.

EVERYBODY'S FLY

One day, most likely in ninth grade, I was sitting in class at Dewey, staring out the window, daydreaming and checking out the Coney Island train yard next door. It's massive—about seventy-five square acres. Graffiti writers love yards like that, where the trains lay when rush hour isn't happening. I got an idea.

I snuck a couple of cans of paint out of shop class and, between periods, slipped out of school, found a hole under the fence, and crawled into the yard. I hit a couple of trains—my name, plus the names of some of my graffiti buddies, like Herb 99 and the 113 Hell Cats. Those were the first trains I ever painted. They ran on the elevated lines up and down Broadway in Bed-Stuy and Williamsburg. Several of my friends back in the hood saw them, and went nuts. *"Yo, that's you, Bull 99! Shit, you did that, Fred!"* The graffiti gave me visibility, and the visibility gave me status. I felt like a celebrity. Talk about positive reinforcement.

I started bombing pretty hard. Graffiti was on my mind day and night. A well-placed wall on a well-traveled corner? In my vandalistic way of thinking, that was something asking to get hit. And hit it I did. I was obsessed. Once I started, there was no stopping.

It's hard to describe the full allure of it, but I think all of us who were drawn to graffiti loved the sheer audacity—the unfiltered rebellion of it. It was a big middle finger raised at any and all who were in charge. It was like, *Catch me if you can, motherfuckers... and I bet you can't!*

Then there was the pure aesthetic fascination. In the '70s, graffiti kept getting bigger, more sophisticated, more colorful. The tags took on weight, shape, shading. Pieces started filling up the entire sides of subway cars. You looked at that and thought, *How do you do that?*

THE COME UP

How much spray paint did it take, and what kind of paint do you need? What kind of techniques?

It was the era of Stay High 149, Super Kool 223, Blade, Dondi, Phase 2—so many others who seemed like gods to me. The first guy I remember doing a really accurate, three-dimensional piece was Flint 707 out of Brooklyn. He hit an F train with it, and it caused a total sensation. Everyone was like, "Oh my God, you gotta see that thing!"

To paint at that level, you needed a shopping bag full of cans—and you had to be super proficient. To get the paint, you'd do what we called racking up: hitting hardware stores and loading up on Krylon and Rust-Oleum. Payment was, let's say, optional. There was an underground network of kids sharing the latest intel: "This store's great," "That one's got this," "That one just put up a cage."

I remember hearing about an artist from the Bronx whose girlfriend would roll into stores with a baby carriage—except there was no baby. Just a hollowed-out compartment where they could rack up mad cans. This was shoplifting on a serious level.

Markers were a huge thing. There was the DriMark marker, with a tip no wider than a quarter inch. The Pilot was thicker—about a half-inch square. Then came the Uniwide, with a broad, flat tip almost an inch and a half wide. Guys started adding two different colors of ink to their refillable Uniwides, which let them create cool, interconnected, multicolored tags. You could actually see the work evolve as these new tools came into the mix. Everyone wanted to know what they were, where they came from, how much they cost. I knew guys who figured out how to make their own jumbo markers using chalkboard erasers—pulling out the felt strips, crafting makeshift cases, soaking them in ink to get thick, gooey, drippy tags. A few even got their hands on that nasty purplish ink supermarkets used to stamp prices on cans. It was messy as all hell.

EVERYBODY'S FLY

The word got out that Pearl Paint on Canal Street in Manhattan was the big art-supply house. They had everything: Uniwides, specialty markers, every kind of ink and paint you could want. When you got off the A train at Canal, you'd see the names of the top writers in the city plastered all over the subway station. The handwriting on the wall literally told you: *This is the place to be.* Soon enough, Pearl Paint got hip to the fact that they'd become graffiti central and started turning kids away. So there'd always be a cluster of us teens hanging around out front, trying to get a grown-up customer to go in and buy for us. While you waited, you'd meet other guys in the graff game doing the same thing. "Hey, man, what you write?" "Yo, I'm so-and-so."

Often, the writers would have their piece books with them—bound sketchbooks used for developing designs and for collecting tags and autographs from the big-name graffiti legends. I wasn't anywhere near that level yet, so I was always blown away when someone pulled out their book. While you were standing around waiting for someone—probably a SoHo artist with an actual loft—to come out of Pearl with your Uniwide, you'd go up to some kid and be like, "Yo, I'm Fred, I write Bull 99, what's up?" And the guy might say, "Hey, I'm Super Kool 223," or "Yo, I'm Dino Nod, Ex-Vandals!" It was like meeting rock stars.

One time I even got to meet the legendary Stay High 149. His "smoker" tag—a stick figure with a joint and a halo, inspired by the one from *The Saint* TV show with Roger Moore—was unmistakable. It always stood out, cutting through the noise of all the other tags. Meeting Stay High was like meeting Michael Jackson. "No shit! That's you, man?" *Okay, wow.*

Sometimes, if you hit it off, a writer might say, "Yeah, man, check out my book." And that might turn into: "Yo, let's hook up. Let's go writing together."

Pearl Paint was a big-time meeting place—where you could connect with guys who hit different trains and worked different layups in the Bronx, Manhattan, Queens. Another famous spot was the Writer's Bench at the 149th Street–Grand Concourse station in the Bronx. A ton of writers would go there just to hang out, watch trains, and meet other writers, getting their black books tagged. That's also where you'd hear that the trains also laid up in tunnels during off-hours.

If you wanted to hit one, you had to get inside the tunnel—walking on the catwalk, with a train maybe two feet in front of your face. Super dark. Super crazy. Someone would always be yelling, "Yo, watch out for the third rail!" That shit was high voltage—six hundred volts of electricity ran through those rails. You touched it, you were gone. Fried. Just thinking back on it now—it's scary shit.

And because trains are always grinding—metal wheels on metal tracks—there was a fine, dark dust everywhere. It coated everything. Doing graff meant being dirty and dusty all the time. Your clothes, your hair, your sneakers—filthy. You'd have paint all over your palms and fingers, and the paint and ink didn't come off easy. Not exactly a great way to impress girls. You just looked a mess—like Pig-Pen from *Peanuts*.

I wasn't trying to be king of the line with loads of burners. But I hit my share—mostly tags inside and out on the A line and some throw-ups here and there: big, soft letters lightly filled in and outlined. We'd just stand at the end of the platforms and tag trains as they came and went, occasionally hopping on for a few stops to hit the insides. I was in some tunnels and layups. I knew the deal. I was learning, trying to improve my skills, trying to find my thing, always remembering that the third rail had six hundred volts that would fry you to a crisp if you touched it.

There were more than a few times I had to haul ass out of a layup in the middle of the night when I saw the beam of a cop's flashlight coming. As time went on, the city went deeper into panic mode over the evil graffiti scourge, a full-on moral crisis about spray paint. But for writers, that only added to the thrill. It was rebellion. It was about being seen. It was hitting back against the powers that be.

I think Norman Mailer was exactly right when he wrote in his essay "The Faith of Graffiti": "You hit your name and maybe something in the whole scheme of the system gives a death rattle."

3

Many will come, but few will be chosen

In the media, Bed-Stuy was often painted as a "bad" neighborhood. The newspapers would call it a slum or "the ghetto." But at its core, Bed-Stuy was—and still is—a middle-class and working-class Black Brooklyn neighborhood. There were those fancy houses in Stuyvesant Heights, kids playing games in the street, families being families.

But New York in the 1970s had a jagged edge. Some of the kids I hung out with in the hood, it didn't turn out so great for them. That was also Bed-Stuy.

Among the various hustles, Black Brooklyn was known for its stickup kids—tough teens who'd rob you of your money or your cool clothes with a knife or a small-caliber pistol. Boosting—shoplifting—was another big hustle. Some folks were into B&E—breaking and entering. There was gambling. The older folk had numbers or policy—a homegrown, illegal lottery you could play for nickels, dimes, or dollars. If your three-digit number was picked, you could win five hundred bucks on a one-dollar bet. That was a major racket. The state eventually snatched it up in the early 1980s when it added numbers games to the New York Lottery.

There was bootlegging too—selling cheap ghetto wine and vodka on Sundays—and the drug thing: weed, cocaine, and heroin. Some guys slipped into that world and never got out. They either OD'd or went to jail, some getting what we called "football numbers," after the numerals on jerseys—25, 34, 40. Whenever somebody got sentenced to a long prison term, you'd hear, "Yo, he got *football numbers.*"

Growing up in the hood, the fascination with hustling was strong. Becoming a doctor, lawyer, professor, or learning a trade—that's what your parents wanted, the American Dream. But for a lot of kids in places like Bed-Stuy, it just wasn't in the cards.

The pull of street money—fast, dirty money—was omnipresent. You'd see guys cruising around in flashy cars like Cadillac Eldorados, stepping out with colorful reptiles on their feet, leather-soled lizard-, gator-, and snakeskin shoes. A lot of those cats had taps on their heels. When they hit the pavement, it was *tap-clack, tap-clack.* They had a particular swagger, a bob and a rhythm to their walk, like a soul song in motion. That was a sound you'd always hear on the sidewalks. These guys weren't working at brokerage firms or doing kids' braces. They were number bankers, drug dealers, gambling-house runners, pimps, con men. Crooks.

One of the most notorious drug dealers of all time, Frank Matthews, used Bed-Stuy as his base. He was a fixture—always zooming up and down our block in one of his big, gaudy cars, like a character out of *SuperFly*. As we heard it, he got his drugs straight from Asia, cut the mob out of the loop, and made a shitload—millions and millions of dollars. I once overheard Doris's boyfriend, who knew what he was talking about, tell my mom that Frank Matthews had so many duffel bags of cash piled up in his stash house you couldn't even see the floor. When he finally got busted, he jumped a $325,000 bail—and disappeared forever.

An old friend of my dad's was a numbers banker—basically the head of a policy racket. One day I overheard him saying to my dad, "Fred, *of course* I'm an outlaw. Look at all the racist ways the law doesn't work for us. Like many people, I've decided to feed myself by taking the law into my hands. That makes me an outlaw. And I'm not talking about a Hollywood Western!" They both laughed. My dad might not have approved, but he understood it.

There were plenty of Black folks who owned legit businesses, drove Continentals or Benzes, and lived well. But then there was the other ilk—guys like Frank Matthews and my father's pal—whose businesses were built on illegal shit, hustling. You could see young people getting sucked into it all the time.

The Blaxploitation films of the 1970s took street-hustler characters and glorified them on the screen: Youngblood Priest, the coke dealer in *SuperFly*; Goldie, the pimp in *The Mack*. And then there were those cheap paperbacks you'd find on revolving wire racks at the corner candy or drug store—like *Pimp: The Story of My Life*, by Iceberg Slim, born Robert Beck, once described as the "most-read Black author." His books were like rap records before rap even existed. They captured the underground hustles of the ghetto so well, they felt like blueprints for guys trying to break into the game. (I actually got to hang out with Iceberg in Los Angeles many years later, toward the end of his life.)

To be a true hustler, you had to apprentice under a senior guy who'd school you. There was no other way into the game, whatever it was. A close friend I grew up with who also attended John Dewey dropped out and started pimping and living in Times Square. Hanging out with him, I got a close-up look at the pimp game, but I was more drawn to the comparatively innocuous hustle of three-card monte known as the "red card." Some of the red card players were also trying to pimp, but when their girls ran off, got busted, or chose another pimp, this was a hustle they fell back on. I learned that game: *"Watch it, chase it, see where I place it. It's always that red, never that black. When you find the red, you get paid on the head. When you find the black, you get nothing back."*

The red card guys had slick banter that never stopped as they worked their sleight of hand con. If an undercover cop was spotted coming up the street, someone would yell, *"Slide 'em up! Slide 'em up!"* and the whole crew would kick the cardboard boxes over and scram out of there with a quickness.

There was an older guy on Hancock Street we called Candy Man. He was in the mix with all kinds of hustles. One warm July night, I took the A train to Times Square and was just hanging out when I saw him cruising down Seventh Avenue in a money-green Lincoln Continental Mark IV, windows down, blasting that William DeVaughn song that goes *Diamond in the back, sunroof top / diggin' the scene with a gangster lean*. Candy Man spotted me and waved me over. "Hey, little Freddy! How's it going, my man?"

He must have known I'd been circling some ill shit—getting curious, hanging around the edges of the game. So I hopped in. We cruised through Manhattan, listening to eight-track soul tapes while he talked that talk.

"I'm gonna tell you something about this game, baby," he said, turning to look me straight in the eye.

I was half expecting him to hand me the keys to the hustle kingdom.

Instead, he said, "Many will come, but few will be chosen."

I was puzzled. Candy Man seemed to be talking about me. But what the hell did he mean? That I would be chosen? Not chosen?

I knew I wasn't a violent guy—I wasn't built for the dangerous

THE COME UP

hustles. But I was getting into some hot water. School wasn't working out. It was senior year at Dewey, and I was tanking hard. I'd had a bunch of visits to the guidance counselor, a bunch of trips to the principal's office—basically for doing fuck shit. Finally, they said, "Look, Fred, you'd better leave, or we'll have to kick you out."

So I left.

That was rough—dropping out with the finish line in sight. When I was a little kid, my mom used to say, "You don't have to be no Einstein. Just do your schoolwork, because you're definitely no dummy." Now she and my dad were extremely—understandably—upset. I felt horrible about it too. Letting them down. Letting myself down. I knew I wasn't a dummy, but I just couldn't get with the structure of school. I wasn't sure which way to turn. So I came up with the genius idea of joining the navy—probably because they had the coolest uniforms of all the service branches. Thankfully, that didn't work out. But everything was suddenly going from bad to worse.

My mother said, "You'd better take your ass upstate, Frederick, and work with Pickles."

Pickles was sort of an uncle, a play uncle, if you will. A family friend about my dad's age. Slick as motor oil—sharp clothes, streetwise. He spoke with a classic New Yawk accent, flavored by hip Black slang and a dash of James Cagney.

We knew he'd been living upstate, in Monticello, working for one of the big Borscht Belt hotels in the Catskills—probably the biggest of them all: Kutsher's Hotel and Country Club, the place later made famous as the setting for *Dirty Dancing*.

I called Pickles and explained the situation. He was cool about it. He just said, "Yeah, come on up, man. I got you, baby." So I took a bus upstate to Monticello and hooked up with Pickles, who plugged me into Kutsher's.

In one swing, I'd managed to find a way to get some cash in my pocket, catch a glimpse of the Borscht Belt while it was still raging, and escape another hot Bed-Stuy summer.

And those sweltering, sticky summers—those were the times when my dad would sometimes boil over. Everybody was hot under the collar when the thermometer was rising and the humidity was pushing 90 percent. Few had air-conditioning, and sometimes crazy shit might erupt on the streets. It was hard to sleep, and when you finally dozed off, you'd be jolted awake by the scream of sirens or the blaring horns from the firehouse at the end of Hancock Street.

My dad and his friends could sense danger in the summer air. "I think Nat's comin'," one of them might say—meaning Nat Turner and his infamous slave rebellion. For my dad, all the brooding over racism and injustice would start to eat him alive. Summer made him unpredictable, irritable, a little erratic. I remember one broiling summer when he'd dragged a speaker over to the front window and bathed Hancock Street in the voice of Billie Holiday and other jazz favorites.

It felt good to be escaping to the country.

I had been lucky enough to spend several summers at a Black sleepaway camp in Farmville, Virginia, called Pine Ridge. I remember hating the idea at first, but once I got there it was heaven: trees, fresh air, a ton of other kids, the whole thing. Kutsher's felt similar, in a way. It was surrounded by mountains and lakes, but this time it was well-off Jewish families on vacation—swimming, golfing, drinking martinis. To me, it was incredible. Super-duper nice. I was grateful my mom thought of it, and grateful Pickles had set it all up.

He connected me with a middle-aged Black guy at the hotel named Jimmy, who told me what was what. There were two jobs available: dishwasher or lobby porter. The porter gig meant wearing a uniform, sweeping up, emptying ashtrays, doing whatever needed to get done. I chose porter. I didn't want to be cooped up in a kitchen all summer.

So I had my uniform—matching dark-green slacks and shirt—my broom, and my dustpan, and I went around keeping the lobby tidy. The ashtrays were the worst, because people would spit in them. They were fucking filthy.

After a few days on the job, I ran into this white kid from Dewey—a guy I was friendly with, someone who had actually been in my homeroom. He was working at Kutsher's too, and he looked sharp in his bellhop uniform: khaki shorts and a white T-shirt with the Kutsher's logo. A definite step up from lobby porter.

He saw me and lit up. "Yo, Freddy! What's up? What are you doing here?"

I was standing there in my ugly green getup, holding my broom and dustpan.

"Well... I'm a lobby porter."

"Man, we're doing this bellhop shit. I gotta get you doing this—it's way better than being a lobby porter, and the tips are great."

It did sound good. You got to greet arriving guests, help with their bags, bring them to their rooms, schmooze them up, collect tips. I'd be great at that.

So my friend put in a word with the boss. "Hey, this kid Fred's a friend of mine. He's great. He should be a bellhop." But deep down, I already knew it wasn't going to happen.

I had noticed it from day one: the bellhops were all white, even though everyone loved to talk about how basketball legend Wilt Chamberlain had once been a bellhop there. The hotel clearly had different jobs earmarked for different races. A lot of the waiters were these handsome Brazilian dudes. People on staff would whisper about how they were eye candy and boy toys for the female clientele. The bellhops were white kids. The lobby porters and dishwashers were mostly Black.

So my friend struck out on getting me a bellhop gig, but somehow I ended up on management's radar. I got invited to work part time in the nightclub, which, in my opinion, was the best place to be at Kutsher's.

I loved it. Helping out behind the bar, preparing garnishes and mixers, mostly just taking in the scene. And what a scene it was—classic, old-school Borscht Belt entertainment. They had big-name stars rolling through: singers like Vic Damone, Jerry Vale, and Mel Tormé, comics like Joan Rivers and Don Rickles, the insult king himself. In earlier times, they even booked jazz legends like Duke Ellington and Louis Armstrong.

This was classic shit. I would see people I had been watching my whole life on *The Tonight Show*. I remember one comic stuffing a sock down his pants and pretending to be Tom Jones. It was like Vegas—but tucked in the middle of nowhere, surrounded by pine trees.

On the weekends, I would head into Monticello to hang with Pickles, usually at a bar on Broadway. He was still slick as ever, full of street energy, a real cool dude. Maybe I shouldn't have been surprised, but it turned out that what Pickles was really doing up there was selling dope.

He said, "Freddy, if your father knew about this.... You better not say nothin'."

He broke the whole shit down for me.

Pickles had worked at Kutsher's for about six months, just long enough to get his operation up and running. Then he left—to deal heroin full time.

THE COME UP

He brought me along on a couple of trips down to Harlem. He would head to 116th Street and buy a few fifty-dollar quarters—each one about a tablespoon's worth. Then he'd cut it to stretch the supply and sell little ten-dollar bags back up in Monticello, mostly to the guys he hung out with at the bar and workers from the hotels.

When we weren't at the bar, he'd take me to the Monticello Raceway—the big harness-racing track up there. He knew the jockeys, knew the angles. He'd tell me it was all fixed and what to bet on.

I was just a fucking kid, and here I was watching all of this go down. It was not exactly the summer my mother—or I—had envisioned.

Meanwhile, there was a weed panic going on. That's when there's no weed available anywhere.

I had run into more guys from Dewey who were spending the summer working at other Borscht Belt resorts—places like Brown's and the Concord—and everyone was looking to buy, but nobody had anything.

A light bulb went off in my head.

That weekend, I went home to visit my parents. While I was there, I talked to one of my dad's friends, who sold me a few ounces of Colombian Gold. I divided it up into nickel bags and brought it back up to Monticello. And just like that, in the tradition of Pickles, I was selling weed and starting to make some money. I thought, *Wow, this is incredible.*

So I came back to the city, grabbed a few more ounces, and repeated the process. Pretty soon I knew I wasn't going to be working at Kutsher's anymore. I moved in with Pickles. I was posted up in Monticello, selling weed.

Then I hatched a plan. I'd head back to Brooklyn for a week around Labor Day, celebrate my birthday, hit the annual West Indian Day parade on Eastern Parkway (a big deal in the hood), pick up like half a pound more weed, then return to Monticello to ride out the fall. The leaves would be turning in the Catskills. It would be beautiful.

I went out and bought myself a little bullshit gold chain. Got my ear pierced for the first time. Copped some suede Clyde Pumas and some fresh wears on Delancey Street. And I had a fat bankroll—a big knot of money wrapped in a rubber band.

It felt really good to be back in Bed-Stuy, seeing my mom and dad, seeing my friends, rolling around like a big wheel. It felt so good I decided to hang around an extra week. A few days before I was planning to head back upstate, my mom dropped some news on me.

"Pickles got arrested."

My heart was beating through my chest.

"What? What happened?"

"We don't know all the details," she said. "But there were drugs involved."

Turns out there had been a sweep in Monticello—a classic buy-and-bust sting operation that had been building for a while. A lot of arrests went down.

Pickles had sold dope to an undercover—which is exactly what I might have done if I had gone back to Monticello when I originally planned.

Pickles got lucky. He didn't get football numbers. He went away for maybe a year. But that was plenty.

I remembered what Candy Man had told me: *"Many will come, but few will be chosen."* Now it sounded like prophecy. I understood that I was not destined to be one of the chosen going in that direction. I'd had my little foray into the game, and the message came through loud and clear. It wasn't for me—and never would be.

I was lucky. I had been given a chance to realize that illegal hustling wasn't my future. What did choose me was what I would eventually do creatively. That's what I was chosen for.

THE COME UP

I didn't know all of that yet. But I knew enough to stay in New York and get my shit together. That fall, I started working on my equivalency diploma from City-As-School. Instead of thinking about nickel bags and hustles, I was back to thinking about art, graffiti, and music—trying to figure out what moves I needed to make to get to a different place

Just like when I was younger, staring at a subway map, tracing the lines and wondering how to get to places I'd never been before.

My next summer job was as a security guard at the massive Woodhull Hospital Medical Center in Brooklyn. The building had recently been constructed—but the city didn't have the money to open it, so it just sat there, empty. I had decided to enroll at Medgar Evers College in the fall of 1978 to study communications. I needed to earn some money.

My assignment was simple: Stand near the sixth-floor elevator, walk up and down a long, deserted corridor once an hour, and check in occasionally on my walkie-talkie.

It was lonely and creepy.

To make those boring shifts go faster, I brought in a pile of used books. One of them was a how-to guide to Super 8 filmmaking. It cracked open something in my brain. Suddenly I was learning about things like the 180-degree rule, persistence of vision, the camera obscura, spatial relationships between characters on-screen.

I started catching myself in everyday situations, thinking, *That would be amazing on film if only I had a camera.* Scenes were composing themselves in front of my eyes. I began to understand the importance of split-second timing, of being in the right place at the right time to capture a moment.

EVERYBODY'S FLY

I had the filmmaking jones now. And studying communications felt like a way to feed it. I started dreaming about being a director, a producer, a camera op—anything that would let me work with moving images and share them with the world.

One morning at the hospital, my supervisor hit me on the walkie-talkie. He said a group of people would be coming to my floor around midday and that I was supposed to show them around. Not that there was much to see. The place was empty, as always. But at least there'd be some people around for once.

Right after lunch, the sixth-floor elevator pinged and the doors slid open. Ten people stepped out. I went along with them as they made their way down the corridor, poking into rooms, taking photos, measuring walls, jotting notes, holding up color chips.

I asked a middle-aged white guy with a Burt Reynolds mustache what was up.

"We're scouting the hospital as a location for a movie," he said.

"What's the movie called?"

"All That Jazz."

I asked what his job was.

"I'm the production designer," he said. His name was Philip Rosenberg—a name I'd remember. He'd end up winning an Oscar for this film. He told me they'd be shooting scenes in the hospital and recreating others on a sound stage.

"Who's directing?" I asked.

"Bob Fosse," he said, nodding toward a guy I recognized from watching Johnny Carson. He'd probably been on the show promoting *Pippin* or *Lenny*, his film about the life of Lenny Bruce.

Then I asked Philip who the cinematographer was. He raised an eyebrow, clearly impressed that I knew the correct term. He pointed toward a guy with a lens hanging around his neck on a lanyard.

"That guy—Vilmos Zsigmond."

THE COME UP

I made a note of the name. Later, I'd find out he was the guy who shot *Deliverance* and *Close Encounters of the Third Kind*.

After about an hour, they left my floor with friendly goodbyes and a round of thanks. I felt dizzy, like I had just stepped out of a dream. My mind was blown: jack shit had happened all summer in that empty hospital—and then, out of nowhere, these film-world heroes showed up, doing preproduction or a tech scout for a major feature film. Exactly the kind of thing I'd been reading about, obsessing over.

It felt like magic. Like a message. A confirmation that being in the right place at the right time wasn't some myth—it was real. Call it luck, kismet, whatever: I was starting to believe that there was a lot of it in the world, and if I kept myself tuned in to the right frequency—open, curious, receptive—I might actually catch some.

Those film guys weren't distant, untouchable names floating by in credit sequences. They were right there, accessible, human, and cool.

Philip Rosenberg actually seemed to enjoy hanging with me, answering my questions. It made the faraway, fairy-dust world I had glimpsed on *Million Dollar Movie* feel attainable. It wasn't reserved for some other type of person. I didn't need to be someone else to get in. I could get there from *here*.

That night, back on Hancock Street, I wrote all of this down in my notebook, sitting in my bedroom with the sounds of Bed-Stuy coming through the window and the summer heat pressing in. I started thinking about chance encounters—how they can come out of nowhere and change everything.

Doors, I realized, aren't always locked. Sometimes you just have to be willing to push them open. And if they are locked, you find a way in anyway—even if you have to kick a little. Or stage a straight-up bum rush. Or sneak in sideways, without anyone noticing.

What mattered most was being ready.

Because to get lucky—to be chosen—you had to be willing.

I was daydreaming about how I might become a visual artist—someone who could bring street graffiti into the art world. I was lit up by the fact that the Pop artists—Andy Warhol, Roy Lichtenstein—had drawn from the same visual language we did: comic books, advertising, big colorful product logos. I loved reading stories about the camaraderie of radical European art movements: the Futurists, the Impressionists, the Surrealists. They felt like gangs, like graffiti crews—groups of artists held together by a common vision.

Having come close to slipping off the edge and getting sucked into the hustle, I was thinking more about the kids in my orbit—graffiti writers and DJs—as the young creatives they really were. They were artists.

And I was starting to think we needed a whole new story about who we were and what we were doing. The media kept painting Black and brown New York City youth as threats to decency and order—crooks, delinquents, menaces. I wanted to change that narrative, to show that what we were building was something else entirely: a vital cultural movement. Loose, wild, and still underground—but powerful.

One day, while browsing through my dad's books and magazines in the cellar, I came across an article about art that quoted the Tuskegee-educated writer and philosopher Albert Murray. He said that for a culture to be complete, it must have its own music, dance, and visual art—an interconnection among three elements. I filed that away.

On Hancock Street, my friend Frank—the guy who'd first put me on to Bob Marley's "I Shot the Sheriff"—had a little basement at his house across the street where we would hang out, smoke weed, listen to records, and shoot the shit. We started calling it our "studio."

Frank had a 35mm camera and was getting into photography; I

was working on my painting. Together, we'd flip through *Interview* and fashion magazines, studying the photos, talking about how we could stage our own shoots. Looking back, I guess we were just two young cats playing around with the idea of being actual *artists*—trying to imagine what it would mean to be part of the art world. How do you make that happen? What would it even look like?

I got a small taste of it when Frank connected me with a shop over at Fulton and Nostrand that sold Santeria candles and needed somebody to design new labels. I came up with a graff-style concept called "Lucky 13." They gave me a hundred bucks for it. My first real piece of commercial art! I kept the candle thing going for a couple of years.

One summer night, Frank and I were chilling on the block with some folks when he said to me, "Hey, I'm working on something in the studio—I want you to check it out."

He handed me the key. I walked over, opened the basement door... and there she was. A beautiful girl, lying nude on a bed, looking like Tyra Banks, playing naughty. I was shocked beyond belief but managed to keep it cool—at least for ten minutes—until Frank walked in, cracking up. He and the girl had totally set me up. They had been doing a kind of boudoir photo session, and this was their idea of a punch line.

Anytime I ran into Frank on the street or got a call from him, it was, "Yo, Fred, come over to the studio!" It always sounded good. The studio was a space we wanted to be in—a space for creativity, camaraderie, and ideas. If we weren't "real" artists yet, at least we could act like it. The basement was our staging ground for figuring shit out.

I talked to Frank all the time about the connections I was seeing between graffiti and the art world. He was always like, *"Oh, yeah!"* If one kid on Hancock Street could see it, I figured maybe others could too.

Frank's older brother Josh seemed to get it. Like Frank, he was a total music head—and a DJ. He had a system set up in their house, and when he got that thing going, the windows rattled. Whenever Josh was working a party, Frank and I would carry records for him and get to watch him work. That was how you got in with any kind of DJ crew—you carried crates. Every DJ had at least five, sometimes ten. Big metal crates packed with albums. It was a heavy lift.

It was through Josh that we finally stepped out beyond the Brooklyn basement house parties and park jams and got a taste of downtown Manhattan—an actual disco, and not just any disco. One of the greatest of all time. He'd been telling us about this new joint, way west in SoHo, on King Street between Hudson and Varick. It was called Paradise Garage. And it was known as a gay club.

The gay thing was pretty new to me. There was a ton of homophobia growing up in a place like Bed-Stuy. You would always hear that there were gay people in Manhattan, especially in the Village—and it was usually followed by some variation of, *"Man, one of them come near me, I'm gonna whip their ass!"*

Bed-Stuy was a fairly comfortable Black neighborhood, but you were still conditioned to expect that jail could be in your future. It just came with the territory—wild cats doing wild shit, getting into trouble, and often getting more than their fair share of justice. *Football numbers.*

And the stories you'd hear about jail—those were the real horror shows. The older heads would talk about guys in prison trying to "take your hood"—meaning your manhood, rape. That was the most feared thing. So you had to be on top of your knuckle game, just in case. Because if you ever ended up in the joint, somebody might try you. And then it was gladiator time, submit or fight.

That logic bled into the streets. You'd hear guys bullshitting, like, *"Yo, them homos get near me, B, I'mma beat them down!"* That was real. That was the mindset. The paranoia about gay people in the hood was connected to that fear of prison, of emasculation, of being made vulnerable. It's an attitude you still encounter today, sadly. And not just in the hood.

But Josh had a different outlook. He was open-minded and led the way. He told us, "Yeah, there's a lot of gay people there—but some hot chicks too. And man, these people *party*! The music, the lights, the sound—everything is all good, it's next level. It's totally cool!"

He said the DJ was a guy named Larry Levan, and that he'd never heard anyone play music the way he did. Frank and I were like, *Let's go!* And so we went.

Discos were the thing in 1978. There were clubs all over. But nothing compared to Paradise Garage. You'd head over to this building on King Street that used to be a parking garage. The block would be dead after hours—except on Friday and Saturday nights, when crowds gathered on that block clamoring to get in.

The Garage was different. For one thing, there was no bar. They didn't want people getting sloppy, drunk, and stupid. And because there was no alcohol, the club wasn't subject to the usual closing-time rules—so the music kept going deep into the next day.

Saturday nights were largely gay; Fridays were mixed.

The lighting, just like Josh told us, was insane. And the sound system—designed by the legendary Richard Long—was state of the art. This was his masterpiece, and he was constantly tweaking it: upping the amplification, adding elements, refining every detail.

There were geometric wooden sound bafflers scattered across the ceiling. Tweeters hung overhead throughout the club. Gigantic bass bottoms anchored each corner. Horns for midrange tones ringed the five-thousand-square-foot dance floor, which was built on a bed of sand and on springs. Richard placed every element in exactly the right spot, and the result was that Paradise Garage became known, rightly, as the place with the best sound in the disco universe.

It was members only, but members were allowed to bring three guests. So we'd hang around outside and ask people if they'd walk us in. Sooner or later, somebody would say, "Okay, come on."

Since the club had once been an actual garage, you entered by walking up a driving ramp. There were lights on either side—like airport runway lights—strobing in sequence up and down. As you approached the front door, you'd hear it: the low, rumbling thump of the sound system, like an approaching subway train, getting louder and louder as you climbed the ramp. At the top, you would pay and go in.

And then—you felt it. This... *vibration*. It was like, *What the hell is this?*

There was a lounge area, a locker area. The hardcore Garage people would change into dancing gear—biker shorts and tank tops for the guys, halter tops, shorts, and tights for the gals. And then you'd reach the main dance floor—pure energy and abandon. Tribal, almost spiritual.

The man responsible for that was Larry Levan himself, the most exalted club DJ of all time. The way he played music—it was mystical. He could build a dozen incredible records into a single long arc of sound, mixing them in a way that brought the entire crowd to a frenzy. It was like what the mobile DJs did back in the parks—but Larry had something deeper. And nobody, not a single park jam anywhere, had a sound system like that.

You could *feel* it: *Oh my god, he's building us up to something.*

And then—boom—it hit.

You had no choice but to let go. People would scream on the dance floor. Some would call out, "Larry!" He might drop Diana Ross's "Love Hangover," which starts slow and midtempo and then shifts uptempo—throbbing wildly, lifting everyone to higher ground. Then he'd bring it back down to catch-your-breath mode, and all these people, soaked in sweat and joy, would finally exhale. Sometimes they'd burst into spontaneous applause, as if they were at a live show. Which, in a way, they were.

Thanks to Larry Levan, the Paradise Garage wasn't just a club. For many, it was a transformational experience. The entire rave and EDM scenes that blew up decades later—you can trace a straight line back to Larry, spinning records at the Garage.

There was a back room, a kind of a cool-out area, where you'd find pitchers of fresh juice, bowls of orange slices, and jugs of ice water. In another chill-out room, they screened cult and sci-fi films. You might not catch all the dialogue over the thumping sound system, but the vibe was clear: *This is cool. This is downtown.*

The Garage might have been mainly a gay club, but it was great for meeting girls. In fact, some of the most incredible women I'd ever seen were there on Friday nights. Gay men, it must be said, tend to have hot female friends. At the Garage, when you danced up close—pelvic winding and grinding, as you do—they'd quickly figure out you were straight. So I met and had big fun with some fantastic women there. It was like an inside secret: The club's gay reputation kept most of the male wolves away, but we knew the hotties were ready to play. I'd had a girlfriend for a while, a great girl from Trinidad, but the Paradise Garage opened me up to new horizons.

That extended to substances too. It felt essential to be high on something at the Garage. I had already experimented with LSD—Orange Sunshine, to be exact—back at Dewey. That was *real* acid, the kind that lasted for hours and hours. At the Garage, it was mostly weed, uppers, and psychedelics like shrooms. The first time I ever did mescaline was at the Garage. Later, my first time with MDMA—Ecstasy—was at the Garage. And since we're talking about the late 1970s into the '80s, there was always some blow going around.

I can't tell you what Josh was taking at the Paradise Garage, but I will always be grateful to him for bringing me into that world. Later on, he fell into one of the biggest hazards of growing up in the hood. He gave the coke trade a try. He went down to Haiti on a cocaine mission and was never seen or heard from again; he'd clearly been murdered down there. His older brother, so I heard, also tried his hand at dealing. He got busted and went away for something like twenty years. *Football numbers.*

Their brother Frank, my studio buddy, always kept it clean, as did their younger brother Mark. When I later started making moves in the art scene, I was always trying to get Frank involved, to be part of that journey with me. But he wouldn't come along. I knew there was a lot holding back guys from the hood like Frank—societally, politically, and psychologically. I had always been looking to bust out, push back, go further. But not everyone was equipped for that, even those talented enough to make a real go of it.

Few will be chosen. So Frank preferred to kick it in the hood, doing his thing as I began to make my moves.

4

Fuck it, let's move this to galleries

Most graffiti was, to put it plainly, teenage rebellion and vandalism. But everywhere you looked, innovations of style and structure were emerging—turning a lot of kids who weren't even thinking about being artists into artists. (Same with the creators of the Uptown Sound: They didn't think of themselves as musicians, even though they were making something brand-new and uniquely their own.)

In terms of sheer expressiveness and impeccable technique, there was one guy who hit the radar of everybody in the graff game. That was Lee.

He was a standout in the super-impactful Fabulous 5 crew, along with Slug, Doc, Mono, and Slave—legends who worked the IRT #5 Lexington line and painted whole cars. One of Lee's most famous murals stretched across an entire train car: A sunny landscape that said "HEAVEN IS LIFE" in huge block letters, featuring a character who looked like Jesus himself. Its companion piece, "EARTH IS HELL," was equally powerful. Another one of his classics was a *Soul Train* mural, with a funky locomotive chugging across the side of a car. The second you saw it, "TSOP," the *Soul Train* theme, would start looping in your head.

Lee's work just popped. It made your eyeballs dance—but it also made you think.

The Fabulous 5 even painted an entire ten-car train, an insane achievement that landed them on the cover of *The Village Voice*. Beyond the skill and vision, Lee had big-time ambition. He was always trying to top himself, always trying to stay a step ahead. He was the maestro.

Around the time I started at Medgar Evers, I heard people talking about a Lee piece that had shown up on the Lower East Side. You had to see it.

It turned out to be a huge mural, stretching across the full length of a handball court in the playground of Corlears Junior High 56, on Henry Street. It featured Howard the Duck, the Marvel Comics misfit, dressed in his trademark blue blazer and polka-dot tie, perched on the rim of a garbage can, holding the lid like a shield. Behind him loomed a massive, red, amoeba-like splotch filled with stars and planets—and jagged purple lettering that read "LEE."

The piece exploded with color and form. The shading was intricate, the lines masterful. It was the most vivid and dynamic example of graffiti I had ever seen. And because it was stationary, you didn't have to chase it like a passing subway train—you could just go visit it, like a public sculpture or a fresco.

As with many of Lee's pieces, he tucked a tribute to "Mom" into the composition. And in the upper-left corner, he added a line that would become legendary: "Graffiti is a art and if art is a crime, then let God forgive all."

It was a triumphant piece—nothing less than a perfect, giant Pop Art painting. I remember thinking, *That's another level of graffiti.* Lee had figured out how to move from the long horizontal canvas of a New York City subway car—about ten by sixty feet—to the towering, rectangular expanse of a handball court, something like twenty by thirty feet. The effect was monumental.

The energy of the piece reminded me of great Mexican muralists I was digging at the time—Siqueiros, Orozco, and Rivera. Rivera in particular felt like a badass kindred spirit: The way he tried to slip Lenin into his Rockefeller Center mural struck me as bold. His murals spoke directly to the people, defied authority, and championed the poor against the forces that oppressed them. Lee, to me, embodied that same rebel spirit.

I thought that if I could just get with this kid—with his insane skill level—and talk to him, maybe we could lay the foundations for a new kind of art movement. I knew he'd be into the ideas I was forming about graffiti's place in the larger story of art.

So I decided to hunt him down.

The thing was, he wasn't just the most visionary guy doing graffiti—he was also the one most wanted by the MTA's antigraffiti squad, led by two cops known on the street as Hickey and Ski. Which meant Lee operated deep in the shadows, by necessity.

About eight years earlier, Mayor John Lindsay had declared a "War on Graffiti." In 1976, Mayor Abraham Beame poured $20 million into buffing subway cars—a toxic chemical cleaning process that wiped away graffiti. Now it was Ed Koch time. In the years ahead, the crackdown would escalate: Koch talked about unleashing dogs—and even wolves—in the layups and surrounding train yards with razor wire to keep people like me and Lee out. There were furious antigraffiti editorials in *The New York Times*.

Outside our immediate community, no one saw graffiti writers with any respect. There were many white kids doing it, but we were predominantly Black and brown, and our art was treated as a stain, a symbol that the city had lost control. The heat was on, and Lee was in the crosshairs. I even remember a wanted poster going around with a sketch of his face. This was not a person who wanted to be seen or to be found. I had no idea where to start looking.

Then one day I got lucky. I was walking around the Lower East Side when I saw a big LEE piece on the wall of the J.B.J. Pet Shop, a spot on the corner of Eldridge and Houston that sold scooters and minibikes alongside birds and fish. I stepped inside and asked the owner, John, who the artist was. He told me the guy's name was Lee Quiñones. John said he was a teenager, that he sometimes worked in the shop, and that he went to high school around the corner, at Forsyth and Stanton.

I walked over there. I was in one of my usual looks—trench coat, sunglasses, brimmed hat—like a character out of *The Maltese Falcon* or *The Big Sleep*. I was borrowing half this shit from my dad's closet and putting it together in a style that was a little bebop, a little Humphrey Bogart, a little New Wave, with the skinny ties.

I walked straight into Lee's school, went to the office, and said, "I'm trying to locate a student named Lee Quiñones to talk about an art project." They sent me to a classroom. I knocked, a teacher came out, and after I gave my pitch he told me I could wait and talk with Lee after class.

So I stood out in the hallway. A little while later, the class emptied out, and the teacher and Lee were the last to leave. "Yo, Lee!" I said. He looked scared shitless, like I was a cop coming to bust him.

He was cautious with me at first, understandably. But I could tell right away he was sharp: observant, aware, and very smart. He had a great sense of humor, and after he realized that I wasn't there to arrest him, he let out a huge laugh. It was impossible not to love Lee.

He told me he was born in Puerto Rico and raised on the Lower East Side, doing graffiti for about four years. Howard the Duck, he explained, was his mascot, his alter ego—loud and outrageous, the opposite of how Lee moved: stealth, shadows, one step ahead. If Howard was a renegade, graffiti-ready version of Donald Duck, Lee was the ultimate graffiti renegade.

I got a master class in painting from Lee. He knew everything backward and forward, inside and out. He taught me about paint, technique, color. I remember him explaining the virtues of Rust-Oleum, which had built-in rust protection and more pigment. If you did a piece with Rust-Oleum and it went through the buff, more of it would survive. Other brands would wash away easier. Nobody painted better than Lee, and here I was, learning from the best.

While Lee schooled me on technique, I gave him a crash course on art history, an earful about the stuff I was obsessive over: Pop Art, museums, comic books, graphics. I told him how I'd fallen in love with Warhol and his Campbell's Soup cans, with Lichtenstein and his Ben-Day dots. I couldn't stop thinking about how Pop and graffiti were coming from a similar place. I brought a couple of my art books to show him, and he instantly understood what I was laying down—that we, the graffiti writers of the 1970s, were looking at comics and soapbox ads with bright colors just like the Pop artists of the 1960s had been.

I went even deeper: the Futurists, Dada, the old art gangs that were all about rebellion. Lee hadn't heard of those movements, but the moment I laid it out, he got it. The blueprint I was sketching made total sense to him: we could take this movement—our movement—and push it somewhere new, somewhere bigger. We could turn the art world on its head. All that '70s conceptual art felt dry to me, overly academic and corny. What was needed was rhythm, color, urgency. And it was already here—in New York graffiti. This was an art-making movement that was sprouting straight up from the street, not from the art schools.

The more we talked, the more aligned we became. Lee said he

wanted the trains to be like a rolling MoMA—an ever-changing museum open to the public, twenty-four seven.

Another thing: Lee and I were both tired of being seen as juvenile delinquents, vandals, criminals. I was especially sensitive to that perception now that I was in college. It mattered deeply to me that no one define what we were doing as "primitive," "self-taught," "outsider," or "folk art"—the usual terms used to describe artists of color who hadn't come through the art-school system. We weren't hobbyists or anomalies. We were artists. So we said: Let's move this into the galleries, into spaces where people can appreciate the power of what we're doing.

Lee introduced me to the other members of the Fabulous 5. They were stepping away from the scene, basically retiring, but I wanted to connect and share my ideas—about how we could take the street energy of graffiti and the legacy of their crew into a new arena. I met Mono, Doc, and Slave, all original members. (It turned out that Slave was from Brooklyn.) I also got on the phone with the group's founder, Slug, or Dirty Slug, one of the earliest whole-car painters. He was moving on too, but he liked what I had to say. He gave me his blessing to carry the Fabulous 5 tradition forward with Lee into new realms.

So I became Fred Fab 5. Or Fab 5 Fred. And soon enough, Fab 5 Freddy.

Shit was popping. You could feel it in the air.

That fall, I was talking with Lee about the Uptown Sound. I had a few party tapes, and I figured he would love them as much as I did. "Yo, money, have you heard any of this new music?" I asked, hitting play. As the beats kicked in, I gave him the rundown: how the mobile DJs had paved the way, how MCs were now getting up there doing their thing, spitting out rhymes to keep the party going. And how guys uptown—like this one DJ, Grandmaster Flash—were taking the whole thing to another level.

Lee lit up. "Oh yeah! There's a local guy around here bringing out his sound system for jams in the park. And I've heard about Flash from one of the graff dudes I know. He's really into it."

That's when Lee introduced me to this friend of his named Caz who had an actual Flash tape. This was before the Furious Five; at that point, Flash was rolling with the Furious Four. The sound quality was terrible, like it had been dubbed numerous times, but what I heard blew my mind: There was so much going on—it was like nothing I'd ever heard. I had a million questions. *How the hell is he doing this?* This, right here, was the coolest thing I'd ever encountered.

Then came the kicker: Flash was going to be spinning at a party right in the Smith Houses, the projects where Lee lived on the Lower East Side. Lee showed me the flyer. I had spent a few years chasing the Uptown Sound, and here it was, right in front of me.

The jam, as I recall it, took place in the community center at the Smith Houses—a gym, basically, still thick with the smell of sweat from pickup games and practices. And then Flash and his crew walked in. I still remember what they were wearing. Each guy was decked out head to toe in a single color: red Lee jeans, red mock neck shirt, red Kangol hat (the bell-shaped type LL Cool J would later popularize), and red British Walker brand shoes. Blue, green, yellow—each member of the crew had his own full-color look. Flash himself was in all black. They looked cool enough to freeze hot water, like some futuristic street gang out of a comic book. A whole new style, very street and of the moment.

And then they started. Flash was propelling everything forward from behind the twin turntables while the MCs rapped about how great he was. Precise, fast, and focused, he moved from one turntable to the other, snapping the mixer switch back and forth, changing one record and smoothly mixing it in, then the other—never missing a beat, keeping it steady for his MCs to rap. I can't remember all the records he was weaving together that night, but it was stuff like "Take Me to the Mardi Gras" by Bob James, "Son of Scorpio" by Dennis Coffey, "It's Just Begun" by the Jimmy Castor Bunch, "Last Night Changed It All" by Esther Williams, "I Can't Stop" by John Davis and the Monster Orchestra. Flash—and other DJs like him—were always hunting for records with those perfect drum breaks, the ones that lit up a party. They'd even soak and peel the labels off to guard their secrets. This was years before breakbeat compilations would let the cat out of the bag.

Watching Flash spin only deepened the mystery. Lee and I were like, "Oh man, look at this guy!" Seeing Grandmaster Flash in 1978 was like watching a mad scientist at work. You could tell he had an engineer's brain. He had a whole process down, and he seemed to have invented it. Every move was specific, fast, and precise. He was obsessed, clearly, with getting everything right. And he got it right. The way Flash moved on the turntables was freaking amazing. It was art, science, and magic—it was the future.

Flash had been on a quest to find the right turntable that would let him extend the breakbeat seamlessly—the needle-drop thing that Kool Herc had been chasing when he started doubling records at parties at 1520 Sedgwick Avenue, then the Hevalo club in the Bronx. The question was how to keep that beat going and going in perfect, seamless, rhythmic sync. Flash ran through the available gear: Numark, Gemini, then Pioneer and Panasonic turntables, all belt drives that weren't fast or precise enough. Then came the Technics SL-23. It was a direct-drive turntable, the precursor to the now-legendary Technics SL-1200, and it changed everything, becoming a kind of gold standard among DJs. Flash made that turntable do unprecedented things. Thanks to the SL-23's drive, when Flash would manually release a record, it would be instantly on beat—it got up to speed that fast. Unlike other turntable mechanisms, there was no lag, no drag, just precision.

THE COME UP

The innovations didn't stop there. Factory turntables came with rubber slipmats that caused too much drag. Flash made his own out of felt, cutting it to the size of a twelve-inch LP and starching it stiff so the record would glide. He called it a "wafer." That invention alone changed the game. He scouted endlessly for the perfect needles, hunted for rare breakbeats on old and obscure records like buried treasure. And when he got his hands on a Vox V829 Percussion King—the original solid-state analog beatbox with individual buttons for kick, snare, bongo—he figured out how to drop drum hits live, in real time, right into the mix. The crowd would lose its mind. He had figured out how to create breakbeats on the fly. His MCs had a special buildup to the moment, rapping, *"It won't be long till everybody's knowing that Flash is on the beatbox,"* and he'd begin to tap out digital drumbeats to the crowd's delight. Grandmaster Flash wasn't just a DJ. He was a one-man R&D lab for a sound that was beginning to be called "rap."

Between sets, I walked up to one of the MCs—Melle Mel, from the Furious Four, who would later also crown himself Grandmaster. I said, "Yo, man, what's up?" I told him I had been listening to their party tapes and tracking this Uptown Sound for a few years. I was like, "Hey, are you aware of how big this thing can be? You guys need to put out a record!"

He looked at me like I was crazy. "Yo, who would buy it?"

It was a legit question—there was no such thing as a rap record.

"Well, the people coming to these parties, to start," I said.

He just shrugged. This was clearly not about selling a bunch of records. It was about doing it yourself, making a name, having a good time, and getting with the fly young ladies. The couple hundred bucks they might each make at one of these weekend jams—that was actually real money for teenagers still living at home.

That night at Smith Houses lit a fire. Every time I left one of those parties, I'd get handed four or five flyers for upcoming events—guys posted up outside making their own kind of hustle. Those flyers connected the dots: where you needed to go, who the featured acts were, what was what, and when it was happening. They had wild lettering, eye-catching imagery, a whole aesthetic. (A lot of them are collector's items now.) Names popped off the paper: DJ Ed La Rock, Lovebug Starski, Mean Gene, Grand Wizzard Theodore and the Fantastic Five, Sonny Gee, Doug E. Fresh, and the occasional mobile-disco veteran like Pete DJ Jones. The venues were all over the Bronx and Upper Manhattan—the Police Athletic League at 183rd and Webster, Evander Childs High School, the T-Connection, the Ecstasy Garage, the Celebrity Club, Harlem World, and the Audubon Ballroom, where Malcolm X was assassinated. The admission prices were two bucks, maybe three or four. *Oh my God, that's all it costs?*

Flash's manager, Ray Chandler—a six-foot-four ex-cop with presence—was there too. I got his number, got a couple others. I was now tapped into the scene.

At Medgar Evers, I was more or less hanging on. Being an alleged communications major meant I had license to indulge my real interests, so I spent as much time as I could thinking and talking about music, art, and filmmaking. Maybe those things could connect somehow. As much as I enjoyed learning, I was starting to feel that old Dewey dread creeping back in. I even wrote on the cover of one of my notebooks: SCHOOL OF HARD KNOCKS.

I filled that notebook with thoughts on television and film... and radio. The best part of Medgar Evers was the launch of its college radio station, WMEC, a legit FM signal you could hear citywide. I developed a show called *Business Briefs*, focused on small business and opportunities in the hood. But my bread and butter was another program I cohosted with my friend Michael Pilgrim—a cool Caribbean guy—

called *The People's Beat*. It was all reggae, dancehall, and dub: Dillinger, Burning Spear, Big Youth, King Tubby, U-Roy, and Bob Marley.

My tastes were expanding. Because of my interest in Pop Art and Andy Warhol, I became a religious reader of *Interview* magazine. At the back of every issue there was a music column called "Glenn O'Brien's Beat." Glenn O'Brien wrote about everything cutting edge and cool and contemporary—punk, New Wave, funk, disco, and dancehall reggae. His writing was passionate, informative, funny. And totally accessible.

He also had a way of tying it all together—music, art, fashion, politics. For a young kid trying to connect the dots between seemingly separate scenes, this was a revelation. *Interview* became a major window into the whole downtown New York scene: the music, art, and culture that was not being discussed in the mainstream but was shaping the future. I was getting some serious lowdown.

I went out and bought some of the records Glenn wrote about, like Bob Marley's *Punky Reggae Party*. I was like, *I really dig this*. I'd already gotten hip to Marley thanks to my neighbor, and here was another angle—this bridge between reggae and the punk stuff I'd been curious about. Thanks to Glenn, I was getting into Brian Eno and the Clash, Culture, and the B-52s. I was locked in, hunting down new sounds. "Glenn O'Brien's Beat" was shaping my musical taste the same way Frankie Crocker had done on WBLS.

Glenn's knowledge of reggae and dancehall was especially deep, and because he seemed so genuinely passionate, I figured he might come out to Brooklyn and be a guest on *The People's Beat*. I cold-called *Interview*, somehow got connected to Glenn, and told him what we were up to at the station. He was into it—and he came out to do the show. (I'd also schemed to get Peter Tosh to come on air, but that didn't pan out.)

I had a ton of questions for Glenn, like, "What is it about your writing, your criticism, if you will, that makes it so different from everything else out there?" Glenn said, "Well, Fred, maybe it's that I only write about what I like." Most critics, like the ones at *The New York Times* or *Rolling Stone*, reviewed whatever came out, whether they liked it or not.

We talked about how he'd grown up in Cleveland, a Catholic school kid like me, and ended up at Georgetown, where he and Bob Colacello had been tapped to help run *Interview*. He told me what the magazine was like in its early days, a true underground publication about underground artists and filmmakers. He shared stories from the Factory—characters like Jack Smith, who acted, did photography, and made experimental films, always walking the line between genius and madness. We went deep on reggae. Glenn was a real fan: Trinity, Dillinger, Dennis Brown, U-Roy, Lee "Scratch" Perry, all of it.

It was an eye-opening conversation. After the show ended and I gave our sign-off—"You have been listening to... *The People's Beat*"—I walked Glenn back to the subway so he could head home to Manhattan. On the way, I started sharing some of the ideas I'd been kicking around: "Hey, I do graffiti and I think it should be treated like a form of art." "There's this new kind of music in the Bronx where they rap over the rhythm parts of hot tunes." I was riffing about how graffiti, rap, and punk shared a rebellious spirit, all of it bubbling up off the radar, straight from the streets.

Glenn listened. "Oh man, that sounds great," he said. "In a couple of months, I'm starting this public-access TV show on Manhattan cable. You should come on and talk about all of this."

Cable was new back then, something I'd only vaguely heard about—mostly that you could get away with nudity and cursing. It sounded exciting. "Yeah," Glenn said, "I'm going to have this show, and I'd like you to be a guest."

I was like, *Yo!* because TV and film had been on my mind constantly. I was always talking about the production side of things. Lee would laugh and say if we ever stumbled across a film crew on the street, I'd be the guy rolling up to ask: "What are you working on? Who's the director? You shooting on sixteen or thirty-five millimeter?"

THE COME UP

So I said to Glenn, "Hey, I'd like to be a cameraman on your show!"
"Have you ever done anything like that before, Fred?"
"No."
"Well, I couldn't have you be a cameraman then."
No harm in asking.

The aesthetic of New Wave was beginning to define itself—growing out of punk, which had been the dominant force. Punk got the big headlines: the bands, the music, the safety pins, the ripped-up clothes, performers spitting onstage and fans spitting back at them. All that shit was happening. I was picking up on it through Glenn's *Interview* columns, for sure, but also from the wide world—TV, radio, *The Village Voice*. Hard news stories in *The New York Times*. It was the zeitgeist.

That little store in Bed-Stuy, The Snowball, where we got snow cones in the summer, always had a rack of weird-looking magazines—punk zines with wild covers. I figured they must have been dropped off by mistake. I remember thumbing through one and being like, *What the heck is this? Who are these people?* So I began to read, and that was what first got me hip to the New York Dolls, the Ramones, the Sex Pistols, and the Clash—beyond all the freakout headlines in the mainstream press and the tabloids. Let's not forget: Punk was hyped up as the end of Western civilization. Grown-ups were freaking out, panicking. So obviously I was drawn to it.

The punk bands looked wild. I had always been a Stones fan—*Gimme Shelter* was my favorite documentary film. Of course I knew the Who, smashing their equipment onstage, and the Beatles. The punk movement felt like a return to what those bands were like in the beginning—raw, loud, and fun. Short songs, fast songs.

I was starting to learn about the new bands; their names were insane, like the Sic Fucks and Dead Boys. *The Village Voice* was full of ads for shows at CBGB, Hurrah, Max's Kansas City, and a million other hole-in-the-wall joints. Night after night of nonstop music, with bands from around the world and from right down the street. A lot of the bands would do their own wheat pasting—slapping up posters all over the city. Posters *everywhere*, every intersection in Lower Manhattan. It was graffiti-esque.

There was a do-it-yourself vibe to punk that reminded me of the mobile DJs and this rap thing that was going down. In my mind, they were two sides of the same coin: 1970s urban youth going against the grain, inventing their own culture, creating their own fun, responding to the world as it was.

I would take the A train to West Fourth Street in the Village and pick up vinyl at Bleecker Bob's on MacDougal, just off Eighth Street. That's where I bought my first punk records—Suicide, Sex Pistols, Richard Hell and the Voidoids. When I first heard Hell's "Blank Generation," I thought, *This is genius, a great song!* I picked up a copy of "Sperm Bank Baby," by the LA punks Black Randy and the Metrosquad, and cracked up every time I played it: *"Sperm bank baby, lookin' for my dad / Sperm bank baby, lonely and mad."*

Bleecker Bob himself was a trip, an only-in-New York character, rude as hell to every customer. "What do you want? I told you, it's over there! Go get it!" You'd be like, *What a character!* But he always seemed to have what you were looking for.

I had started going out to shows. CBGB was raging. I remember seeing the Cramps there, with James Chance and the Contortions opening. James Chance was notorious for punching people in the audience—starting fights mid-show was part of the whole routine. That night, he hit a guy from a Brooklyn band; I think they were called Straight Edge—hardcore outer-borough dudes who did *not* play. They beat the shit out of him, real quick. James got right back onstage, bloody nose dripping and all, and finished the set. I was like, *Holy shit, who is this guy?*

I loved the Cramps, with their psycho-R&B, rockabilly-horror-movie aesthetic. When the lead singer, Lux Interior, came onstage, it was literally kind of scary. That was a revelation: *Wait a minute, a band can scare you?* Yes, that was part of the weird magic of it: *This shit is intense.*

I felt a bit like a Black secret agent on a mission, since the crowd at CB's and most of the other punk clubs was blindingly white. But I'll never forget the first time I went into the bathroom at CBGB: graffiti was *everywhere*—literally everywhere—on the walls, on the mirrors, even *inside* the freakin' toilet. I had this flash of recognition, a major moment of vindication: *Yes! There* is *a connection here between the aesthetics and feel of punk and the rambunctious energy of hood culture.*

There were other connections, synergies. The Specials came onto the scene. They were a killer English band, with Black and white members, putting a punk spin on ska, the musical forerunner to reggae. The first Specials album pushed me to dig deeper into ska and start filing those records alongside my reggae and dub albums. The Specials also got points for perfecting the two-tone, rude-boy style—sharp black suits, porkpie hats, thin neckties. It was not unlike the jazz-inspired vibe I was already rocking myself.

When I saw Grandmaster Flash at jams, I'd watch what he was doing with vinyl and think, "Man, that's punk." The energy he brought, the way he handled the turntables—*Yo, money, you're not supposed to do that!* Putting your fingers and hands all over the vinyl? *Criminal!*

The cardinal rule of owning records was: *Don't ever touch those grooves!* Vinyl was precious. But Flash was like, *I don't care. I'm doing this. Are you with me?* He was breaking all the rules, which was the most punk thing you could do.

Rap and punk: They were both so wrong they were right.

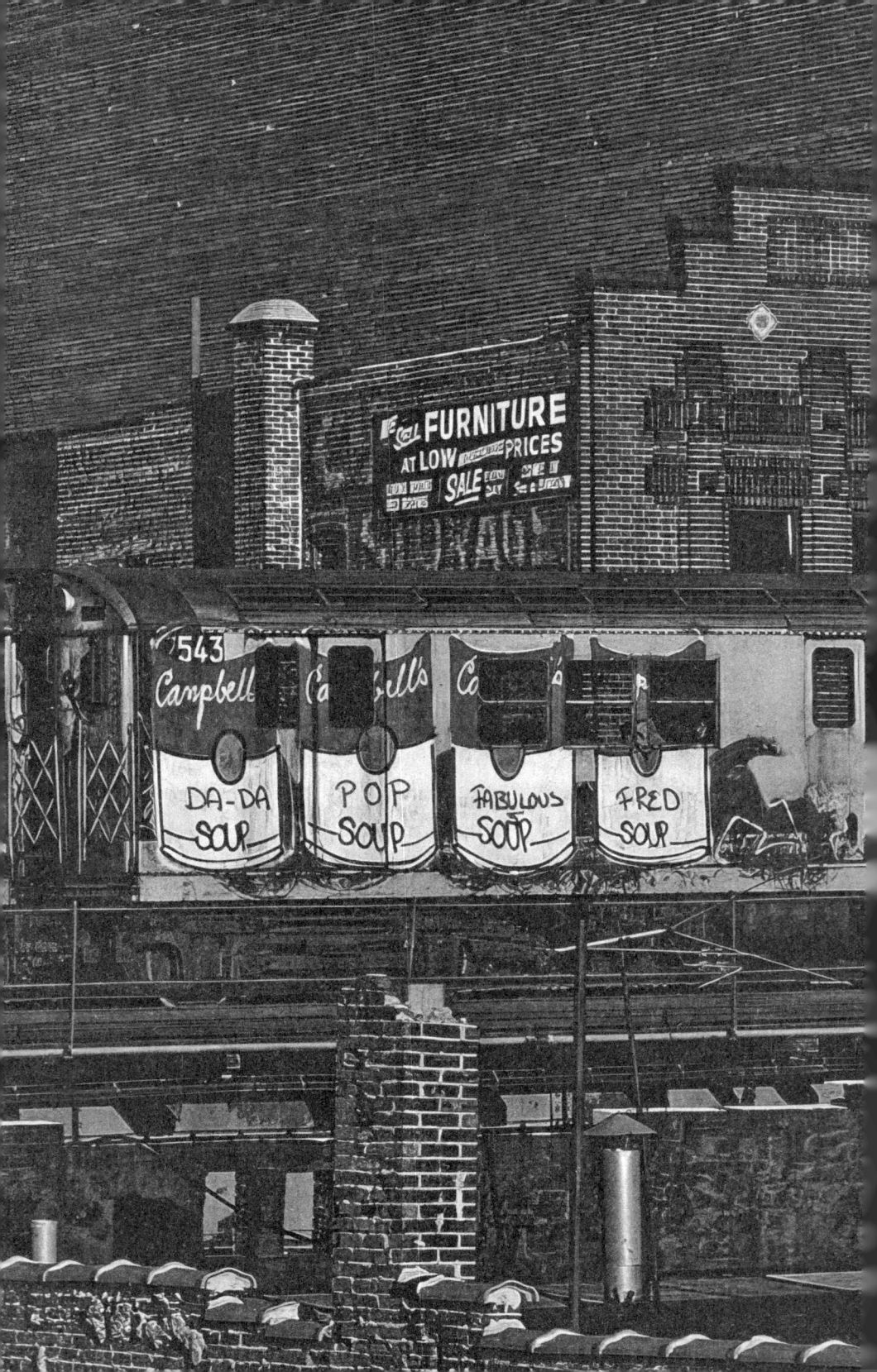

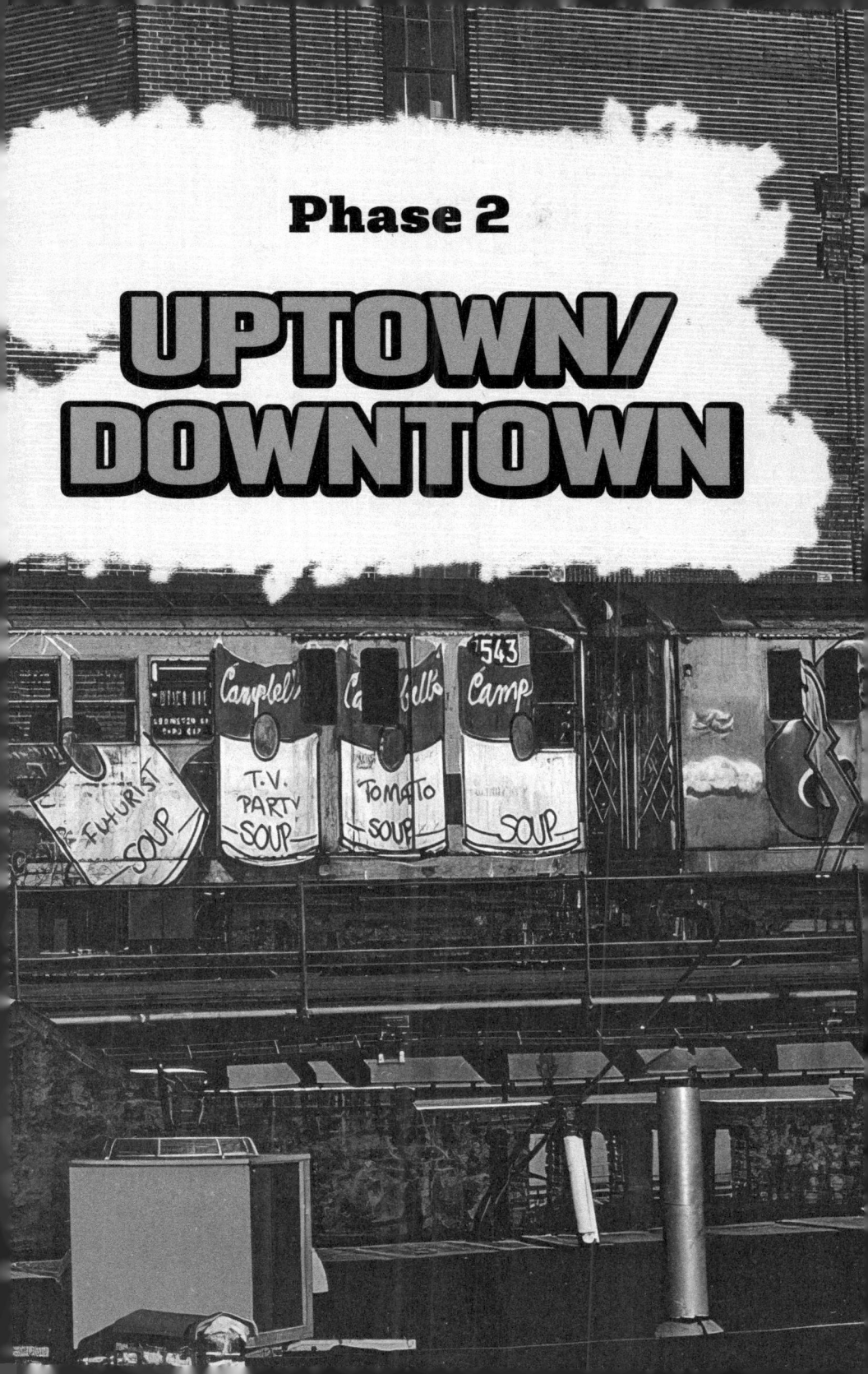

5

Be resolute, fear no sacrifice, and surmount every difficulty

Glenn called me up. His late-night cable-access show on Manhattan Cable Television was going to be called *Glenn O'Brien's TV Party*, and it was set to debut right around Christmas. He was cohosting it with Chris Stein from Blondie. "I want you to come on and talk about graffiti and rap music," he said, "or whatever else you feel like talking about." The show would broadcast live from ETC Studios (short for Experimental Television Center) at 110 East Twenty-Third Street, just off Park Avenue. Glenn told me to meet him and the crew at eight thirty, across the street at the Blarney Stone bar for a preshow hang. We would go on air, live, at ten. I was like, *Wow... TV!*

On the appointed Tuesday night, after a few cheap drinks, we made our way across the street. The studio was tiny, and the set was bare bones. A few director's chairs for the hosts and guests. Behind them, Glenn had pinned up pictures of Lenin, Mao, and Marx. There were maybe twenty chairs for the audience, a couple of vintage video cameras on tripods, and a control room that looked like it had been borrowed from mission control in a 1950s sci-fi B-movie about space exploration. The cameras shot in black and white, adding to the low-fi, time-warp vibe. Still, it was a real television studio—and I was about to be on a real television show.

The director was Amos Poe, the underground filmmaker who'd made *Unmade Beds*, starring Debbie Harry. He was running the switcher in the booth. The guy who owned the place, Jim Chladek, looked like Mister Rogers—who, for the record, I'd always liked as a kid. Jim ran around the studio shouting, "You can smoke joints, but no cigarettes, please!" That was the vibe. Glenn and Chris would roll joints and light up on the air, passing them back and forth. Who watching at home could say whether it was real weed or not? But trust me—it was real weed. And it was high quality, easily the best I'd ever smoked. This was when high-grade weed was first starting to circulate in New York, and those two were next level about it, just fanatical. Glenn and Chris sparking up on camera was the equivalent of whatever was in those mugs on *The Tonight Show*.

Glenn, with his cropped hair, trim suit, and bow tie, was the perfect master of ceremonies. He was deadpan funny, the living parody of a smooth-operating talk-show-host schmoozer. He'd often say that *TV Party* took its inspiration from *Playboy After Dark*, Hugh Hefner's old televised cocktail hour. At the top of each show, Glenn would offer his signature greeting: "Welcome to *TV Party*, the TV show that's a cocktail party, but which could be a political party." It sounded like a joke, but Glenn was serious. Behind any on-air anarchy, *TV Party* had a purpose. It was part cultural happening, part political act.

Later, Glenn put it this way: "I liked the idea of mixing entertainment with some kind of political discussion, because it was the Carter and Reagan era, and things were bad politically. The interest rates were about 20 percent. New York was broke." As I've said before, New York had a jagged edge in those days.

Chris Stein—who played the Ed McMahon sidekick character, though way cooler—shared that same sense of mission. He believed *TV Party* could compete with *The Village Voice* in terms of informing people, showing them what was really going on in the underground.

For me, just being on set was wild. The fact that people would be watching—live—was almost too hard to believe. I was beyond nervous; I was practically terrified. But when I asked around, nobody thought I looked it. As we ticked down the minutes to airtime, it became clear that one of the camera guys wasn't going to show. Glenn looked my way and said, "Fred, get on that camera!"

So now I was both on-air guest and a cameraman. As I remember it, the guests on that first episode of *TV Party* were me, the performance artist Robert Delford Brown, who'd founded something called the First National Church of the Exquisite Panic, Inc., and the artist David McDermott, one half of the art duo McDermott & McGough. David and his partner were flamboyant downtown fixtures who lived, dressed, and painted as if it were still the nineteenth century.

I remember Glenn introducing me as "Freddy," saying I would be talking about what was happening in Bedford-Stuyvesant. That pretty much captured it. Robert Delford Brown waxed poetic about his philosophy of "Pharblongence." McDermott announced that he was planning to remake *Gone with the Wind*. He glanced over at me, and I shot back, "Yes, I'll gladly play the Rhett Butler role!"

I'd gone into the studio nervous as hell. But *TV Party* made me realize I could actually be confident and cool on camera. What helped most was the atmosphere: a big, happy, dysfunctional, underground family. To me, it felt like enrolling in Downtown Hipster University—at the PhD level.

EVERYBODY'S FLY

As *TV Party* became a regular Tuesday-night ritual, I found myself fully immersed in the Lower Manhattan bohemian world. Glenn and Chris. Debbie Harry. John Lurie of the Lounge Lizards. Klaus Nomi. Robert Mapplethorpe. James Chance and his girlfriend, Anya Phillips, and his Contortions bandmate Pat Place. Nile Rodgers and Robert Fripp and the Brides of Funkenstein. The writer Cookie Mueller, who'd acted in John Waters's films and came on air for a special heavy-metal episode to chat about the actual heavy metals that were discovered in her blood. You never knew who might show up. One night, I brought the Bronx rapper Kool Kyle the Starchild onto the show, and he freestyled with the TV Party Orchestra, led by the multi-instrumental genius Walter Steding (a former janitor at Warhol's Factory), accompanied by the funky drummer Lenny Ferraro, who sometimes played a stack of magazines instead of a drum kit, and Chris, who sometimes played guitar.

David Byrne from Talking Heads might pop in and perform, or Tuxedomoon, or even George Clinton, my Parliament-Funkadelic hero, straight from the Mothership, who declared what we were doing "Anarchy Howdy Doody Guerrilla TV." (Glenn was a fan of the writer Ishmael Reed and believed there was a real connection between Reed's vision and George Clinton's cosmic funk.) Eventually, even David Bowie came through.

The audience at *TV Party* was the cream of the downtown crop—painters, musicians, photographers, writers, fashion models, and underground film people. It made sense, given that the aesthetic of the show was pure underground cinema, grainy black-and-white video, moody lighting, and with Amos back there in the control room, giving me direction on the headset while punching between the cameras in a way that must have made viewers at home feel dizzy.

I got to be pals with a lot of the regulars who showed up week after week, shouting from the sidelines or just soaking up the chaos.

UPTOWN/DOWNTOWN

There were photographers like Steven Meisel, William Coupon, and Kate Simon. There was the poet and critic Rene Ricard, a real downtown legend. Lisa Rosen, a model-actress-everything type with presence for days. The curator and writer Edit DeAk. The sculptor Jo Shane. Arthur Weinstein, the nightclub impresario. Claudia Summers, dominatrix and downtown cool girl, who'd record an underground dance hit, "The Dominatrix Sleeps Tonight." These were all heavy heads in the scene—and major inspirations for me.

Every week, once the show got rolling, Glenn and Chris would open up the phone lines. That's when the real madness started. Calls poured in, and Glenn loved it. The more unhinged, the better. People would dial in just to curse us out: "You're a fucking bunch of commies!" "I'm going to come down there and kick your ass!" "It looks like a fucking dope house!" "I'm going to fuck your mother in the ass!" "You suck pud!" "You're a bigger bunch of assholes than the assholes on commercial television!" On and on.

It was like *TV Party* became this pressure valve for New York's pent-up late '70s fury. We got bombed with the n-word too. That was heavy. But Glenn and Chris would just throw it back, clowning the callers or hanging up on them. And if Debbie Harry was on that night? Forget it. "Debbie, show me your—" *Click.* Sometimes they got to the cutoff in time. Sometimes they didn't.

The pictures of revolutionaries on the walls of *TV Party* reminded me of my father and his deep reverence for those figures who dared to challenge and overturn oppressive systems. Back in the 1950s, while studying to become an accountant, my father had to learn about the economies of the world and their histories. That was the Jim Crow era, with racial inequity everywhere you looked. The

Civil Rights Act was still a decade away. As a young Black man with intellectual curiosity, my father went searching for alternatives to American-style industrial capitalism.

On paper, socialism offered something else—a more just, communal structure—and to him, that sounded like hope. He immersed himself in the writings of Marx, Lenin, and especially Mao. The Chinese Revolution fascinated him, as did the Haitian one. By the late 1960s, when the Black Panthers were espousing Maoist principles, it was no surprise that Huey Newton's words echoed something my dad already believed: "Chairman Mao says that death comes to all of us, but it varies in its significance: to die for the reactionary is lighter than a feather; to die for the revolution is heavier than Mount Tai."

That image—of the mountain—had deep meaning for my dad. He wasn't a militant like the Panthers; he was far more of an armchair activist. But he believed in their ideals. One of the books I remember him reading to me as a child was *The Old Man Who Moved a Mountain*, a Chinese children's story that had been translated into English. He'd read it aloud to me at bedtime in his engaging, resonant voice.

The story—based on a Chinese folk tale that Mao often cited—was about a ninety-year-old man who was fed up with the massive mountain he had to walk around every time he needed to go anywhere. So he decided to dig it away, one bucket of dirt at a time. Naturally, everyone thought he was nuts. But the old man insisted: He might not live to see it done, but he'd get a good start. And his children—and their children—would continue until the mountain was gone.

To my dad, and later to me, that was a powerful metaphor. Revolutionary change didn't happen overnight. You needed to keep digging, even when the mountain towered high above you.

In our household, Mao's image—and the reverence for him—held a place not unlike the Jesus myth in other homes. Where most of the Black households I knew in Bed-Stuy had that iconic, European-looking portrait of Jesus hanging on the wall, ours did not. Down in my dad's man cave, you'd find posters of Mao and other revolutionaries, along with copies of Mao's *Little Red Book*, stuffed with dense passages of quotations. I would flip through it now and then as a teenager. One quote that stuck with me was this: "Be resolute, fear no sacrifice, and surmount every difficulty to win victory." I later realized it came from that same speech where Mao invoked the story of the old man and the mountain. I took that as a kind of motto.

I remember Mao also writing about the importance of staying connected to the people—to really know what the masses were thinking and feeling, to be attuned to the pulse of the historical moment. That idea stuck with me. Seeing that Andy Warhol painted giant portraits of Mao also resonated.

By the start of 1979, rap was still a wild child of the streets. Nobody had made a rap record yet. When I brought the idea up to Melle Mel, he looked at me like I had two heads. But I couldn't stop thinking about the massive crowds showing up every weekend—not just in the Bronx, but in Brooklyn, Queens, and Manhattan—gathering purely through word of mouth in the ghetto neighborhoods. The mainstream knew zero about what was going on. But I remembered that quote. *Okay,* this *is what the masses of my generation are into.*

I was sure rap could—and would—grow into something big. Maybe even a revolutionary force, something capable of moving mountains, if the planets aligned just right.

I was by no means a Mao expert, let alone a Maoist, but the little exposure I'd had to his teachings gave me a way to take a broader view of what was happening around me. I started to see the same kind of energy—radical, expressive, collective—at the rap parties, in the train layups with the graffiti writers, and on the sidewalks where the B-boys were breakdancing. They'd throw down sheets of cardboard and start flipping and twisting right there on the ground in front of you.

And I remember thinking: All of this, every bit of it, had the markings of a brand-new *culture*. A culture created, developed, and nurtured by New York urban teens. One that was bubbling up from the street. Maybe even unstoppable.

On certain Sundays, I'd head into Manhattan, taking the A to Broadway-Nassau to catch up with Lee when he and his family got home from church. Sometimes we'd hang out at his apartment, have a meal, and maybe listen to the latest party tape I'd gotten my hands on—like one from Frankie D—or we'd just walk around the hood together. Sometimes we'd go check on *Howard the Duck*; it was great to see kids running around that handball court, slapping the ball off Lee's mural, which looked as colorful and surreal as ever. Handball was a quintessential NYC sport, played year-round, and so many playgrounds had those enormous handball walls. We would walk by them, and Lee would say, "Man, I'm gonna paint these things." They were giant, empty canvases, including the opposite side of *Howard the Duck*, where he would later paint the *Lion's Den* mural in 1980. That winter, walking around the Lower East Side in our hats and coats, Lee shared with me his plans to execute it and paint other courts. He was deep into it in his piece book, sketching everything out.

I was telling Lee what was happening with Glenn and *TV Party*, which had opened the door to downtown for me—and, I hoped, for Lee. I felt like that crew—Glenn, Chris, Debbie, Amos, and their friends—were the gatekeepers of an underground culture developing in New York that was so expressive of that time and place. They became my mentors. I would bounce ideas off them, like the ones I'd shared with Lee about graffiti and its place in the story of art, and they'd be like, "Oh, yeah, that's cool, Fred! You should do this and do that and meet this person and meet that one." Lee, being a guy who had literally traveled the entire length and breadth of the city for years doing his work, understood. Just as he had been aware of the rap parties, he'd also been noticing the emergence of the punk aesthetic and this new downtown vibe.

One day, while talking with Glenn about what Lee and I were trying to do—our planned assault on the art world and the cultural chess moves I wanted to make—he said, "Fred, what you need now is some publicity. You and Lee need to get exposure. Talk about what you're doing in the press."

"Yeah, sure. But how do I do that? Where do I go?"

"*The Village Voice.*"

My head snapped back. Everybody downtown read the *Voice*.

Glenn told me about a writer named Howard Smith who had a regular column called "Scenes," and said we might hit it off. The name rang a bell. Glenn explained that Howard had directed the Oscar-winning documentary *Marjoe*, about the evangelist and former child preacher Marjoe Gortner, and had been writing for the *Voice* for years. He was the only journalist reporting from inside the Stonewall Inn during the riots ten years earlier. I knew his "Scenes" column better than his byline—it was this funky weekly feature that highlighted fringy, countercultural stuff. Glenn said, "This guy's perfect."

I can't remember if I called Howard or he called me, but Glenn did the initial intro. Howard said that he and his collaborator, Cathy Cox, wanted to write a column about me, Lee, and the graffiti scene. I was like, *Let's do it!* Lee, though, wasn't into it. He didn't want to be seen or heard at that point. It was part of his whole stealth thing. So I said, "Well, I'll go out and represent us."

Lee was cool with that, so I went solo and met Howard at *The Village Voice* offices downtown. He turned out to be a character: big, frizzy hair, thick mustachio. I showed up sporting my jazzy New Wave look, laid out some images, and gave him my spiel. I told him that Lee and I represented the Fabulous 5, that we were artists, and that we were willing to offer our expert mural services for people's homes at five bucks a square foot.

Lee and I had discussed the economics beforehand. "How should we price this?" Five dollars per square foot sounded fair. An average wall could add up to several hundred bucks, easy to knock out quickly. I told Howard we were open to storefronts, sides of trucks, "boring" lobbies, whatever people wanted. We'd already gotten a few inquiries, I said. A rock star had even commissioned us to do his ceiling.

That last part was a bit of a stretch. David Bowie had been interested, but our go-between—a British guy who floated around the *TV Party* scene—disappeared and the job never panned out. Still, it made for a decent talking point. "You name it, pay us, we'll paint it," I told Howard.

I could tell that he was sympathetic to what Lee and I were up to. But I had braced myself for the kind of question I knew was coming—and it came.

"Are you kidding?" Howard said. "Most people I know in the city are trying to get *rid* of you spray-can freaks."

"It's that kind of attitude I have to fight," I told him. "I think it's time everyone realized graffiti is the purest form of New York art. What else has evolved from the streets?" I explained that we were just taking graffiti out of the subways and bringing it above ground.

Howard asked to see some work. I'd brought a few paintings on paper and some sketches I'd made and snapshots of a few of Lee's whole cars. He seemed genuinely impressed that the artwork wasn't just scrawled tags—it had depth, style, range. In the eventual column, he called them "flashy futuristic fantasies" and praised their "vibrant technical imagination." I said we were inspired by Warhol, Crumb, and Lichtenstein.

When the story came out in February, it included a photograph of me standing in front of Lee's *Howard the Duck* mural (Lee was still lying low), along with my Hancock Street mailing address and seven-digit home phone number. This was back when you didn't need to include an area code.

The phone at my parents' house started to ring—which was interesting, especially to my mother. She had known for a while that I was tagging. I'd tagged the inside of my closet with my name, the same style she'd seen around the neighborhood, so there wasn't much mystery. It wasn't a big deal to her. Later, when I started hitting the yards with other graffiti cats, she was the one I'd come home and share my exploits with. And as I started to make those cultural chess moves, she became my sounding board.

But now, seeing her graffiti-artist son in *The Village Voice* and fielding calls from strangers—this was a whole new level.

Lee and I started getting commissions. We began making a little money here and there—several hundred bucks at a time. It was a start.

Working alongside Lee, I was truly learning how to paint. I was not at all at the level of Lee and the Fabulous 5 guys—no way—but I came loaded with ideas, concepts, and a game plan. While I was putting that into effect, I was apprenticing under the spray-can maestro himself. Lee showed me the finer points of can control: how to angle the spray can and how manage the flow, how to finesse each stroke at proper speed: technique. He was even smuggling in European paint—colors you couldn't get in the US—and that was a huge lesson for me in pigment. Then there was all of the detail stuff: trimming characters and letters, outlining, building depth, achieving three-dimensionality.

EVERYBODY'S FLY

Piece by piece, under Lee's guidance, I was learning, developing, and stepping up my game.

The phone kept ringing. One night, it was a teenager from Far Rockaway who called himself Rammellzee. He said he was into graffiti and rap. We stayed on the phone for a solid hour while he went off about how all the arrows you see in graffiti actually represented nuclear missiles—what he called "the armament of the letter." He talked about something he called Ikonoklast Panzerism. He brought up Gothic Futurism. I was like, *What the hell is this?* It was fascinating, but was it for real?

A week later, Ramm came to visit me on Hancock Street. He brought drawings for some of his pieces and handed me a nineteen-page essay he'd written, with a title I will never forget: "Ionic Treatise Gothic Futurism Assassins Knowledge of the Remanipulated Square Point One to 720°." What also struck me was how he dressed. No jeans, no sneakers, no athletic wear. His style was dapper R&B playa: blazer, slacks, tie, sharp shoes.

The one and only Rammellzee and I would end up seeing a good bit of each other in the coming years, as I took him under my wing, schooled him, and eventually introduced him to the art scene.

Soon after, I got a message that someone named Claudio Bruni Sakraischik had called. He was a *Voice* reader who'd seen the article—and, as it turned out, he was the owner of Galleria La Medusa, a prestigious art gallery in Rome. *Holy shit!*

I hit Claudio back. In a heavy Italian accent, he said he wanted to meet with me and Lee as soon as possible. I explained our plans, mentioned that mural commissions were starting to come in. He said he had some canvases for us and invited us uptown to his townhouse on East Seventy-Second Street. The place was stunning—filled with major blue-chip art. Right away I spotted a bronze sculpture by Umberto Boccioni, one of the Italian Futurists I'd read about. It was called *Unique Forms of Continuity in Space* and it reminded me of three-dimensional wild style graffiti—those wild corners and impossible angles. The Futurists' emphasis on speed, modernity, and machinery felt totally in sync with New York subway graffiti.

Claudio's place also had massive paintings by Giorgio de Chirico, the metaphysical Italian painter whose estate Claudio managed and whose catalogue raisonné he was working on. (De Chirico had just died at the age of ninety.) There was a life-size, ultra-real Duane Hanson sculpture of a cop, and a few pieces by Warhol and Lichtenstein—the Pop artists whose work I already saw as spiritual antecedents to the whole graffiti movement.

Lee and I had never been in a space like this. It felt like stepping into MoMA or looking at a spread in *Architectural Digest*. I was art-nerding big time. I thought, *Okay, this is another level.* Claudio was a scion of the Bruni winemaking family—his social circle included top-echelon Italian families like the Agnellis. He had residences not only in New York and Rome but also in Brazil and Morocco. And yet, this aristocratic, globetrotting Italian guy preferred taking the subway when he was in New York. He rode the 5 train regularly and had fallen in love with graffiti. So when he saw the *Voice* story, he was already primed.

Claudio got to the point. He gave us a roll of pre-primed canvas and a few hundred dollars for spray paint. The canvas was fifty inches wide, and we had enough for three four-foot-long sections. I did one that said *Fred*, in red that faded down into orange and yellow, on a background of light blue and four-inch green diagonal stripes. Lee did a couple, including a *FAB 5* in light blue on a green splat over an orange background.

A couple of days later, we brought the three canvases back uptown to Claudio's townhouse. He was blown away—he loved the work. He bought all three for a thousand dollars a pop and told us he wanted to show our graffiti-inspired art at his gallery in Rome that fall.

EVERYBODY'S FLY

I had flown down a few times to Barbados, and Lee might have gone to Puerto Rico when he was a kid, but neither of us had really traveled, let alone to Europe, to Rome. This was a huge leap. At a time when most of the press about graffiti was negative, when hardly anyone outside our scene saw any validity in what we were doing, here was this suave, art-world insider from Rome who fully got it. He immediately saw the connection I'd been trying to make between graffiti and Pop Art. We could hardly believe what he was saying, let alone the respect and encouragement he brought to the table.

This being 1979, the stories coming out of Rome were intense, all about the Red Brigades militant group terrorizing government officials and high-profile Italians. Just the year before, they had kidnapped and murdered Aldo Moro, the former prime minister who had been poised for reelection. Their signature move was kneecapping—drive-by shootings that targeted the knees and legs of their victims. Brutal stuff. Their political graffiti was splattered all over Rome.

I remember thinking, *Damn, so graffiti is a radical, political thing in Rome right now. Claudio Bruni might be exactly the kind of person on the Red Brigades' hit list.*

When Lee and I left Claudio's townhouse and were walking to the downtown 5, I turned to him and said, "Yo, man, this Rome trip is going to be wild and historic. When they hear about us, those Red Brigades cats might show up at the gallery!"

On a Wednesday night in early March, I headed over to Lee's apartment in the Smith Houses. What I remember most about that place was the *Star Wars* mural Lee's parents had actually let him paint on one of the walls. I sometimes crashed there when we were hanging out or working late. That night, while waiting for Lee to get ready, I chatted with his mom and his buddy Caz. Lee finally emerged with his sketch and his cans, getting ready to hit a handball court not far away.

He was a little on edge. His father had voiced concern about the job, worried that this might finally be the one where Lee got caught. And the weather had been tricky. It rained the day before—there were even floods in parts of the city. But now the skies were clear. More rain was expected over the next couple of days, so it felt like the right time to strike.

We walked through the neighborhood in the damp chill, down Cherry Street. Spring was technically around the corner, but it still felt a long way off.

It was around nine when we got to the playground at Mechanics Alley, tucked next to the Manhattan Bridge. The kids had all gone, just as Lee had hoped. Only a few night porters were lingering, cleaning up. We rapped with them for a bit, and they gave us the go-ahead.

I hung with Lee for a few minutes while he prepped and got set up. Then I split. He needed to go it alone, as always. On my way back to Bed-Stuy, I pictured Lee in the cold, mapping out his outline on that enormous wall, then slowly filling it in, layer by layer, while the temperature dropped by the hour.

When it was done, the entire wall was transformed into a space-themed mural, like an exploding nebula of color and form. There were stars, Saturns, and a cascade of red bubbles drifting against a deep-blue background. Near the top, Lee had written "Here I go again," a nod to his earlier *Howard the Duck* piece—and just below it, "The Fabulous Five for old times," tipping his hat to the crew that had brought him up. As usual, there was a "Mom" tucked in there somewhere.

And in the lower right-hand corner, painted in red, was a shout-out to me: "FRED."

But the centerpiece—what felt like a call to arms—was a phrase that seemed to rise from the surface like molten space rock, rendered in three-dimensional lettering that shimmered with intensity:

"GRAFFITI 1979."

6

This is what's popping now

The year 1979 was when I started scribbling things like "It's good to put yourself in the position to meet people who can help you do the things you want to do," and "I should start creating an aura about myself," and "Make them want to see more of me by letting them see too little of me" in my notebook. I was thinking like that—self-mythologizing, plotting, pushing myself forward. It was the year my friendship with Glenn deepened, and I started meeting people who would actually help me do the things I had been dreaming about.

I was in full art-nerd mode. I was burying my head in books like *American Pop Art* by Lawrence Alloway, *The Age of Avant-Garde* by Hilton Kramer, *Social Realism: Art as a Weapon* by David Shapiro, *Art in America: A Brief History* by Richard B. K. McLanathan, *The Visual Dialogue* by Nathan Knobler, *The Painted Word* by Tom Wolfe. The library at Medgar Evers was loaded with art history

EVERYBODY'S FLY

books and I was feasting on them. Who knows how many I actually returned.

I was still doing my college radio show and loving it. I got Frankie D, one of the local Bed-Stuy DJs I revered, to come on the air with me, and Glenn made a return visit. But I began to be like, *I don't need to be enrolling in school anymore.* The puzzle pieces were starting to snap into place. I was ready to go hard in the paint.

Lee and I had already booked our first gallery show—in Rome, no less. The commissions were trickling in. I had Grandmaster Flash's number in my book. I had Glenn's, and Chris and Debbie's from Blondie. Thanks to Glenn, I even had Warhol's number.

Things were beginning to happen. I was riding out the spring term at Medgar Evers—and when it was time to register for the fall, I just didn't show up.

Graffiti was everywhere, and it was hitting new levels. Writers like Seen, Dondi, Revolt, Zephyr... the trains were getting more elaborate, and the work was becoming more expressive and individual—not just in the subways but on the streets. That year, everyone started noticing these strange new tags downtown: in the East and West Villages, in SoHo, all over Lower Manhattan. They stood out from the other graffiti. They were visually spare, and their tone was satiric, kind of philosophical:

SAMO SAVES IDIOTS AND GONZOIDS.

SAMO 4 THE SO-CALLED AVANT-GARDE.

SAMO AS AN ALTERNATIVE 2 PLAYING ART WITH THE "RADICAL? CHIC" SECT ON DADDY'$ FUNDS.

UPTOWN/DOWNTOWN

They usually ended with the copyright symbol—SAMO©—and sometimes included a three-pointed crown, clean and simple. The graffiti scene, as I've said, was a network of friends, rivals, names you knew, reputations you followed. But this was different. Nobody I knew seemed to know who SAMO was. He—or maybe she?—wasn't hanging out in front of Pearl Paint or the writer's bench at 149th and the Grand Concourse. This was like some outlaw SoHo artist hitting the streets with phrases and statements rather than a traditional graff writer.

As I spent more time in Lower Manhattan, with Lee and with the *TV Party* crew—always taking the A train back to Hancock Street in the early morning—I kept noticing more and more of these SAMO tags. And then, suddenly, SAMO IS DEAD was everywhere.

I thought, *This is interesting. Who the hell is this guy?*

Lee and I got another break when, again thanks to that piece in the *Voice*, a couple of downtown dudes—Michael Holman and Stan Peskett—reached out. It was Michael who first called my folks' place on Hancock Street. He said he was a musician, and that his friend Stan, an English artist, had a loft on Canal Street they were turning into a downtown art hub called the Canal Zone. "Stan wants you guys to come over," Michael said. "He wants to meet up." And we did.

The address was 533 Canal, and it was way, way west—practically at the Hudson. The space was massive, a huge open loft, maybe five thousand square feet, with a double row of fat columns running all the way through. Michael turned out to be a really interesting cat—smart, glasses, thoughtful, mixed-race. He'd been an auxiliary performer with the Tubes, the outrageous glam-punk band from San Francisco, part of their extended troupe. I knew them from a *Midnight Special* TV performance. Recently, he'd moved to New York for a job at Chemical Bank. Talk about range.

Stan was older, intense and passionate, around forty, and had this wild London art-world pedigree. Back in the '60s, he'd been part of a scene with young British Pop artists like David Hockney and Derek Boshier. Since I was deep into Pop, that definitely got my attention. Stan made murals, and he'd basically designed the interior of Fiorucci, the ultra-hip Milan boutique that had opened a shop on Fifty-Ninth Street in Manhattan. Everyone dialed in knew Fiorucci as the coolest boutique in town, where hot chicks went to get these brand-new, sexy, ultra-tight "designer jeans."

So they were telling us what they were up to with Canal Zone—this experimental downtown space for art and music—and I was laying out the mission Lee and I were on: how we were pushing graffiti into the galleries and connecting the dots to Pop Art. Since they were both music heads, I also started preaching the gospel of rap. Michael nodded but said, "I see a coming resurgence of that Motown thing, man. *That's* the energy we need." I was like, "Yeah, all that was cool. But this is what's popping *now*."

Stan said he wanted the Canal Zone to feel like a Warhol Factory for the new generation—a place where artists could collaborate, show work, stage performances. He was even talking about franchising the idea, expanding it to other cities around the country and in Europe, turning it into something big. This sounded a lot like the kind of energy I'd envisioned.

And then it got even better: Stan and Michael said they wanted to kick the whole thing off by inviting the Fabulous 5 to create murals for the Canal Zone launch—a big happening full of downtown tastemakers and creatives. These guys seemed connected, no doubt, and I was feeling the vibes.

In my conversations with Lee about taking our art into new spaces, I kept coming back to the idea of materials. If we were pioneering a new medium with spray paint, why were we sticking to the same old canvas that painters had been using for centuries? I tossed out various alternatives—sheets of metal, plywood—and eventually Lee and I landed on thick plastic sheets. Drop cloths, essentially. They were huge, cheap, and flexible. Paint would dry fast, and once we finished a piece, we could roll or fold it up and move on to the next one. I pitched the idea to Stan, and he loved it.

Stan went out and bought a bunch of ten-by-twenty-foot plastic sheets. Lee and I hung them from the ceiling of Stan's loft, two at a time, set up our colors, talked through the imagery, and got to work. I remember Stan and Michael standing there, watching in awe. We sprayed those sheets with wild explosive images, filling every inch with loud, bright colors. Stan was ecstatic. We'd leave them hanging up for a few days to dry and be photographed, then swap in the next round, and the next.

The Canal Zone party happened on the last Sunday in April. Lee and I arranged the plastic murals around the loft to create an immersive graffiti environment. The place started to fill with cool, groovy, artsy downtown types. Michael weaved through the crowd with a microphone, doing play-by-play while a friend filmed everything on video. At one point, Lee sprayed a big Fab Five tag in red paint while Michael riffed: "I'm Word Man, ladies and gentlemen... Look at the moves! Look at the moves! You seen it here at the Canal Zone!" Stan, fully in the spirit, sprayed "Z-RATED" on the back of Michael's white jumpsuit.

The whole thing turned into a blowout. People were doing crazy shit with spray cans while music blasted from Stan's massive stereo system. The Tubes, or some semblance of them, made an appearance. A tall model who Stan was dating, named Roanne Rogers but billing herself as Mistresse M, floated by and whispered to Michael, "I am everywhere, in everything. I'm absolutely everywhere." There was some ketamine going around, and I stood there watching the scene unfold, trying to clock the energy. Was this it? Was this what a real downtown happening felt like? This Canal Zone affair had the right ingredients, but it felt a bit contrived, a bit performative. I kept thinking about Warhol's Exploding Plastic Inevitable, trying to place this within that lineage.

And then I noticed another young Black guy in the room. He looked like a teen street urchin—caramel complexion, hair shaved into a wild kind of mohawk, full punk-rock energy. He had on a white T-shirt with GUMBY IS BAD scrawled across the front. Nobody seemed to know who he was. He hadn't been invited, but somehow he'd caught wind of the Canal Zone party and showed up. He checked out the murals Lee and I had made and, with a warm smile, asked Michael and Stan if he could join in.

They handed him a can of red spray paint and tacked up a massive sheet of photo-grade paper. He started writing: WHICH OF THE FOLLOWING IS OMNIPRZNT? Then he added multiple-choice options—little checkboxes with basic lettering. I was like, *What's going on over here?* Lee and I leaned in to get a closer look. Next he sprayed LEE HARVEY OSWALD, followed by COCA COLA LOGO, and then GENERAL MELONRY. As a final flourish, he sprayed out S-A-M-O and the copyright symbol, ©.

There was an audible gasp. This was the moment—a downtown mystery unveiled—when Samo finally revealed himself to the world. His name was Jean-Michel Basquiat.

Jean and I vibed instantly. He had come up like me: from Brooklyn, raised in a brownstone over on Pacific Street in Boerum Hill. Like me, he had island roots—his dad was Haitian, his mom Puerto Rican. His father, like mine, was an accountant. His time at Edward R. Murrow High School in Midwood mirrored my own stretch at Dewey. He bailed. (I later heard that before he left Murrow he attended a graduation ceremony and hit the principal in the face with a cream pie.) Just like me, he wound up at City-As-School. In his case, he dropped out.

When I met Jean, he was basically living like a starving artist. He was staying somewhere on Eldridge Street, but he was mainly couch-surfing from friend to friend downtown, as I was too, whenever I wasn't hauling back out to Brooklyn on the A train. Jean already knew about me and the Fabulous 5, and I knew about SAMO; *The Village Voice* had run stories on each of us. We were kindred spirits and bonded right away.

Like me, Jean had spent serious time in museums and was hip to art history—from Caravaggio to Delacroix, from Franz Kline to the Abstract Expressionists, Johns, Rauschenberg, and Warhol. He knew his stuff backward and forward and had already formed a sharp, distinctive point of view. Here was another Black kid who came from where I came from and knew all this stuff, and yet neither of us could really talk about it with the kids back in the neighborhood. They'd look at us like we were crazy.

Jean told me that he and his friend from City-As-School, Al Diaz, had come up with SAMO. It stood for "Same Old Shit." But after they had a falling out, Jean got tired of the whole thing. That's why he'd started writing SAMO IS DEAD everywhere.

One thing Jean didn't know about was this rap thing, which was still deep in the hood—underground culture all the way. I hipped him to my rap party tapes, playing them on my boom box.

On the music tip, Jean was hip to punk and New Wave and was like, "I play some guitar and clarinet and keyboards." Basically he meant that he made abstract sounds with those instruments—he wasn't formally trained, but his confidence was solid, and that was a total punk requisite. Being in a band was the cool thing to do back then, and according to the punk-rock playbook, not knowing how to play was no problem. Being cool, stylish, and confident—that's what counted.

That night at the Canal Zone, Jean and Michael, who played a little drums, hit it off and decided to form a band. They ended up calling themselves Gray. Jean invited me to join too. Since I didn't play an instrument—and hadn't touched the drums since I was a kid—I said, "Hey, I'll do scat rapping." Jean said, "Hell, yeah!"

I was at Gray's first rehearsal, but I soon dropped out. It wasn't quite my cup of tea, and I didn't feel like I had much to contribute to the sound they were after. But they kept it going. I remember Michael giving Jean this weird little Wasp synthesizer; Jean would get the craziest sounds out of it. The whole idea of Gray seemed to be that each player would attack his instrument like he had no idea what it was originally designed to do. There was nothing like the noise they made. It was avant garde, atonal jazz... with a hardcore-punk attitude and New Wave energy.

When Jean and I first met at the Canal Zone, Stan actually tried to stir shit up between us. He was like, "Fred, what do you think? SAMO is here—*and he's Black*," like some kind of playground taunt. Maybe he thought the two Black graffiti guys were going to get into a rivalry or some nonsense. He didn't understand what was up; it was clear from the second we met that there was never going to be any hating between me and Jean.

Stan figured that out pretty quick too. His Canal Zone party had gone well enough that he invited me and Lee to keep coming by the loft on the regular to create more artwork, and he offered up other connections to help us make a little money. Jean was invited too.

Stan was excited to see what Lee and I could do, so he hooked us up with a paid gig to do some work at the Unique Clothing Warehouse, on Broadway and Waverly Place, in what we'd later start calling NoHo. Unique had been around since 1969, a cool, vintage-clothing pioneer and downtown landmark. You could snag a Harris tweed overcoat for under twenty bucks. Alongside all the used stuff, they would take denim jackets and jeans and dye them these bright and crazy colors. It was cheap, hip fashion, and it seemed like everybody shopped there.

Stan introduced us to the owner, Harvey, who wanted us to update the store's image. The idea was for us to repaint the sign out front with some graffiti flair and add embellishments throughout the space. Lee and I brought along Slave from the Fabulous 5—and Jean too.

Lee, Slave, and I worked on the signage outside, while Jean focused on the interior. At one point, we had just come down off the scaffold to take a break when we heard Jean yelling from inside. Something had gone down. He stormed out the front door, ranting: "Fuck them! Nobody talks to me like that. I quit!" Apparently, as he was painting inside, doing his thing, one of the bosses yelled at him, telling him how he *should* be painting. For Jean, that warranted a "Hell no!" and a "Fuck off!" He might have been broke but wasn't about to take shit from anyone. He told them to kiss his ass—and just like that, he was gone.

It didn't seem to bother Stan, who told us he was heading to Italy for a few weeks to drum up support for his Canal Zone idea from the Fiorucci backers. Which meant that, all of a sudden, the three of us had this massive downtown studio to ourselves. A total dream. To have a place like that to come to every day and make art? It was like, *Yo, we're real artists now, with a studio in SoHo, for real!*

Stan asked Lee and me to keep turning out more pieces like the ones we'd been doing; he'd folded up a few of the big plastic murals to bring with him to Italy. My street sense wondered if he was filling our heads with pie-in-the-sky promises while trying to seed a downtown-culture plantation at the Canal Zone—something he could brand

and export. The commercial vibe, which sounded kind of exciting at first, was starting to bug me. But I wanted to see how it might all play out, especially if it meant we could keep using that giant loft. At least until we could lock down a space of our own.

So Lee and I kept at it, putting up those big plastic panels, painting the shit out of them, letting them dry, and then folding them up and setting them aside. We had also created a little spray room, plasticked off as a separate area to work on pieces for the show in Rome.

I asked Jean if he wanted to help out. He didn't come from the traditional school of subway graffiti, but the ethos had clearly filtered into his work. I handed him a can of red Rust-Oleum with a special fat cap nozzle on it. A fat cap makes the paint come out in a wide spray, like three or four inches; it's what you use to fill in large areas. I demonstrated on a small patch and tossed him the can: "Here you go, Jean, keep the can moving, just don't let it drip."

Jean shook the can and stepped up to the plastic sheet, then started spraying. I ducked into the bathroom for a minute or two, and when I stepped out, Jean was still in that same spot, just going back and forth with the can over the same area. The paint was dripping everywhere, like a red waterfall. "Jean, stop!"

While Stan was away, he left his studio assistant, Jennifer Stein, in charge of managing the place. She was a young artist, cool as hell, always around, sometimes helping us out. She and Jean clicked instantly. What I remember most is the work they started making together—these amazing postcard-style collages, which might have been some of Jean's first works that weren't graffiti on walls. They'd fold a regular sheet of paper into four quadrants and make small images in each of those. Then one of them would head over to Jamie Canvas on Spring Street to get them color xeroxed—this new, kind of futuristic technology that artists were just beginning to mess with—and they'd mount the prints onto cardboard to make individual art cards. Some had pictures of Jean and Jennifer, like photo-booth snapshots of the two of them goofing around.

At the studio, I always had music playing on my Sanyo boom box—loud. I would play my live rap-party tapes, which hardly anyone outside the most dialed-in cats had ever heard. I broke it all down for Jean: what the parties were like, how the DJs were mixing and spinning tracks you couldn't hear anywhere else. One of my go-to jams then was Captain Sky's twelve-minute disco-funk opus "Super Sporm"—it had an incredible break, and the DJs were spinning it nonstop back then.

Every time I played it, Jean would drop whatever he was doing and we'd all have to stop and go into dance-party mode. If Michael Holman was around, he'd jump in too. As much as Michael was more of an old-school Motown and soul guy, he soon turned himself into a full-on B-boy, one of the earliest adopters of the entire rap way of being. Jean's dance style was, well, something else. He'd seem totally off beat and perfectly on it at the same time. Just a wild, cool dude. Every time we locked eyes while dancing, we'd both bust out laughing. The energy level at 533 Canal Street was sky-high.

One day, looking over the postcards he and Jennifer had been making, Jean announced that he was going to go walk around SoHo and see if he could sell some of them on the street. A little while later he came back: "Yo, man, I sold two cards to Andy Warhol!" I was like, "What? No way! Wow!"

He'd spotted Warhol through the window of a restaurant called W.P.A. on Spring Street near West Broadway, having lunch with Henry Geldzahler—the curator from the Met and New York City's Commissioner of Cultural Affairs. He walked right in and up to their table. Geldzahler, who eventually became friendly with Jean, looked over the pieces and said, "Too young." But he and Warhol still bought a couple, probably just to give Jean the brush-off.

EVERYBODY'S FLY

But to me, that moment was electric, and so *Jean.* Walking up to Andy Warhol and Henry Geldzahler like it was nothing, showing them his stuff, making a sale. It felt like a victory for everything I was trying to build. The kid was fearless.

T he graffiti giant Dondi came through the Canal Street studio one day with Slave. Dondi was digging the big plastic-sheet pieces we had hanging up—the whole idea of painting on plastic really caught his eye. I said, "Yo, money, let me show you some more stuff we've been doing."

I went and grabbed one of the folded-up pieces from the growing pile. Lee and I cleared some space to unfold it, excited to show it off. But as we opened it up, we heard this weird sound, like something tearing. Lee and I exchanged looks: *"What the hell is happening?"*

As we got the mural spread out on the floor, we realized that the paint had not properly adhered to the plastic. The tearing sound was the paint itself peeling off in huge sheets. The image was destroyed—chunks of color sticking to the opposite side, zigzags of peeled paint breaking up the composition. A total freakin' nightmare.

Lee and I stood there in disbelief, stunned. Weeks of work—all of that paint, time, and energy—now peeling off in chunks. And then, after a beat, we looked at each other and laughed our asses off for about ten minutes. *This* was what Stan had packed up and flown to Italy to impress potential investors, showing them how he'd corralled some *major* NYC graffiti painters who would spit out these instant murals all day long for his Warhol Factory–like Canal Zone concept.

You'd think Stan, the trained artist, the guy with decades of pigment knowledge, would have clocked this—that he would have tested the material or checked a panel before crossing the Atlantic. We were just graffiti kids figuring things out as we went. We should have known better too, but we didn't. We had no idea that the spray paint was just sitting like a skin on top of the plastic. Lee and I explained to Dondi and Slave what had happened—that Stan had taken a bunch of these things to Italy—and pretty soon they were cracking up too.

Sure enough, when Stan got back to New York, he was in a dour mood. Lee and I immediately knew there had to have been a problem in Italy, but we decided not to let on.

"Hey, Stan!" I said, bright and cheerful. "We've been waiting to hear how the trip went!"

He sat us down and sighed. "I don't think this is going to work out," he said.

"What's not gonna work out?" I asked.

He was not pleased. You could feel it instantly. Stan looked around at what was going on and just wasn't having it anymore. His Canal Zone dream was dead on the vine, and with it was the warmth he'd shown us before. The energy shift was night and day. He also knew that Claudio Bruni had given us some money to work on pieces for our Rome show at Galleria La Medusa, which we'd been steadily plugging away at while he was overseas.

So he pulled me and Lee aside and said, "Look, I'm going to have to start charging you guys if you want to stick around here."

Just like that, it was over. No more talk of global franchises or creative incubation. The Canal Zone had become just another downtown loft—and we didn't have rent money. So we packed up our stuff and took off, saying goodbye to those magical weeks on Canal Street.

Stan gave Jean and Jennifer the boot too. I got the feeling he didn't like whatever was going on between them, artistic or otherwise. So it was: "All of you guys, you gotta go."

I was sketching out a campaign I called "Summer Assault 1979." Lee and I still had to finish the pieces for the Rome show, scheduled to open on November 30. There were more connections to make, more alliances to solidify. I was deep in my daydreams about the link between Pop Art and graffiti—and how the two could speak to each other across the cultural divide. And then one day, an idea hit me: Why not do a whole-car piece in tribute to Andy Warhol's Campbell's soup cans?

I grabbed a notebook and blue ballpoint pen and started sketching it out: six Campbell's soup cans in a row, tagged with "Fabulous Five." I was convinced this would be the perfect message to New York City that we—or at least someone—in the graffiti world actually knew about art history and the art world. That we, as artists, were just as viable and "real" as the art-school types who showed their work in galleries.

The palette would be simple: lots of white, lots of red, some black, a little gold. I would need to start racking up. Lee told me that fifteen cans of paint would do the job, but maybe we could get away with eight. I showed him the sketch, and he loved it. Locking in on the Pop connection, Lee came back with a next-level idea: doing a loaf of supermarket bread as a whole car. No, scratch that: it should be *two* whole cars! Lee would do Taystee and I would do Wonder Bread—*Tayst-Lee* and *Wonder-Fred*.

Subway cars were even shaped like loaves, so they would practically be moving sculptures. More white and red, with hits of blue and yellow. The pieces were designed to go on what writers called a "married couple," a pair of subway cars permanently connected. (Lee's incredible *Stop the Bomb* is a perfect example of a married-couple piece.)

UPTOWN/DOWNTOWN

Every time we talked about this project, we'd end up cracking up. This was always the sign that an idea was worth doing: laughter meant we were onto something, because we knew the kind of reaction these cars would provoke when they rumbled down the track—pure disbelief and delight. The white-bread express, art history-bound!

I was tempted to call up Henry Geldzahler at the Met to tell him the big news—that the Fabulous 5 was prepping rolling tributes to the Pop artist whose book *The Philosophy of Andy Warhol (From A to B and Back Again)* had been a revelation. That book was a treasure, absolutely transformative, a blueprint for me and for so many of the younger artists I was coming up with. One quote from Warhol burned itself into my brain and became a phrase to live by: "They always say time changes things, but you actually have to change them yourself."

An idea sprouted between me and Jean to start our own museum club. We'd both been deep into going to art museums when we were kids, and now we had the time and focus to take it seriously. On occasional Wednesdays, schedule permitting, we'd set off on field trips—mostly to the Met, but also to MoMA, the Frick, the Whitney, the Guggenheim, wherever the art called us. The Met was our favorite. We'd wander all over the museum, soaking in everything from Renaissance and modern to Egyptian and African art. Then we'd head to the dining room, grab a late lunch, and talk through what we'd seen. One day on the ground floor, Jean stopped in front of an ancient bronze Roman belt buckle and just stared. He was transfixed. "Man, it's so beautiful," he said. You could tell it was being filed away into his internal visual archive. We always carried sketchbooks and pencils with us, pretending we were art students learning from the masters.

One artist we got deep into was Caravaggio, who would be given a huge exhibition at the Met in 1985. In the early 1600s, he became the most famous painter in Rome—brilliant, violent, and short-lived. We had read about his wild life and loved how he invented creative emotional lighting in paintings, and we were struck by one detail: He carried a sword. This wasn't some costume-drama thing—back then, carrying a sword meant you were ready to use it. It was *gangster*. Caravaggio got into constant fights, including one in which he killed a man named Tommasoni—reportedly while trying to castrate him, which, as we learned, was a common way to punish a man for dissing another man's woman in seventeenth-century Italy. One account described Caravaggio as "ever ready to engage in a fight or an argument, so that it is most awkward to get along with him." We thought this was hilarious.

I was always throwing ideas at Jean, just like I did with Glenn and Lee. "Yo," I told him, "Lee and I were thinking about going into Leo Castelli's gallery and spray-painting something beautiful right on the wall—we'll have somebody there to document it, shooting stills and film. They'll freak out, call the cops, and we'll get arrested. But then they'll read about why in the news, our manifesto, and realize we're making a radical statement. A demand to be recognized as artists."

Jean said, "Man, I love that idea. I've got something similar. What if we filled up a bunch of balloons with paint and threw them at the Castelli building? Let the colors just drip down the front."

"I like that!" I said.

"Well, if you do yours, let me know. I'm down!"

"And Lee and I will back you up with the paint balloons!" And so it went.

Jean and I talked about being creative across as many platforms as possible—whatever it took to get the message across. I told him about my evolving idea of using film to document these emerging pieces of street culture—rap, graffiti, breakdancing—to show the world we weren't just hustling for fame or crime or flash. We were creators. We were culture. I wanted to counter the negative portrayals we kept seeing in the press. Jean was all in. "Hell yeah to that!" he said. We talked art, music, Gray, underground film, photography, girls, all of it.

We were two of the few Black guys on the scene, pushing at the edges, trying to communicate on a wider level, to a wider audience. We took Malcolm X's words—from the famous black-and-white poster of him holding a rifle to protect his family—to heart: *by any means necessary.*

I knew Glenn would love Jean. I had to introduce them—and so I did. Jean handed Glenn one of his postcard pieces. It featured the face of J. Edgar Hoover, eyes blacked out by a Coke can. (When Jean was a kid, he'd sent a drawing of a gun he'd made to Hoover at the FBI's Washington office. Classic Jean.)

Glenn had been curious about SAMO. His take on Jean's work lined up with mine: This wasn't graffiti in the traditional New York sense. Jean wasn't tagging or bombing trains. What he'd done was absorb the context and attitude of graff and spun it into his own art statement.

Jean and Glenn hit it off immediately, and, pretty soon, Jean got pulled into our *TV Party* world. He became a regular guest—a star, really—a kind of instant underground celebrity. Most of the *TV Party* crew were aware of SAMO, and Jean was embraced warmly—like any other weirdo in our circle. He'd hang out in the control room with Amos Poe, messing with the character generator to create absurdist, Dada-esque subtitles that generally had nothing to do with anything on-screen. One I remember: "DEATH IS ROLAIDS." Another: "GAMMA RAYED PROSTITUTES LOOKING TO A CROWD OF FISH ON BEING A DOG." Pure Dada chaos.

That fall, we did a Halloween episode. I came on set wearing a giant paper bag with "NICKEL BAG (DUST)" scrawled across the chest, and a bag on my head. Glenn interviewed me in character—Nickel Bag. It was ridiculous and hilarious, exactly the kind of public-access weirdness we lived for.

Another night, when Jean was on camera, a voice came over the phone line claiming to be Jerry Wexler—the legendary Atlantic Records producer. It really sounded like him. And if it wasn't, it was someone doing a damn good impersonation. For a second, the studio vibe shifted—this was the guy who produced Aretha. I mean, *Aretha Franklin*! How were Glenn and Chris supposed to handle this, when the standard modes of communication on *TV Party*, especially during the phone-in segments, were sarcasm, heckling, pranks, abuse?

Chris finally blurted out something cynical like, "Well, you're a little late, but there's still a lot of talent left."

Wexler—or Wexler's impersonator—then started talking about how there is, in fact, a *lot* of great talent in this country *and that's what makes this country so great*! At that, Jean grabbed the mic from Chris and yelled, "It makes you fucking money, you art pimp!"

Click.

Whoever was working the phone lines hung up on Jerry Wexler right then and there.

"You could think of *TV Party* as early reality television," Glenn would later say, "but it was a whole different reality."

7

Yo, Fred, I just saw your train!

I was hitting as many rap jams, parties, and battles as I could, piling up a pretty good mixtape collection along the way. The music I was getting into didn't really exist on the radio yet—or barely did—until the World's Famous Supreme Team came through on WHBI, 105.9 on the FM dial. The Supreme Team were two DJs, Sedivine the Mastermind and Just Allah the Superstar, both also Five Percenters. Theirs was probably the first radio show I can remember that served up the real-deal mix flavor. I would record their shows and add those tapes to my stash.

Then, out of nowhere, the Sugarhill Gang's "Rapper's Delight" dropped in the fall of 1979—and landed in the Top 40. This was what I had been talking to Melle Mel about, months and months before. There was still barely any marketing or promotion, just word of mouth, but this record exploded. An actual rap hit!

I was hyped. Rap, which only lived in the hoods and the housing projects of NYC, was busting out onto a bigger stage. There had been precursors, as there always are. Earlier that year, the Fatback Band put out "King Tim III," which a lot of folks see as the first commercial rap single. Bobby Robinson's Enjoy label put out some contenders. Spoonie Gee's "Spoonin Rap" came out that year too. But all of that was still local. "Rapper's Delight" broke through nationally. For a lot of listeners, it was their first taste of this new music.

The record itself was fun... but it left me kind of cold.

If you were going to the parties and you were into it, you *felt* it. It was like, *Man, this is so intense... I love this energy.* When the Sugarhill Gang—a group cobbled together by Sylvia Robinson, the founder of Sugar Hill Records—adapted that vibe to make a record, they built it around the hottest songs the DJs were spinning. In the case of "Rapper's Delight," that meant "Good Times" by Chic. But the vibe felt too clean, sanitized. It was like, *Okay, cool. At least they're hearing rap for the first time.* But if you'd ever been to a real jam, heard a raw party tape, or felt those sound systems cranked to the max, you knew the difference. That texture was *dirty*. In 1979, nobody had figured out how to bottle that grit in a studio. I mean, how could you capture something like that?

For the heads, though, the biggest issue with "Rapper's Delight"—besides the fact that it was cooked up in the Jersey burbs with zero grassroots connection to what I'd first learned to call the Uptown Sound—was that it straight-up lifted rhymes from one of the most revered and gifted MCs in the game: Grandmaster Caz of the Cold Crush Brothers. It turned out that a guy named Big Bank Hank, who had managed Caz for a time, was working at a pizza joint in New Jersey, rapping along to a Cold Crush tape behind the counter. Somebody heard him and asked if he wanted to be part of this new rap group. Hank didn't have rhymes of his own and he wasn't a rapper—so he just reached into Caz's portfolio, grabbed a handful of verses (which he knew by heart), and delivered what became the spine of the track. That included references to "Super Sporm" and even Casanova Fly, one of Caz's aliases. It took years for Caz to receive any recognition for providing the rhymes that propelled "Rapper's Delight" into the history books as the first big rap record, and he was never compensated. He was robbed, straight up.

(For more years now than I can count, I have been reading that around the time "Rapper's Delight" was climbing the Billboard charts, I jumped onstage with the Sugarhill Gang at the Palladium on Fourteenth Street—during a Clash concert, no less, with Chic as special guests. The story goes that we freestyled, goofed around, and everyone had a blast. Didn't happen.)

To me, "Rapper's Delight" being a *song* (even in its extended fourteen-minute version) marked the start of a shift in the rap game—from DJ to MC. The early days were all about DJs: Grandmaster Flash, the father of the quick mix and cutting; Grand Wizzard Theodore, the inventor of scratching; and the early DJ pioneers I loved, like Grandmaster Flowers, DJ Plummer, Maboya, Master D, and Pete DJ Jones. These cats piloted the party. MCs were the hype men, building energy on top of the DJ's foundation: *Come on, clap your hands to the music! Everybody clap your hands!* They were tapping into a long tradition of talk-singing-storytelling that goes way back in Black music, to the blues and early gospel.

Then came Grandmaster Caz, Melle Mel, Cowboy, and others, pushing the whole thing forward. They elevated the lyricism, tightened the flow. Like the DJs, they were remixing—but with words.

There was still a ways to go. I remember thinking: *When rap records start to speak about real shit—what's really going on out there in people's lives, not just the party, but the struggle—that's when people everywhere will feel it and connect with it in a huge way. That's when this thing becomes a force.*

EVERYBODY'S FLY

When Lee and I landed at Leonardo da Vinci Airport, Rome Fiumicino, I could tell that he was nervous as hell. This was the same Lee who'd always guided me through new terrain—subway tunnels, train yards, rooftops. Now, he looked like he wanted to catch the next flight back to JFK.

For my part, I was glued to the window, thinking, *Okay. I'm in Rome for the first time. Wow.* It was the same high I had always gotten from exploration, like riding the subways around New York as a kid.

Our show at Galleria La Medusa was titled *The Fabulous Five: Calligraffiti di Frederick Brathwaite, Lee George Quiñones*. "Calligraffiti" was a word I'd come up with—an idea sparked by the overlap between calligraphy and graffiti. I'd been thinking about how one of the roots of abstraction in global art was calligraphy, how it shows up in everything from Japanese landscapes to Islamic painting. It felt like the perfect note to strike for our debut show—and the first European exhibition devoted to graffiti-inspired art.

We'd brought about twenty pieces from New York, most of them roughly four by five feet, sprayed onto coarse, pre-primed canvases we'd picked up at Pearl Paint and placed on wooden stretchers at the gallery. The surface had this scratchy burlap texture that held the pigment in unpredictable ways as we layered our tags and images.

One piece I remember vividly was Lee's painting of an orange spray can with a cartoon face, letting loose a big yellow plume of pigment speckled with orange dots. Floating beside it, in pink bubble letters, was his signature: LEE. Later on, I found out that Lichtenstein had done a spray-can piece early in his career, which felt vindicating.

Lee and I were put up in a pensione a few blocks from the Spanish Steps and a short walk from the gallery. We were perplexed that there seemed to be two toilets in the bathroom, one of which had knobs, like you'd find on a sink or bathtub. I twisted one to see what was up and got blasted in the face with a jet of water. We later found out that this was, in fact, a bidet.

We spent the first couple of days hanging the show at the gallery, and our evenings at Claudio Bruni's place. If his Upper East Side townhouse had blown our minds, this was another level. More de Chiricos. Caravaggio drawings. Works by Lucio Fontana and Alberto Burri. Photographs by Baron von Gloeden, those stylized, turn-of-the-century shots of Sicilian boys posing like ancient statues.

On our first day in Rome, we had lunch at Claudio's. Lee and I were surprised to find ourselves being waited on by a Black, uniformed staff in white gloves—formal to the max, with table settings that required an instruction manual for the cluster of forks and knives. We were trying to keep it together. Claudio told us he had ties to the African nation of Togo. He knew the president, Gnassingbé Eyadéma, quite well—and that's why he employed an all-Black squadron of servants. At his Galleria La Medusa office, Claudio kept a large portrait of Eyadéma on the wall, a striking black-and-white image of a very dark-skinned man in full military getup, Idi Amin–style, medals gleaming. Claudio nodded toward the portrait and said jokingly, "That's my king." In 1979, Eyadéma had already ruled Togo for a dozen years, and he'd remain in power for another twenty-six. It was a strange and surreal touch to take in, to say the least.

One night, at a dinner party at Claudio's house, again presided over by the white-gloved Black staff, we noticed that all the guests were men. That struck us as a little unusual. At one point, an older Italian gentleman who barely spoke English leaned over and asked if Lee and I were a couple. We looked at each other, startled—and that's when we belatedly realized that Claudio was openly, proudly gay. He had come to visit us downtown once wearing a full-leather motorcycle outfit, straight out of the Village People. And somehow we hadn't figured it out. His partner, we learned, was an artist named Stanley John Allen, though everyone called him Tony.

Claudio was in many ways a larger-than-life character, for sure—but he understood what Lee and I were trying to do. He really saw our work. It reminded me of what I'd always heard from my dad and his friends about how jazz musicians found in Europe the kind of artistic respect that America too often withheld. Claudio saw graffiti not as vandalism but as art, and he treated us like real artists, not just curiosities. He saw graffiti in the context of art history, as I did.

He created a beautiful catalog for the show. In the essay, he wrote: "In New York there are some people who want to rub out the spray graffiti without realizing that this is the purest form of American popular visual art of the late '70s." He compared graffiti to jazz, which I appreciated, and he had picked up on another of my core ideas: "The Fabulous Five represent the natural and spontaneous result of the fusion between American Pop Art and the innate desire of the people to leave their mark, through graffiti."

It was honestly incredible to see these ideas in print, expressed so clearly and intelligently by someone with Claudio's standing in the art world. He even mentioned other American artists with deep Roman ties, Robert Rauschenberg and Cy Twombly. He compared our use of spray paint to Jackson Pollock and said that elements of our work evoked both Walt Disney and Alexander Calder. He suggested that what we were doing might someday be considered as significant as the early-twentieth-century avant-garde movements in European art.

But what hit the hardest was how deeply he understood the urgency and rawness that Lee and I loved about graffiti and tried to express in our work: "The feeling of aggressiveness that their message conveys is due to the fact that they are on the fringes of a society they want to conquer," one, he wrote, that "is too busy and organized to notice their existence." It was like, *Yo!*

The other catalog essay, by the scientist Adriano Buzzati-Traverso, floated the idea that it would be cool if the mayor of Rome hired me and Lee to paint the Victor Emmanuel II Monument!

Rome was magic. When we weren't at the gallery or Claudio's, Lee and I would just walk the city, often all night, trying to take in everything we could. Around every corner were more ruins, more history, more mystery. One night we hopped a fence and sat on the crumbling steps of the Colosseum, amid hundreds of stray cats. We talked about gladiator scenes from old movies and how it was wild to be here, a kid from Bed-Stuy and a kid from the Lower East Side.

One afternoon, I spotted two attractive girls, both with dark, shoulder-length hair, sitting at an outdoor café in Piazza Navona. They looked weirdly familiar to me. I nudged Lee: "I could be wrong, but I think those two cuties were in the audience at *TV Party* a couple of weeks ago and know Glenn." Sure enough, they were. How crazy to meet two girls from New York on a street in Rome! They became our friends; like us, they were happy to be strangers in a strange land. They were sisters, Cookie and Maria, in Rome for a few days of fun on their way to Barcelona to visit family.

And then, one evening, I saw Federico Fellini walking down the street in his signature Borsalino hat. He lived right in Claudio's neighborhood. I stopped him, and we had a quick little chitchat—me and the director of *La Dolce Vita* and *8½*. Yet another surreal Roman moment.

I'd brought my boom box and some mixtapes, just the dopest shit that no one in Italy had ever heard before. That became our soundtrack as we wandered Rome. It felt wild to be blasting that sound in the middle of a Roman piazza. At home, boom-box culture was really becoming a thing. A major part of what would later be called hip-hop was about putting things right in your face—whether you liked it or not. That was graffiti. That was breakdancing in the middle of a sidewalk. And that was this new music, blasting out of a huge boom box regardless of whether the rest of the world was ready or not. It was about being noticed, being *heard*. Deal with it.

Some of the boom boxes were so huge they needed like twenty D-size batteries to run. Guys who carried them around all the time developed forearms and biceps like weight lifters—I'm talking loud and heavy. My own Sanyo was my baby; it came with me wherever I went.

The Red Brigades were a no-show at the gallery opening, so there was no kneecapping, no drama. But Gianni Agnelli did show up, along with the Fendi sisters. We were introduced to contessa this and contessa that. The women were decked out in colorful fur coats and dripping in jewels—the absolute highest tier of Roman society. Lee and I were treated with total respect and kindness.

Even better, the show was a hit. Collectors were buying; every piece was sold. One of Lee's, a diptych, even fetched an unheard-of price: two thousand bucks.

I had always dreamed of bringing graffiti into what I thought of as another kind of subway yard: the art world. Now we were there.

Word traveled fast through the graffiti grapevine: Lee and Fred from the Fabulous 5 had just pulled off a major first—getting their work into a legit art gallery, even if that gallery was across the Atlantic. At the same time, because Claudio was so plugged into the scene, the art world was now paying attention. For the first time, people were starting to see graffiti in a different context—one where it could be appreciated, not just criminalized. The media had always framed it as a nuisance. But here it was, shown as art.

Some folks worried that we were trying to "clean up" graffiti by bringing it into the respectable realm of capital-A Art. But to us, putting on a show at Galleria La Medusa wasn't some act of compromise—it was a major outlaw statement. We did it our way, on our terms. And people noticed.

When we got back to New York that December, I knew it was finally time: the Campbell's soup cans train had to happen. (Lee and I never did get around to doing *Wonder-Fred* and *Tayst-Lee*.) The whole-car tribute to Warhol wasn't just an homage—it was a statement about contemporary art, about NY graffiti being on a continuum with Pop. The streets and the galleries were more connected than anyone realized.

Late one night, with the temperature plunging, we rode the 5 train up to the Baychester Avenue layup in the Bronx, loaded down with cans. We worked through the night, layering red, white, and gold. As the sun started to rise, we packed up and scrammed. The response was instant. Subway riders noticed. The Campbell's soup can train got an immediate response from riders, and the graff community buzzed.

And then it was gone. Buffed in a matter of days.

Suddenly, it was the 1980s.

Lee and I didn't wait long to take another swing at a whole-car, top-to-bottom Campbell's soup can piece. This time, we targeted the Morris Park IRT station in the Bronx. A mile-long tunnel there served as a layup, and we figured it was the perfect spot to go big. We reassembled the Fabulous 5—or most of it: Mono, Slug, and Doc rolled with us, bringing their expertise and, as usual, plenty of hilarity. Lee was tense, worried they'd goof off too much and bring heat down on us.

I was nervous as hell myself. That tunnel was long, cold, dusty, and pitch-dark. The five of us posted up, all in a line, to get the thing done. I had brought the red and white paint, and Lee came strapped with a full spread of colors. The other guys were working on their own pieces. Lee was also working on his own whole-car piece that night—running back and forth between both cars, troubleshooting, sketching, monitoring the progress, suggesting fixes, and helping me out with the proportions and any other issues that came up. He later called the night a "catastrophe." It really was a lot to handle.

We had upped the ante, big-time, with a revised design. Instead of four cans, we'd do eight. Lee had the idea to tilt one slightly, which added a whole new dynamism to the design. We planned to anchor the center with a bold "FRED" piece and fill the background with a fiery mix of red, orange, yellow. The cans came first; the background and lettering could wait. Those eight soup cans took forever to fill, even with fat caps. To make things slightly more manageable, we simplified some of the details, ditching the fleur-de-lis pattern at the bottom of each can and leaving the medallions as plain gold circles. With all five of us spraying away, the fumes in that tunnel got brutal fast. The air was thick. You could feel it in your chest, and I hadn't brought my respirator. The sound in there was eerie, echoey.

On the eight cans, I sprayed: DA-DA, POP, FABULOUS 5, FRED, FUTURIST, T.V. PARTY, and TOMATO. The last can, all the way on the right, I left blank—I never got the chance to write anything there. We didn't finish the background either, or the big FRED in the center. Before we could finish, the train started rolling out of the station. We grabbed our shit and took off.

An unfinished piece—every writer's nightmare. But even in its incomplete state, it became my calling card, my manifesto. It was my way of saying, "Check, check it out, art world—I'm hip to you, and we're coming, hard!"

Word spread fast. I heard people were clapping when the car rolled into stations. I loved imagining some curator from the Met or MoMA or the Whitney stepping onto that train on their morning commute, seeing our tribute, wondering who the hell would do something like this.

Somehow, the MTA let that second Campbell's soup can car stay in rotation for a long, long time. No buff, no repaint—it just kept rolling. I'd get calls or run into people: "Yo, Fred, I saw your train!" or "Hey, I rode your train today!" I was amazed it hadn't been taken out of service. Lee had a theory: There were MTA employees—track workers, conductors, whoever—who were down with what we were doing and kept certain cars away from the buffer. They protected it.

That train got serious exposure. For a while, it was paired up with another classic: Blade's swinging-letters car. As Lee put it later, the Campbell's soup can train "helped a lot of cats in the scene. Helped them realize and actually see that there was something bigger than this little cocoon that we had built for ourselves."

That was exactly the point. And it felt good that the Fabulous 5 crew came along for that ride. It was our last roundup—the end of one phase and the beginning of another. As 1980 got going, you could feel the cultural attitude around graffiti shifting. Claes Oldenburg, another of my Pop Art heroes, even said he liked it. To him, graffiti was "a big bouquet" sprouting all over the city.

I had a little Instamatic 110 snapshot of the first Campbell's soup can train—the one that got buffed—that I sometimes carried around. One day, I happened to be in Manhattan, walking past 860 Broadway, on the block between Union Square and East Eighteenth Street. As a devoted reader of *Interview*, and someone who'd read everything

I could about Andy Warhol, I knew this was the headquarters of *Interview* and the latest incarnation of Andy's Factory, where he'd moved the operation in 1974. I'd thought about tipping Henry Geldzahler off about the soup can train. But here I was, right at the source.

I hung around for just a moment. And then, to my amazement, the man himself came walking out the front door, accompanied by his assistant, Ronnie Cutrone, who had famously contributed his own urine to Andy's then-recent *Oxidation* paintings.

I walked up: "Excuse me, I'd just like to..." I introduced myself, said I was friends with Glenn O'Brien and the *TV Party* gang, and pulled out the photo of the soup can train.

"Oh my god, Fred," Andy said, in his Andy way. "This is so incredible." He took the photo from me, pulled out a pen, signed it, and handed it back.

I was like, *Um... okay.*

I had finally met Andy Warhol.

8

I was born and raised on planet Mars

Chris Stein and Debbie Harry of Blondie remember first running into me at CBGB. I remember first encountering them on the set of *TV Party*. Either way, we just hit it off. They started buying some of my and Jean's paintings, and we got pretty tight.

For long stretches, Chris and Debbie would be AWOL—always off on tour somewhere, gone for weeks at a time, crisscrossing North America, Europe, wherever. It seemed like they never stopped working. When *TV Party* kicked off, Blondie's *Parallel Lines* album had come out and was *everywhere*. As a commercial force, Blondie had blown way past the punk scene downtown, but they were still connected to the underground.

The big single from *Parallel Lines*, "Heart of Glass," was massive; you couldn't escape it. That electronic pulse reminded me of Kraftwerk, the German proto-techno band that was hugely popular on the DJ circuit and in the rap scene. Kraftwerk's "Trans-Europe Express" was always getting spins—and would later get sampled all over the place. So much music connects back to those guys.

Blondie's next album, *Eat to the Beat*, kept the momentum going with "Dreaming," "Atomic," and "The Hardest Part." If you check the video for "The Hardest Part," you'll catch an elaborate graffiti backdrop that Lee, Jean, and I painted—including one of my Campbell's soup cans, "ART SOUP."

And then, at the start of the new year, came "Call Me"—just as huge as "Heart of Glass." It had been recorded as the theme song for *American Gigolo*, the hit Richard Gere movie, and it was everywhere. Chris and Debbie had officially crossed over. They were now full-on rock stars.

Whenever they were back home and stationary for a minute, I'd head up to their prewar penthouse at 200 West Fifty-Eighth Street. I loved seeing that "PH," the top button on the elevator door, after the concierge got the okay for me to go up—it gave off this aura of palatial Manhattan living, like something out of an old movie or glossy magazine layout. But the apartment itself was just a classic three-bedroom, nothing flashy. No over-the-top rock-star stuff.

Chris or Debbie would open the door and be like, "Hey, Freddy! Can we get you something? A drink? You hungry?" That was always the vibe—warm, domestic, generous, totally at odds with how huge they were at that moment. They were sky-high pop stars, but always down to earth.

We'd hang for hours, just talking about everything that was happening—music, art, film, politics, whatever crazy stuff had gone down on *TV Party* that week. I'd bring up graff and how I wanted to take it somewhere new. They were amazing sounding boards when I was planning the Campbell's soup can trains, especially since they were tight with Warhol. We'd talk punk and New Wave, and I would explain that what I was seeing in the rap scene wasn't that different. I'd break it down—the DJs, the MCs, the B-boys, the slang, and the style.

UPTOWN/DOWNTOWN

"Yo, here's what goes on," I'd say. "There are fly guys and fly girls. This cat Flash is the fastest DJ, and that really means something because..."

By then I had a handful of raps, in case I found myself on the mic at a block party. I wasn't trying to be an MC, but I had one rhyme I rapped for Chris and Debbie—just to give them a little flavor:

> *I was born and raised on planet Mars,*
> *where I used to chill and rock with the stars.*
> *One day I got bored and decided to split.*
> *I came to Earth on a rocket ship.*
> *I crash landed in this park.*
> *It was a full moon out and very dark.*
> *Somebody was rapping upon the mic.*
> *It sounded kinda good and they rocked all right.*
> *So I moved a little closer to see how it was done.*
> *They said, "Grab the mic and have a little fun."*
> *So I grabbed the mic and rocked them all.*
> *I made them beg, scream, cry, and crawl*
> *to my vicious beat that's so unique.*
> *I made all the fly girls want to tap their feet.*
> *I made them throw their hands in the air,*
> *rock to the rhythm like you just don't care...*

And that was my little sci-fi fantasy rhyme about a man from Mars.

Chris and Debbie were naturally inclined to be fascinated by everything I was telling them. They had come out of the counterculture, they were in touch with the street, they had encyclopedic musical taste, they had friends in the art world, and they had do-it-yourself energy. (Like me, Chris had grown up in Brooklyn; he ended up at art school, at School of Visual Arts.)

They talked about wanting to make funkier music, something that would really make people dance. As I played mixtapes for them, I could see them becoming true believers in front of my eyes. Aside from "Rapper's Delight," there still wasn't a ton happening for rap in terms of media and exposure—a phenomenon they related to from the early days of punk, when Blondie was still coming up on the Bowery. So this was their first real exposure. And with Chris and Debbie, I always felt like we had major aesthetic synergy.

There certainly was synergy between the two of them. Whenever I was with them, I was struck by how tight they were as a couple—emotionally, intellectually, creatively. Chris may have been the one engineering most of the projects, but Debbie was right there with him. And they wrote most of their biggest hits together. In any conversation, she would speak right up. When they came up with a plan, they implemented it together, 100 percent. When you talked about Chris or Debbie, it was always *ChrisandDebbie*—like a single entity. That's how unified they were, even as they were becoming a huge force in the culture.

Stephen Sprouse, who designed Debbie's stage costumes, lived downstairs. He'd often come up and join these hangout sessions. He was on the verge of blowing up as a designer, cleverly incorporating graffiti elements into his colorful Day-Glo camouflage outfits.

You never knew who might be around at Chris and Debbie's. One afternoon, I had my goddaughter and her younger sister with me—Olu, who was six, and Ramona, who was four. They were the daughters of my father's buddy Jimmy Gittens. We were going to spend the day cruising around Manhattan. Chris and Debbie had asked me to swing by with the girls.

When we got to the penthouse, William S. Burroughs, of all people, was sitting in the living room. I had read *Naked Lunch* and told him so, mentioning how cool it was that he'd been the one to use the term "heavy metal" for the first time in that book. I also started talking about the new wave of DJs—how they were cutting and mixing and scratching—the musical equivalents of the cut-up techniques that he and Brion Gysin had pioneered in the realm of writing. I was always trying to draw these kinds of parallels—finding connections that might help people understand the culture I was bringing forward. Burroughs listened with interest, but I think he was more fascinated by Ramona and Olu, just amusing themselves at the coffee table. I remember him remarking about how kids are always so wrapped up in their own little worlds.

One thing about Chris: He always had a stash of super-sticky, high-powered grass from Cali and Hawaii—well before that level of cannabis became the norm. He collected knives and weird horror-movie memorabilia, and there were piles of weird, cool shit all over that apartment.

I would often sit on the floor of their bedroom while Chris sat cross-legged on the bed and Debbie floated in and out. The bedroom TV was always on. Chris would be flicking the remote, keeping tabs on cable programs that you might say were "competing" with *TV Party*: Al Goldstein's show, Robin Byrd's show, Coca Crystal's *If I Can't Dance, You Can Keep Your Revolution*. It wasn't competition, exactly. The vibe was more like we were all pioneers in a new uncharted space we'd just jumped into headlong. The great unknown.

Chris was into TV in a super-intense, ultra-observant way. Looking back, I realize how much it must have fed his vision. He had a three-quarter-inch U-matic video-cassette deck; we'd watch tapes of *TV Party* together, which was the only way I could ever see the show. (Glenn also had one of those machines.) Chris would talk about the new LaserDisc technology—back then, it was known as DiscoVision—and how music videos were going to be the next big thing. They would replace albums as the way to experience music—you'd see it as well as hear it. He spearheaded a whole bunch of Blondie videos for the new format. They were like little films, each one built around a song.

No surprise, we talked a ton about movies. As always, I was thinking about filmmaking, and I had a vague but growing idea: a movie about everything we were immersed in—graffiti, rap, breakdancing, punk, uptown, downtown. Something that tied it all together and made a real statement.

I kept coming back to something I'd read in that essay I'd found years earlier in the basement on Hancock Street, the one quoting Albert Murray: For a cultural movement to truly be a movement, it needed three aesthetic components. That idea had lodged deep in my brain. And it was clear to me. Graffiti (art), rap (music), and breaking (dance) were together the force. Clearly linked and emerging from the same place and space, same time. The right frequency—one shared, emerging, complete culture. But nobody had defined it yet, and few understood or celebrated it. To me, a film—something raw and stylish, like an underground art movie—would be the perfect way to tell that story and to broadcast it to the world.

Chris and Debbie knew all about reaching a wide audience—and how to do it on their own terms. When they were home, off tour, they weren't chasing paparazzi or playing the fame game. They were low-key, anti-celebrity. That was part of the downtown code. But when it was time to step out—for a show, a shoot, a television appearance—it was like, *Okay, here we go...* Debbie would then turn it up to eleven— throw that makeup on, get the hair just right, and *BOOM!* Suddenly it was... *Blondie.*

It fascinated me. Debbie was "Blondie" in the sense that she was such a focus of attention, playing the archetypal blond Marilyn Monroe–like bombshell in the American pop pantheon. But she and Chris would wear buttons that said "BLONDIE IS A BAND." They were constantly playing to and against type, a fascinating push and pull in terms of their very powerful public image.

Our conversations could go anywhere, and I never felt like I had to hold back. I remember one time bringing up a song I had loved since I was a kid—Bobbie Gentry's "Ode to Billie Joe." They were probably surprised, but to this day, whenever that song comes on the radio, I'm still struck by how real it feels. The dramatic elements always grab me, like, *Yes, this probably happened. Billie Joe MacAllister really* did *jump off the Tallahatchie Bridge.* Or something *like that* happened. I had never been to a place like Choctaw Ridge—a pocket of the Delta probably filled with trailer parks and poor folks, Black and white—but that song gave me a glimpse. It showed me how a "real record" could work: a song about people's actual lives, their fears and secrets, their pain and their culture and their shame. A song that could travel *way* beyond your own little world and hit people right where they live.

I didn't plan on jumping off a bridge or anything, but I would think to myself: *What if there was a song like that about me? Or about Bed-Stuy? About the world I came up in. What if this rap thing could talk about that kind of stuff?* You know: Make it *real.*

After talking for hours and hours, I would say good night to Chris and Debbie and catch the A train from Columbus Circle for the long haul back to the Kingston-Throop stop in Bed-Stuy. Passing a newsstand, I would see magazine after magazine—*Rolling Stone, Interview, Creem*—with Chris and Debbie's faces right there on the covers. I would be like, "Yo, are those really the same people I was just hanging out with?" Yes they are! That's something I learned from them— how to be calm, be cool, be yourself, be normal in the face of fame. That was a huge life lesson for me—one I'd also gotten from my godfather, Max Roach. Like: You can be famous and still be cool as hell—

not a jerk, not a diva, not an asshole, unlike too many people in their situation!

That mattered to me, because, as I once told Debbie late one night at their place, it was inevitable I'd be well-known someday based on the quality of work I planned to do. She smiled, and I could tell she felt my confidence and focused determination.

When I got back home to Hancock Street, my mother would often still be awake. I'd hit her with the major headlines of what I'd been up to: "Hey, I was just with Blondie!" Or, "Mom, I hung out with Andy Warhol!" Or, "I met William S. Burroughs tonight!" I'd be standing at her bedroom door, talking a mile a minute, and she'd just listen, soaking it all in, while my father slept. Our relationship was almost like that of siblings—she never got tired of hearing about my latest exploits, my wildest encounters, all the new plans and projects I was chasing. These conversations would typically end with, "All right, Frederick, you just be careful out there."

After the Tuesday-night *TV Party* broadcasts, we'd head down to this new joint on White Street in Tribeca, in a building owned by the artist Ross Bleckner. It was called the Mudd Club. The location was perfect in the most unlikely way. After work hours, Tribeca and SoHo basically went dark. They weren't real neighborhoods yet. Everything shut down; the era of twenty-four-hour bodegas was still in the future. At night, those streets were empty and eerie, like you were stepping into some kind of nether zone.

The building itself was bland, totally unremarkable. But inside, something wild was happening. Somebody once referred to our downtown scene as the "Fabulous 500," meaning that our extended posse of artists, filmmakers, writers, actors, and art-school dropouts looking for a good time was tiny in terms of the overall population of NYC. We were the original crew at the Mudd Club, before it blew up into the epicenter of New Wave hipster cool.

CBGB was still a staple and Max's Kansas City was always a scene. But both spots felt like they were winding down. The Mudd Club? When it hit, it hit hard. We knew right away: This was ours. This was our place.

It quickly became the hottest club in New York, the total opposite of Studio 54. And it pulled people from all over the city, like a magnet. But if you showed up looking like you were trying to get into Studio 54—all uptown and polished and establishment, not cool and downtown and young—you probably weren't getting past the door. Richard Boch, the guy working the entrance, made sure of that.

When the Mudd Club took off—and it took off fast—Studio 54 was the symbol of velvet-rope exclusivity: "Oh, *you* can come in, but not *you*." "*You're* cool, but not your friend." I went up there once to see what the hype was about. I wasn't trying to play myself, nor get played, so I laid back and watched the frenzy to get in. People begged, cried, and pleaded, getting no love from the rope keepers.

At the Mudd Club, there wasn't some fancy velvet rope—just a flimsy metal chain. But Richard could work that thing like a savage. I will never forget one night rolling up with Jean and a couple of our homies, just as a group of people were stepping out of a limo parked in front of the entrance on White Street. I want to say it was Halston, Paloma Picasso, and some other boring fashion somebody-or-other I can't remember. *That* crowd. They were standing there in front of Richard, assuming they'd be whisked inside. Meanwhile, the sidewalk was packed with punks, fashionistas, artists—the funky downtown melting pot.

EVERYBODY'S FLY

Richard looked right past the limo crew and spotted me.

"Oh, Freddy. Hi, Jean. How many?"

"Four," I said.

"Okay, come right through."

We sailed past the uptown types, who were left standing on the curb. It was a major affirmation: *This is ours, baby.*

Studio 54 was sexy to some—but the Mudd Club was edgy, cool, and *kinky*. It was a lot like *TV Party* (we even filmed a couple of episodes there), but supersized, with a pumping sound system designed by a brilliant tech named Brooke Delarco, based on a napkin sketch from Brian Eno. The owner, Steve Mass, was a film guy—he'd worked with Jack Smith—and had some money to play with. He started the club with Diego Cortez, a curator, and Anya Phillips.

They clearly thought hard about the crowd they wanted at the Mudd Club. That was always key in clubland: You needed a solid core every night to really make a scene happen. At the Mudd Club, that crew was us—every kind of downtown bohemian you could imagine, the edgier the better. We were the ones keeping it lit. So it became a clubhouse. A place where you could have intense, late-night discussions about culture, ideas, and all the crazy projects you were working on. The Mudd Club made being intellectual feel sexy.

Every time I walked in, I would meet someone fascinating— artists, musicians, freaks, misfits—and more than a few infallibly cool, not to mention gorgeous, women. Tina L'Hotsky, who threw outrageous theme parties, earned her crown as Queen of the Mudd Club. And then there was the glamorous Wendy Whitelaw, a top-tier makeup artist and scene-maker in her own right.

The interior had a stripped-down, Bauhaus vibe—which was cool by us, since we were already hip to earlier art and design movements. Unlike most clubs, it wasn't all flashing lights and disco balls. It was raw and minimal. It might've been the first club to have its own gal-

UPTOWN/DOWNTOWN

lery space. There were screenings, fashion shows, and a stage for live performances—the curtain was one of those roll-down metal gates you'd see on storefronts. A genius touch.

I was there one night when Marianne Faithfull rolled in after doing *Saturday Night Live* and jumped up to perform a set. The B-52s played. Talking Heads played. Even the old-school Stax legends Sam and Dave played. And Gray played too, laying down a sound like no other and pulling in the hippest crowd. Soon you started seeing Iggy Pop and Nico checking out the scene. And before long, Andy Warhol and David Bowie were there too. Our scrappy downtown playpen of cool had acquired an international reputation as the place to be.

The DJs—Anita Sarko and Johnny Dynell—spun the wildest mix of sounds: punk, funk, oldies, No Wave. One minute you'd get Bryan Ferry; the next it was ESG, Bauhaus, or James Brown. The latest underground tracks bumping right up against old favorites. As I became a regular, I started nudging them to go even deeper—early rap records, rare disco cuts, the kind of stuff the mobile DJs played. This was still a mostly white scene, so a lot of that music wasn't on the radar yet. But Jean and I were on a mission.

We'd go up to Anita and say, "Yo! Why don't you play this?" And she'd be like, "Well, if Steve sees that you guys are here, he won't mind." And Steve didn't mind. In fact, most of the cooler DJs were ready to get funkier. And they did. (Johnny's original track, "Jam Hot," would go on to become a major club hit just a couple of years later.)

The overlap I'd always sensed between punk and rap was now pulsing live on the sweaty dance floor of the Mudd Club. It was a stunning cultural moment, and for me, it made the Mudd Club feel even more like home.

Steve invited me to do some rapping at the club. He could tell rap was the new thing, saw me as the downtown connection to that culture, and assumed I could rap. And, yeah, I had a few hot rhymes in my pocket. But being an MC wasn't my objective. I was working on being an artist, trying to light the fuse to help set off a movement.

Still, I figured that whatever raps I might throw down would sound cool to that downtown crowd. As hip as they were, they had zero clue about what was actually going down at the parties and jams. They had no frame of reference—no way to gauge whether I was any good. So I said, "Why not?" and decided to go for it. The downtown folks needed a little taste, and maybe it would open a door.

So, in the summer of 1980, I hit the stage at the Mudd Club with Master D, a DJ from Bed-Stuy, billed as "Freddy Fred and the Master D Crew" in a "rappin performance." Glenn, Jean, and a bunch of the *TV Party* crew were on hand to support the effort, adding to a great crowd. Along with my little arsenal of rhymes, I hit them with the standard "Wave your hands in the air and act like you just don't care," and everybody happily complied—grooving along and loving it, as I knew they would. I made sure to give Master D plenty of spotlight moments so he could show off his cutting, scratching, and backspin skills. Jaws literally dropped. Nobody at the Mudd Club had ever seen or heard anything close to what the two of us were doing.

That night sealed it. Word spread. I ended up being credited with bringing rap into the downtown scene.

Of course it went down at the Mudd Club, where the spirit of connectedness reigned supreme—the hippest spot and the most open. Even then, at the height of post-punk New York, a lot of us were still very conscious of the wildness of the 1960s, that earlier wave of creativity and rebellion we'd absorbed as little kids and kept reading about and thinking about: Warhol's Factory, Swinging London, Haight-

Ashbury, the Panthers, all of it. The Mudd Club gave us a way to channel that same electric energy and make it ours—our time, our sounds, our look.

"Last call for alcohol!" you'd hear as four a.m. approached. When the Mudd Club was ready to close and the new day was rising, we'd drift around the corner to Dave's Luncheonette at Broadway and Canal for hot dogs and egg creams or lime rickeys. After-hours conversation would flow, as we laughed about whatever craziness had gone down at the club, debating the latest gallery show or record, or diving deep into bohemian history—the Lost Generation in Paris? The Impressionists? Caravaggio's Rome? One of us would ask, "Did you read *Popism* yet?" "Yes, loving it, and I'm almost finished!"

We were keeping the bohemian flames lit, trying our best to go against the grain. Us against them! Other clubs were crawling with bridge-and-tunnel types. But this was *our* turf, something truly ours. Have another egg cream!

And then it was back to Canal Street, waiting forever for that damn A train, and riding on home to Brooklyn.

When spring was about to turn the corner into summer, two major things happened. First: There was a new addition to the family. Nicole—a bouncing baby girl, my adorable little sister. My mom was happy about being back in mommy mode. My dad was pleased as well. And Doris was right there, excited to help out with her brand-new niece.

The second thing—maybe not quite as momentous, but still a big deal—was that Glenn O'Brien published a massive story in *High Times* called "Graffiti '80: The State of the Outlaw Art." He put it all in there: graffiti's beginnings in caveman times, the omnipresence of Taki 183, the artistry of Stay High 149, the invention of bubble lettering by Phase 2, the "post-pop" flavor of Lee's work, the guerrilla-style messages of SAMO, and the art-world statement of my Campbell's soup can train.

I had been in Glenn's ear about graffiti for more than a year, so it made sense that I ended up as the main voice in the piece. He wrote it with that same razor-sharp, stylish swagger I knew from his *Interview* columns: "Graffiti fights the fascism of design, the ultimate subliminal weapon for grinding down the human spirit, the hideous barrenness of 'clean' urban design."

He saw graffiti as "reminders that there are some things that can't be controlled, thousands of individual identities asserting themselves in wild color and bold hand across the tabula rasa of modern corporate planning." He quoted Lee: "It reminds you that there's some life around you."

Glenn also spotlighted my efforts to bring graffiti into new spaces, mentioning the Unique Clothing Warehouse gig, the work Lee and I did on people's garden walls, and, of course, our Rome show. He captured our mission to "have fun, make money, and brighten things up."

This was easily the most ambitious story about the graff scene since Norman Mailer wrote about it in "The Faith of Graffiti" in the early 1970s. It featured a lavish and colorful layout, which used some of my own lettering and included a photo of the *Graffiti 1979* handball court—updated by Lee to read "Graffiti 1990," because I wanted to signal that this movement had its eye on the future.

There was a sharp photograph of me standing next to Lee, who—for once—had allowed himself to be in the picture. And there was another of Jean, looking fly in a big gray trench coat in front of one of his surviving SAMO wall pieces. A shirtless Mick Jagger was on the cover. I figured that would get some attention on the newsstand.

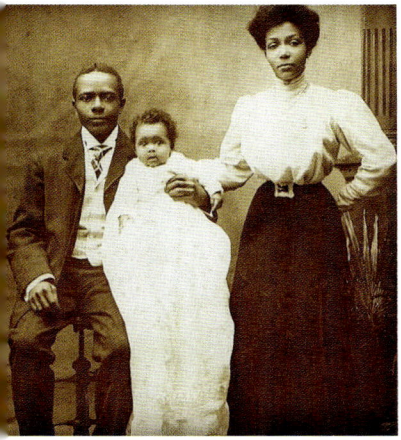

My Garveyite grandfather, Frederick Theophilus Brathwaite, in 1907, with his first wife and daughter, Fredericka, affectionately known as Aunt Freddy, who lived to a hundred and passed on in 2007

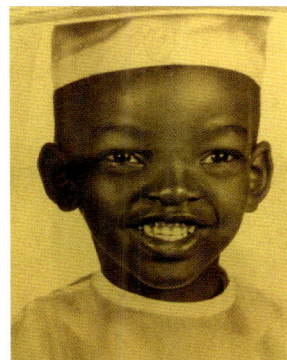

Kindergarten graduation, age five

With Mom and Dad, Theresa and Fred Brathwaite, at the airport, age six

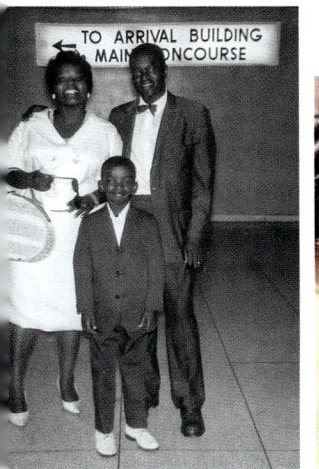

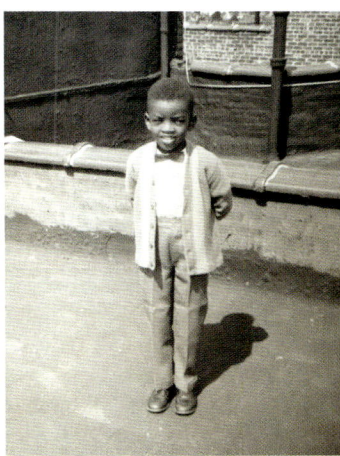

Age five

Outside Holy Rosary Catholic school, age twelve

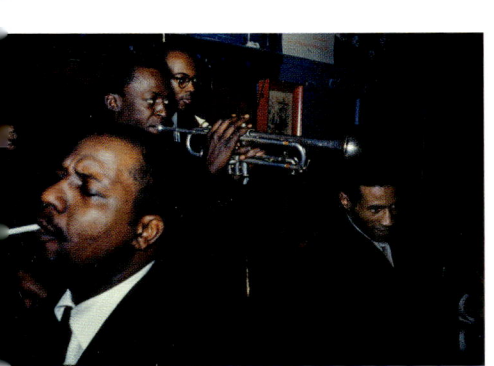

From left to right: Thelonious Monk, Miles Davis, Gigi Gryce, and Max Roach on drums, in Brooklyn at Tony's Club Grandean, 1953

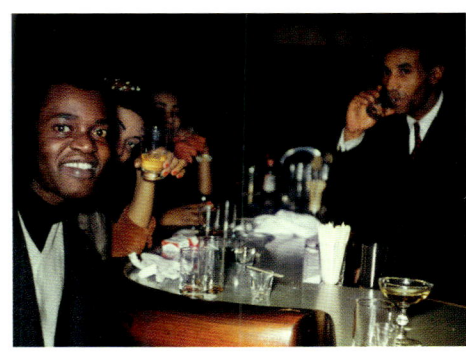

My dad chilling with my godfather, Max Roach, with the Clifford Brown–Max Roach Quintet at the Beehive in Chicago, 1955

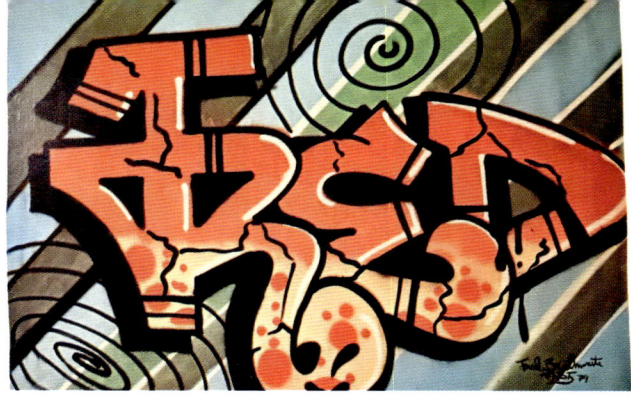

One of my first works on canvas at the Galleria La Medusa, 1979

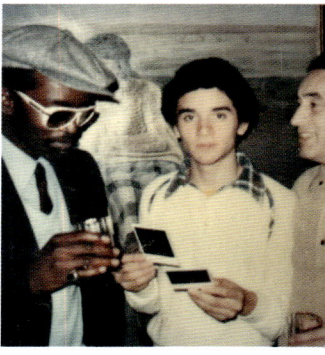

Me and Lee Quiñones at our art dealer Claudio Bruni Sakraischik's house in Rome, 1979

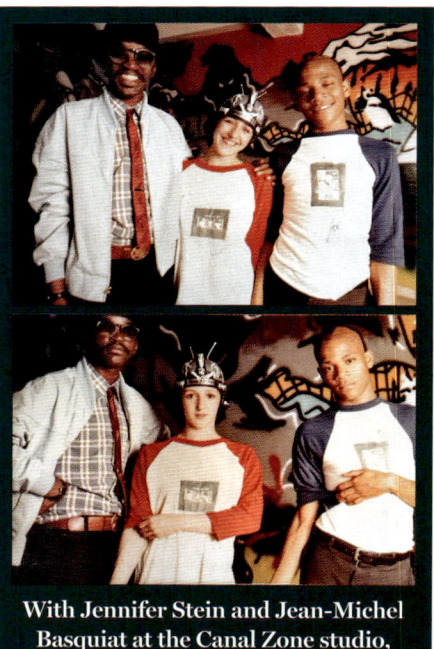

With Jennifer Stein and Jean-Michel Basquiat at the Canal Zone studio, 533 Canal Street, New York, 1979

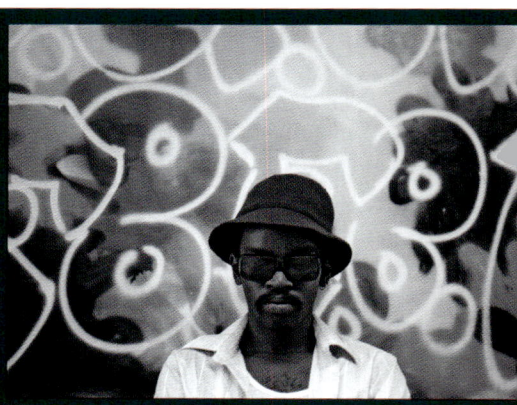

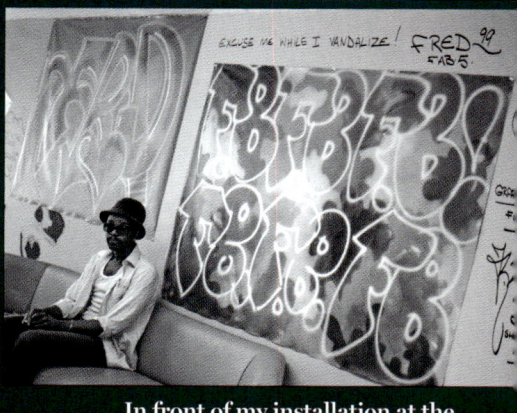

In front of my installation at the Times Square Show, 1980

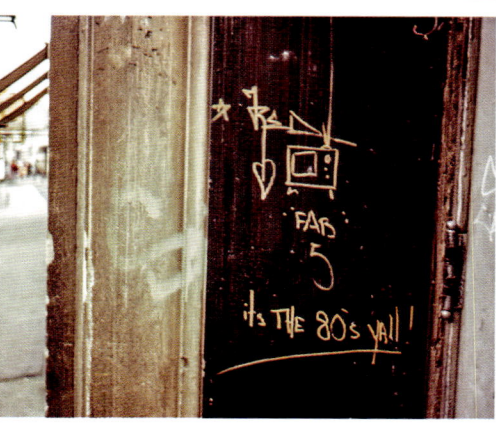

A tag I did: It's the '80s, y'all!

Outside the Times Square Show, 1980

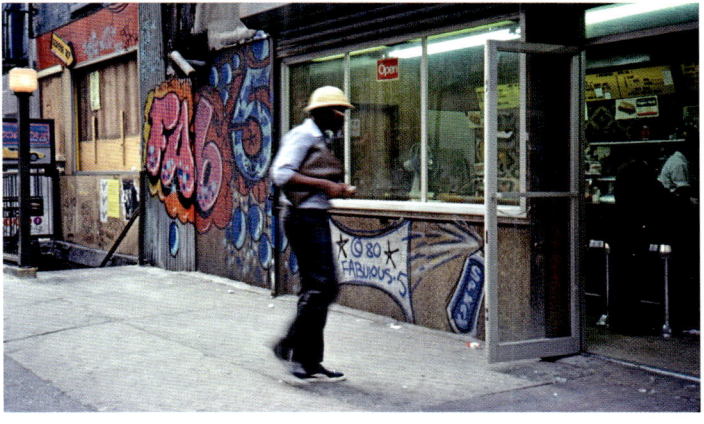

At my apartment/studio at 42 Clinton Street, New York, ca. 1981

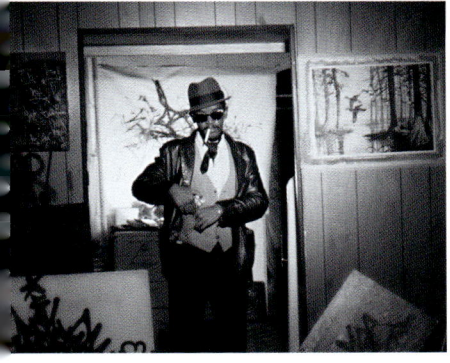

With Lee and Jean on the set of *Downtown 81*

Rammellzee, Kool Koor, myself, Jean, and Toxic at the Fun Gallery, New York, 1982

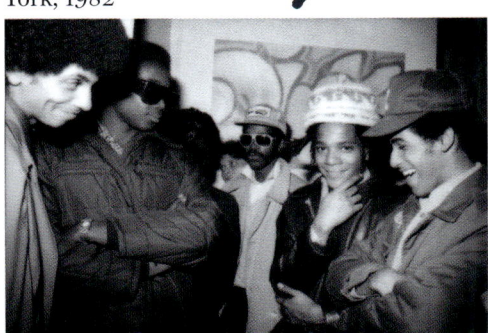

PHOTOGRAPH © ELINOR VERNHES

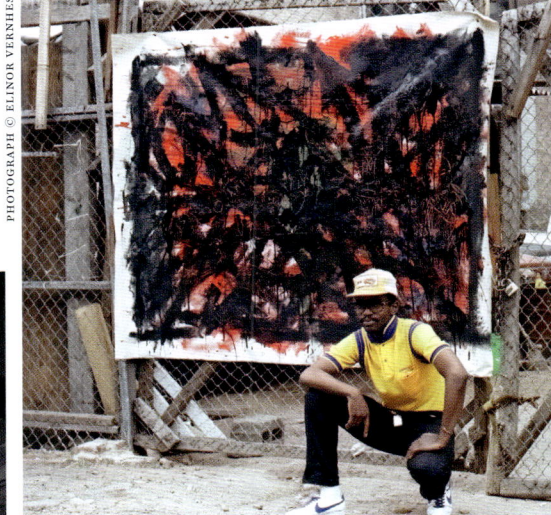

Outside my Clinton Street apartment with a fresh piece I just finished, ca. 1980

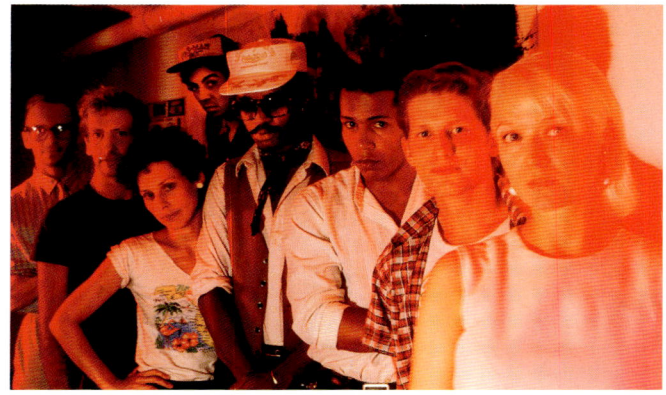

The Fun Gallery crew: Arch Connelly, Kenny Scharf, Jane Dickson, Futura 2000, me, Dondi, Kiely Jenkins, and Patti Astor at the *Radiant Child* photo shoot at the Fun Gallery, 1981

With Arch Connelly and Dondi at the *Radiant Child* photo shoot at the Fun Gallery, 1981

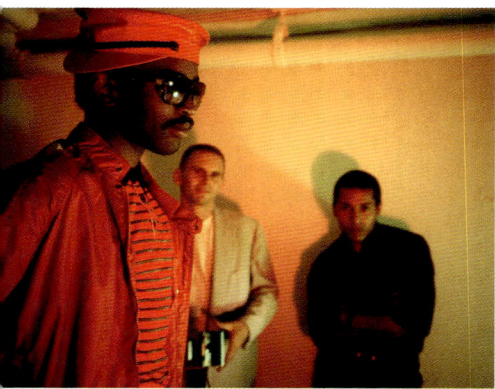

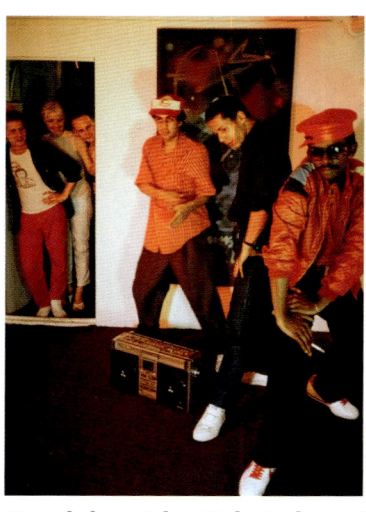

From left to right: Kiely Jenkins, Patti Astor, and Arch Connelly in the doorway and Futura 2000, Dondi, and myself at the *Radiant Child* photo shoot at the Fun Gallery, 1981

Hanging with Joe Strummer of the Clash, Raymond Jordan, and Futura 2000 in Asbury Park, New Jersey, June 1982

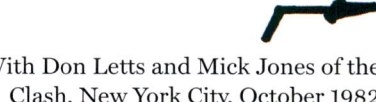

With Don Letts and Mick Jones of the Clash, New York City, October 1982

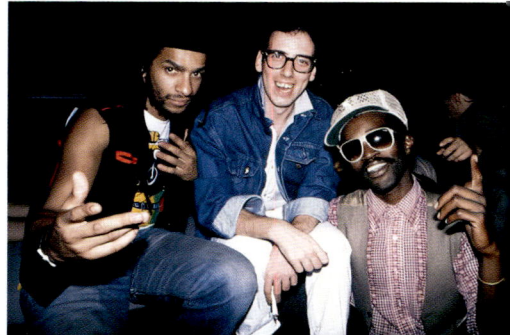

Jean at the turntables on the set of the "Rapture" music video, 1981

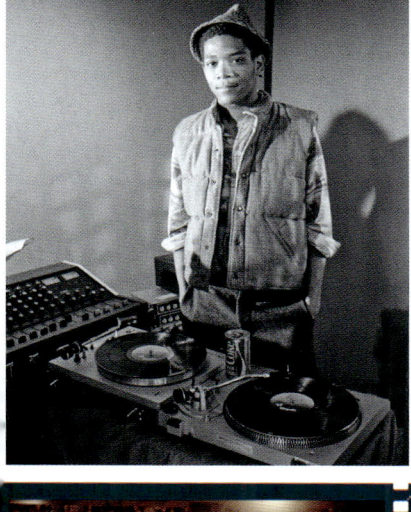

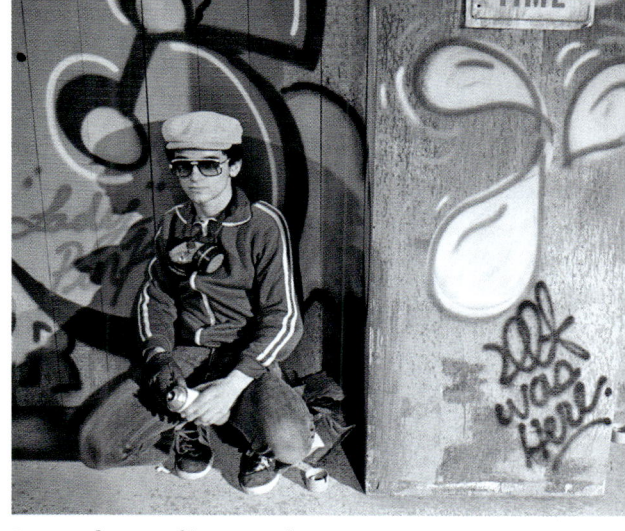

Lee on the set of "Rapture," 1981

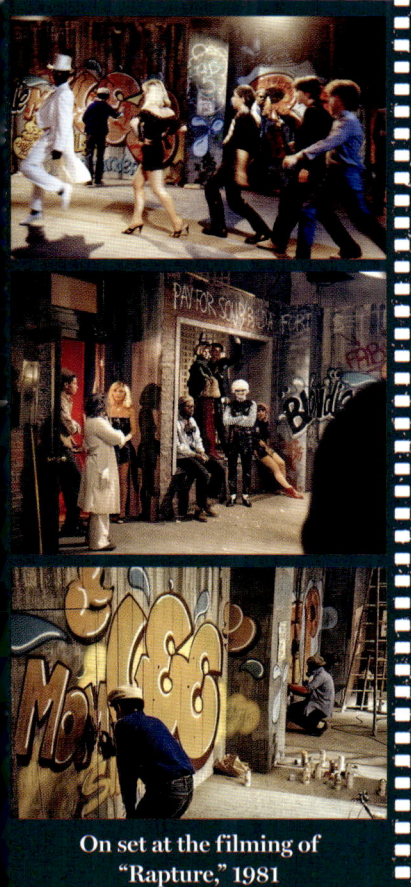

On set at the filming of "Rapture," 1981

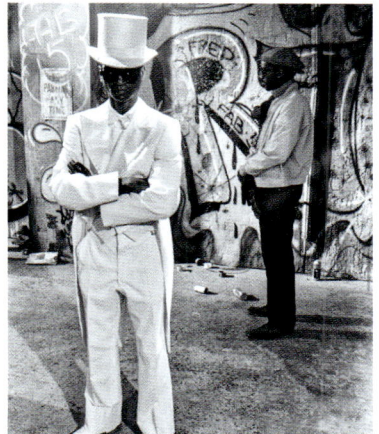

Chillin' behind a member of a Haitian dance troupe on the set of "Rapture," having just painted my *Rap* piece, 1981

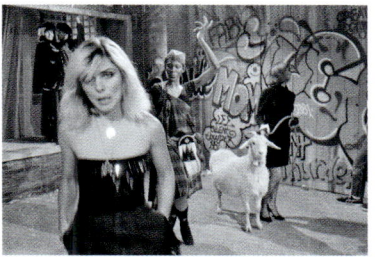

Chee Chee behind Debbie Harry on the set of "Rapture," 1981

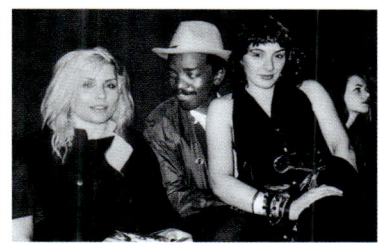

Debbie, me, and Maripol, 1983

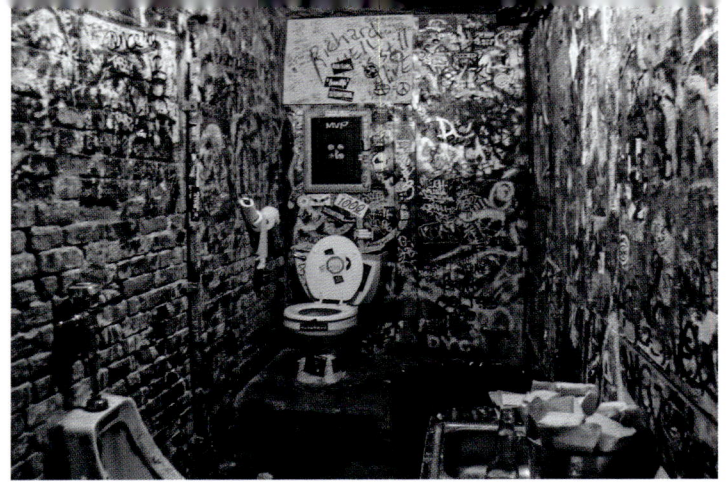

Bathroom at CBGB, 1980

With Max Roach, New York City, 1983

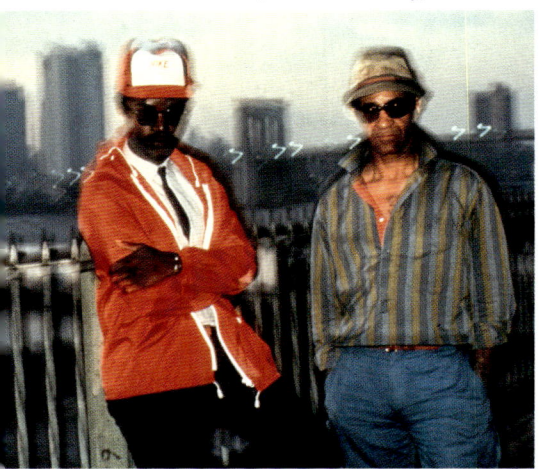

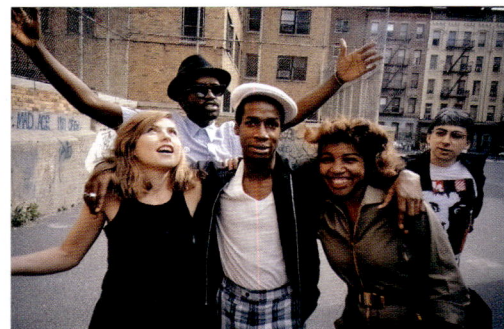

Hands in the air behind Debbie, Grandmaster Flash, Rae Chamblee, and Chris Stein, New York City, 1981

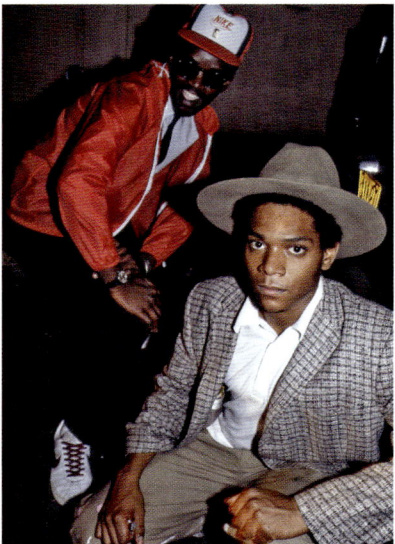

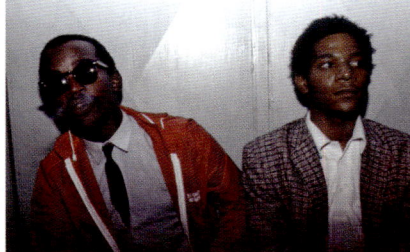

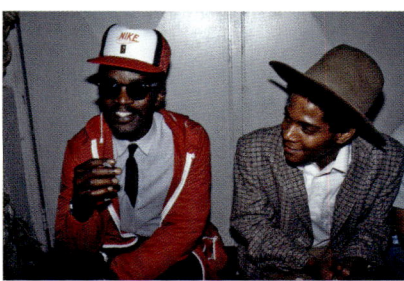

Hanging with Jean, New York City, 1983

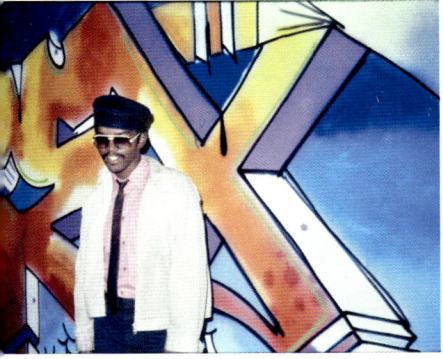

In front of my *Sex* painting at the New York/New Wave exhibition at MoMA PS1, Queens, New York, 1981

Taking a puff after filming of *TV Party*, 1980

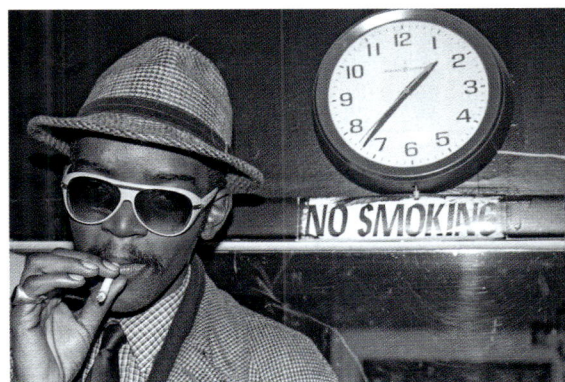

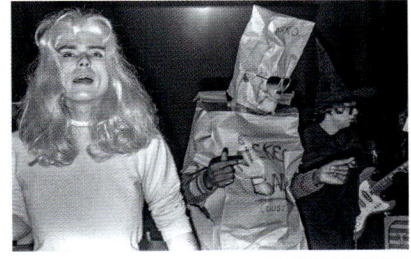

TV Party Halloween costume party with Glenn O'Brien, me (dressed as a "nickel bag of dust"), and Chris Stein, October 30, 1979

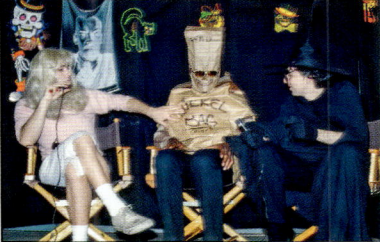

TV Party Halloween party, October 30, 1979

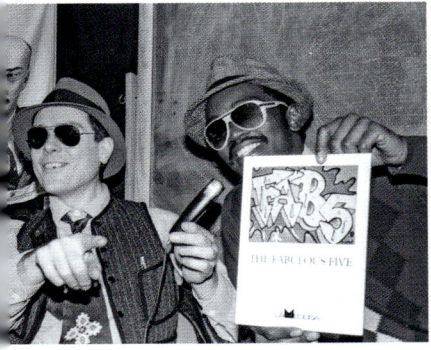

With Glenn at *TV Party*, showing off the catalog from our exhibit in Rome, 1980

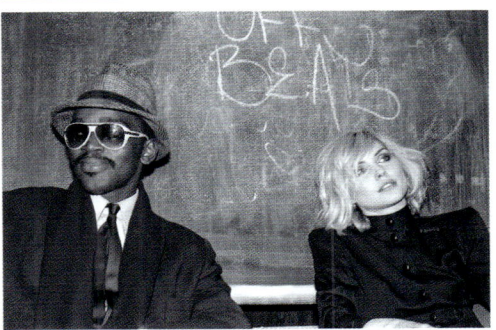

With Debbie at *TV Party*, 1980

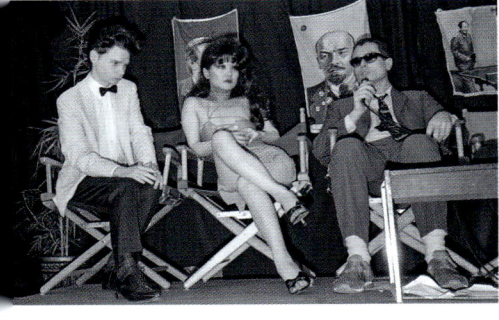

James Chance, Anya Phillips, and Glenn at *TV Party*, 1980

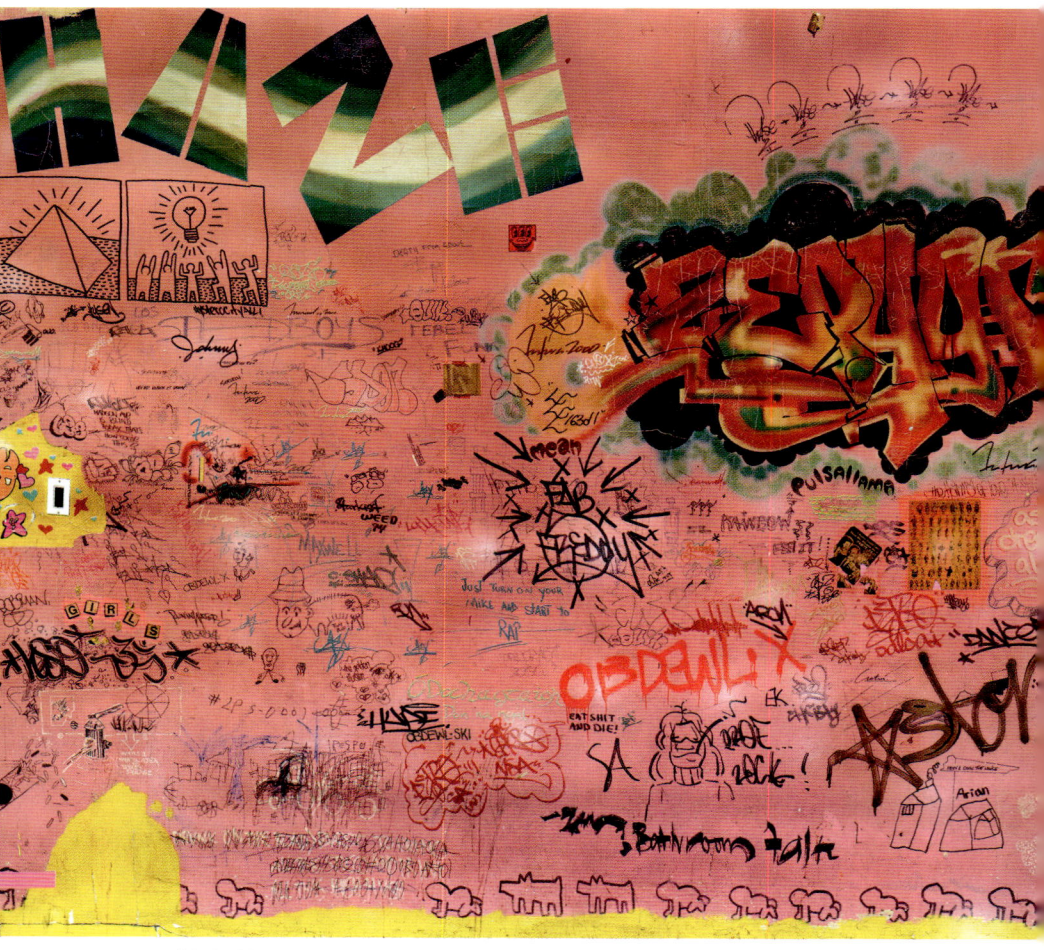

Gerb's hallway wall in his apartment, with contributions from me, Futura 2000, Keith Haring, Jean, Revolt, Zephyr, Eric Haze, Phase 2, LSD, and many more

PHOTOGRAPH © RAINER HOSCH

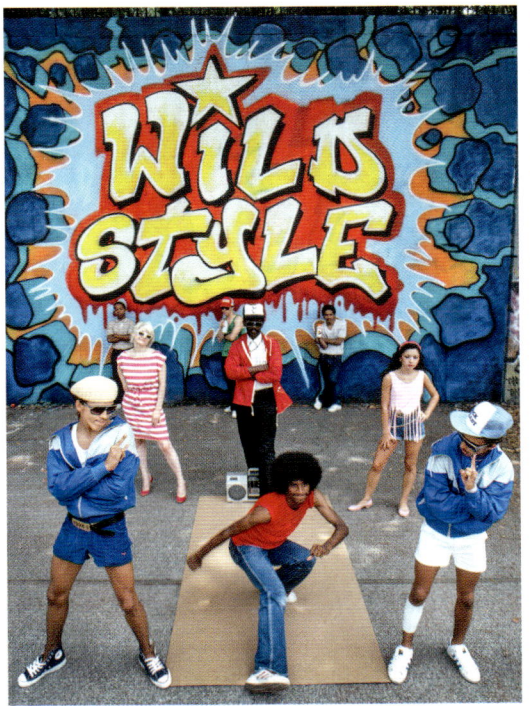

Wild Style mural by Zephyr, Revolt, and Sharp, New York, 1983. Front row from left to right: Doze, Frosty Freeze, and Ken Swift. Middle row: Patti Astor, myself, and Lady Pink. Back row: Lil Crazy Legs, Revolt, and Sharp

Lee Quiñones painting the *Wild Style* amphitheater mural, 1983

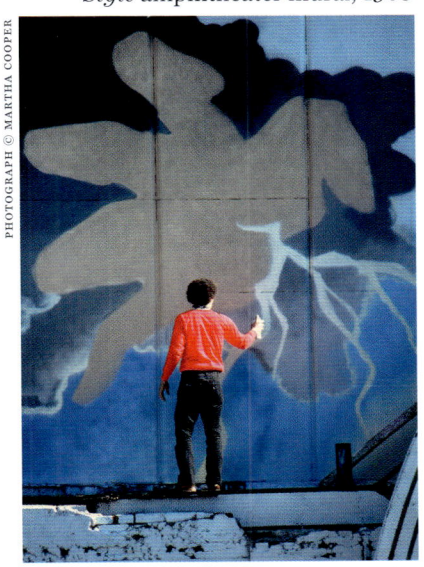

Charlie Ahearn directing the basketball scene in *Wild Style* with the Fantastic Five, 1983

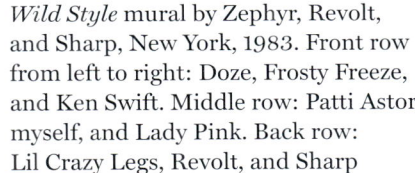

Chief Rocker Busy Bee performing in *Wild Style*, East River Park Amphitheater, Lower East Side, New York, 1982

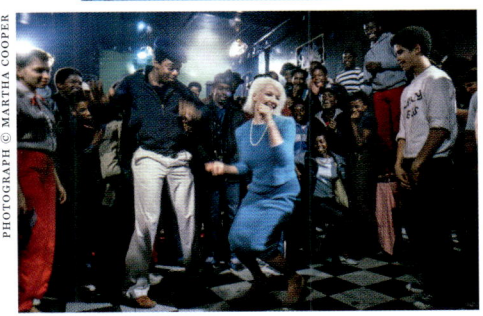

Patti Astor with Crazy Legs from the Rock Steady Crew looking on at the Dixie Club, in a scene from *Wild Style*, South Bronx, New York, 1981

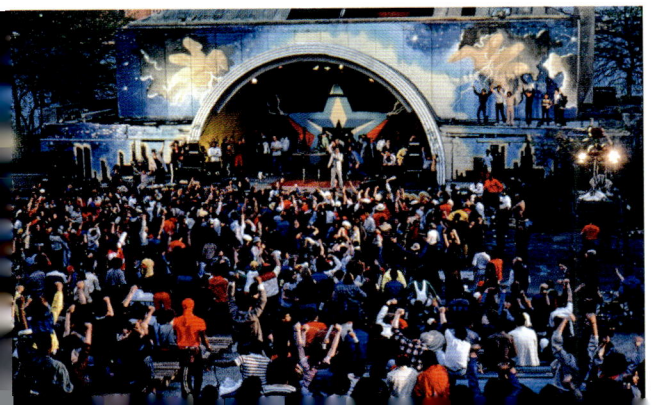

With Patti Astor on the set of *Wild Style*, 1983

Charlie directing me on the set of *Wild Style*, 1983

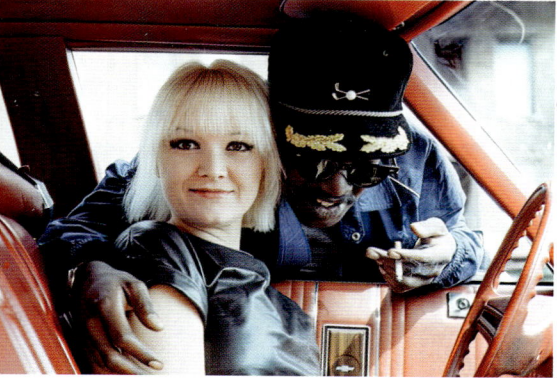

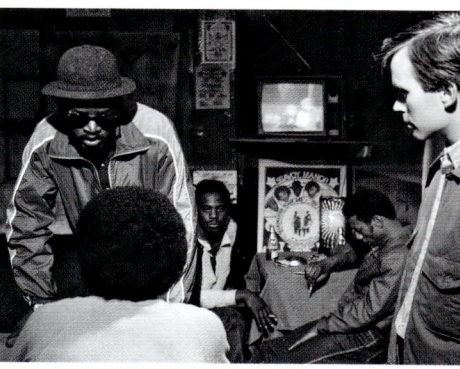

PHOTOGRAPH © MARTHA COOPER

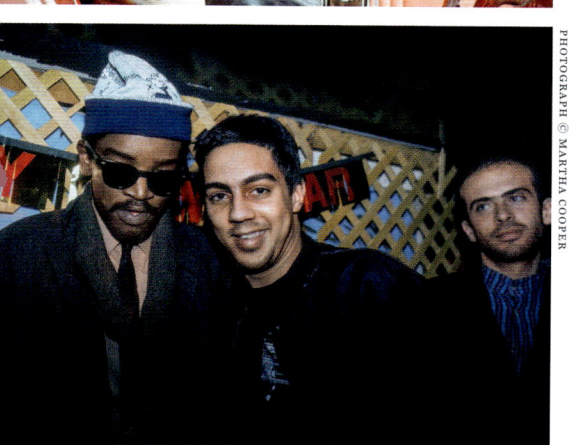

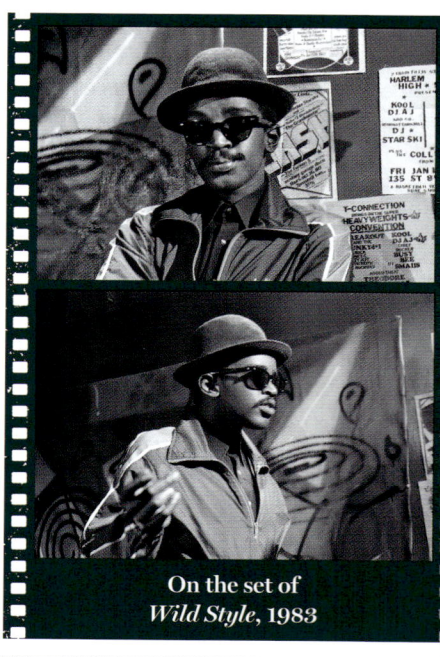

On the set of *Wild Style*, 1983

At Negril with Futura 2000 and Francesco Clemente, ca. 1981

Keith, Bethann Hardison, Grace Jones, and me at the after-party for Keith's Fun Gallery show, 1983

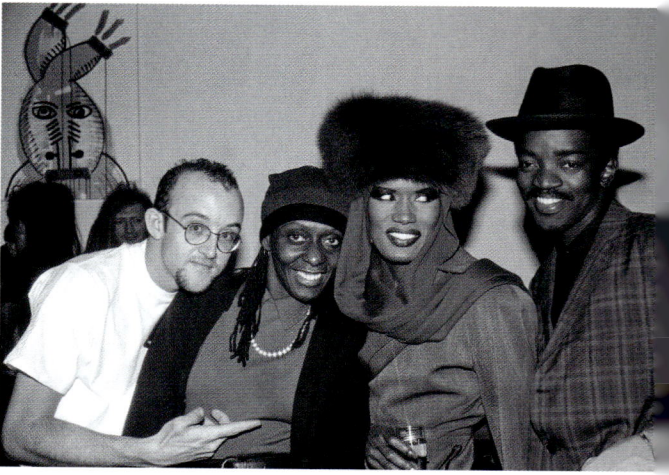

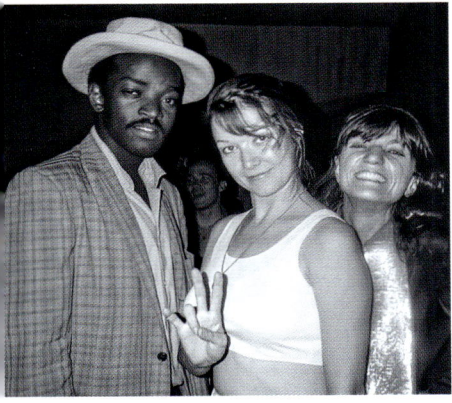

With Patti Astor and Edit DeAk at the Absolut Vodka party for Keith Haring at the Whitney Museum, October 2, 1986

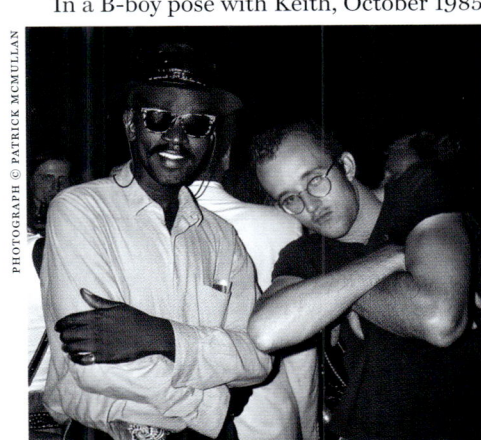

In a B-boy pose with Keith, October 1985

PHOTOGRAPH © PATRICK MCMULLAN

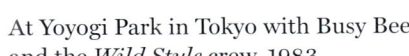

At Yoyogi Park in Tokyo with Busy Bee and the *Wild Style* crew, 1983

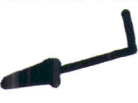

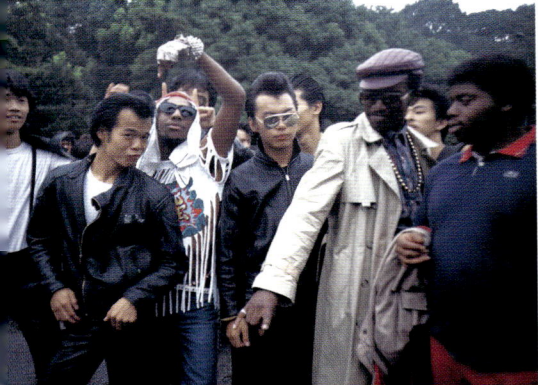

With MC Sha-Rock, ca. 1981

Hanging backstage at Madonna's first Madison Square Garden show with Keith and John F. Kennedy Jr., June 10, 1985

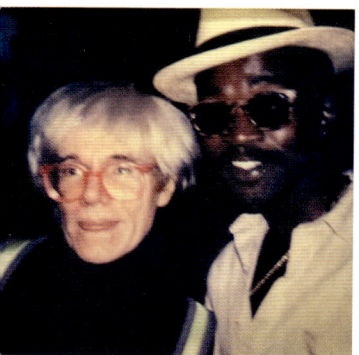

With Andy Warhol at Keith's first *Crack Is Wack* wall on E. Houston Street, New York, 1986

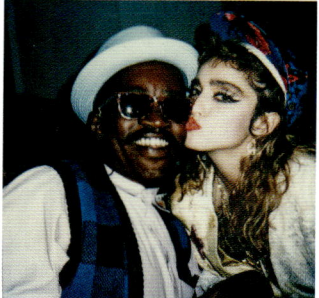

A kiss from Madonna, 1985

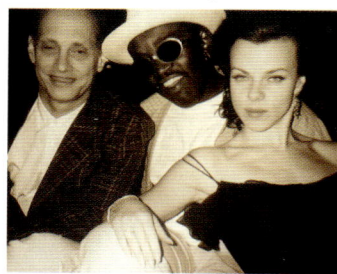

John Waters, me, and Debi Maz at the *Talk* magazine launch par Liberty Island, August 2, 1999

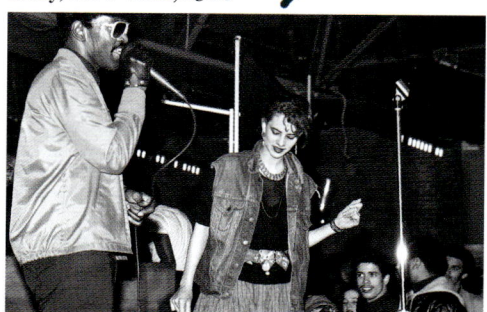

Performing "Change the Beat" with Beside at the Roxy, New York, 1983

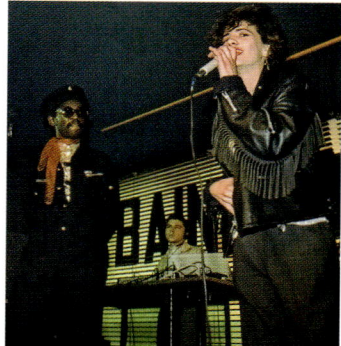

Performing "Change the Beat" with Beside at Les Bains Douches in Paris, 1983

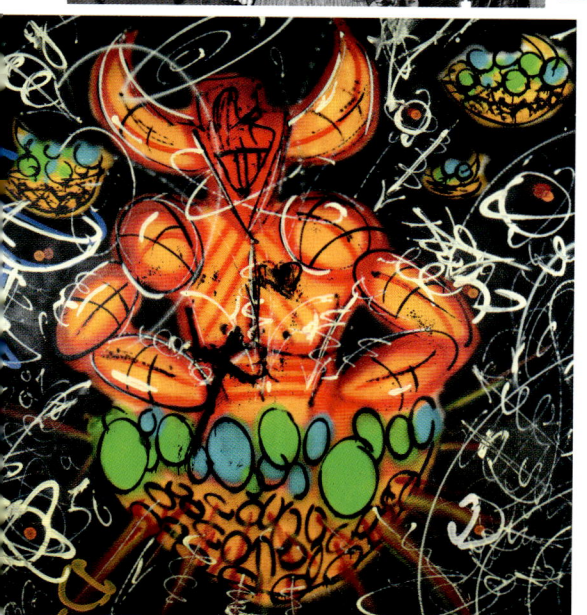

One of my favorite works, *The Return of God to Africa*, 1984

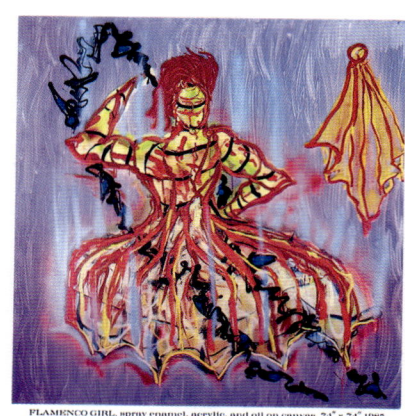

Invitation to Holly Solomon exhibition featuring *Flamenco Girl*, 1985

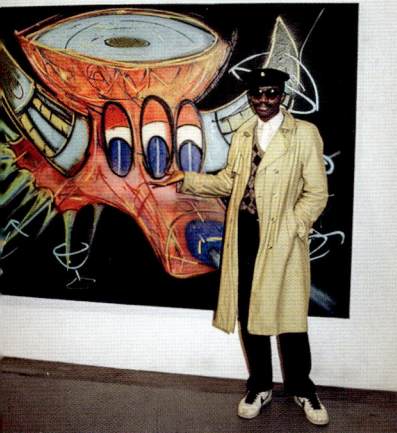

In front of my *Sacred Cow* piece at the Fun Gallery, ca. 1983–84

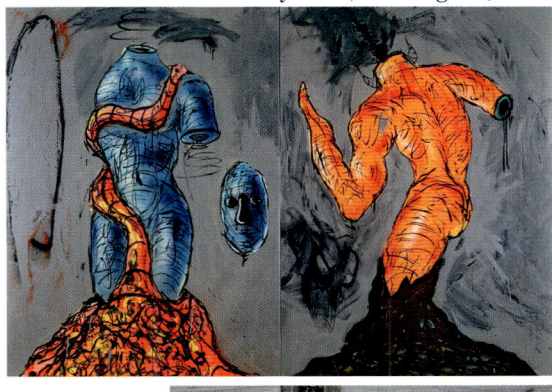

Prince Looking In, from the Flow Ace Gallery show, Los Angeles, 1986

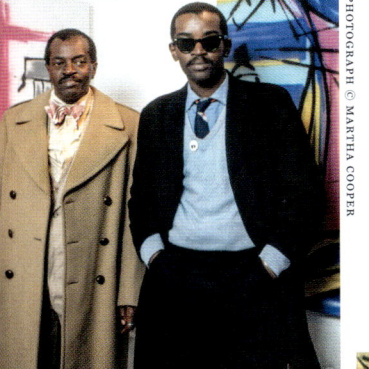

PHOTOGRAPH © MARTHA COOPER

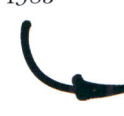

Taking a break to sit for David LaChapelle, 1985

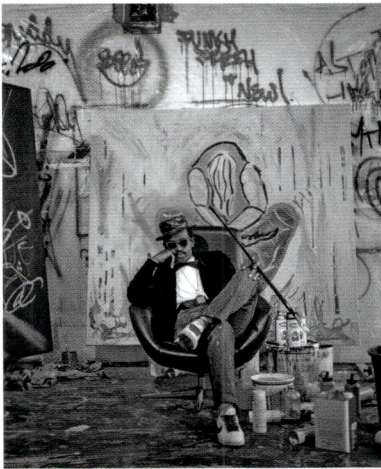

With Pops at my first Fun Gallery show, 1981

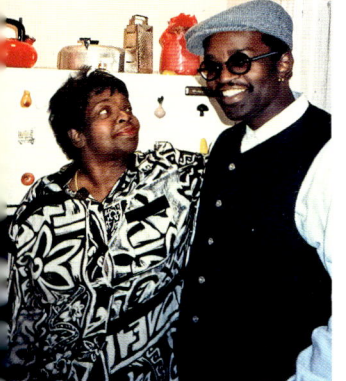

With Moms—Mother Theresa—1990

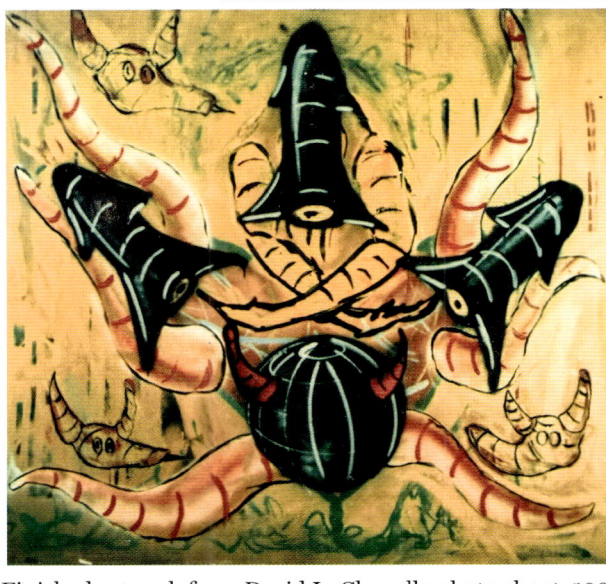

Finished artwork from David LaChapelle photo shoot, 1985

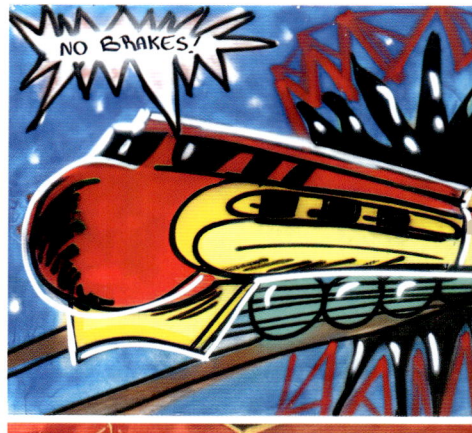

No Brakes!, 1979

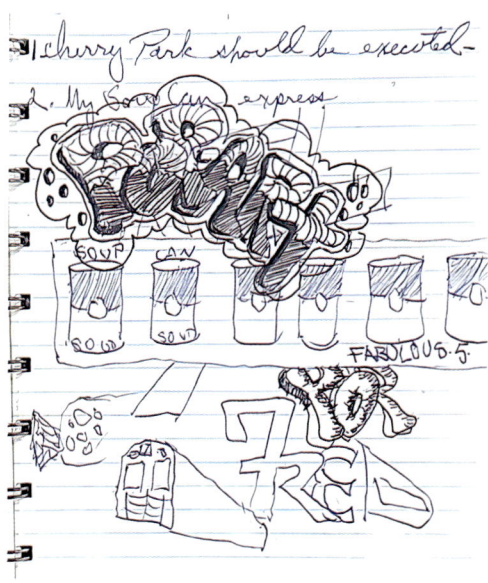

Sketch of soup can train, 1979

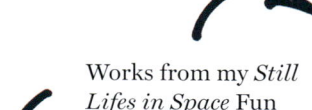

Works from my *Still Lifes in Space* Fun Gallery exhibit, 1984

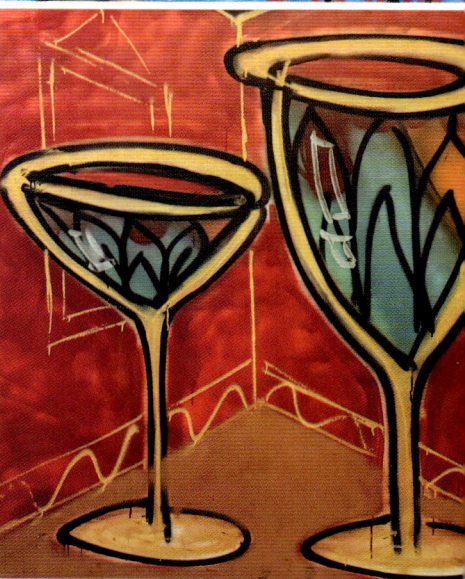

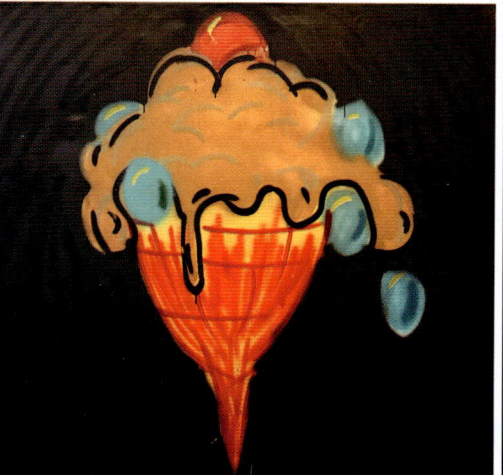

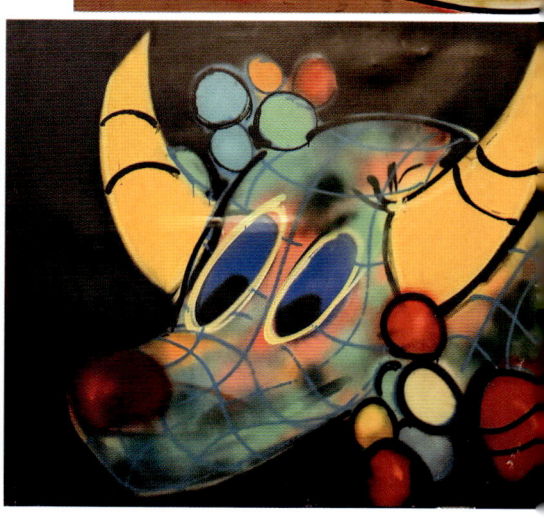

From my Rag Tag series, *Rag Tag #8*, 1983

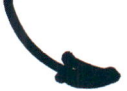

Vanessa Countessa, 1986

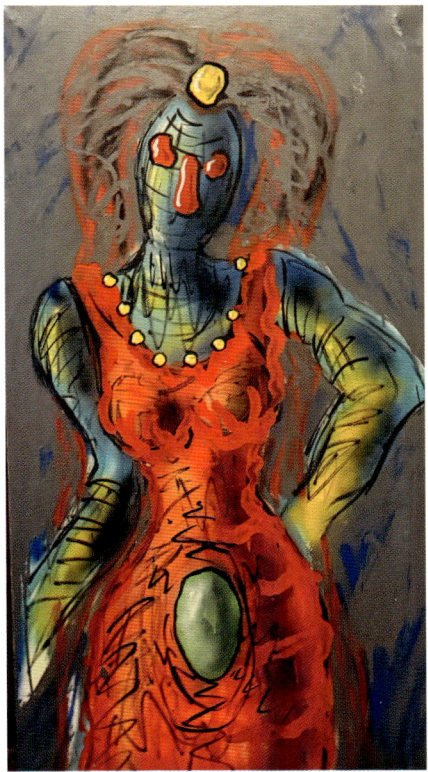

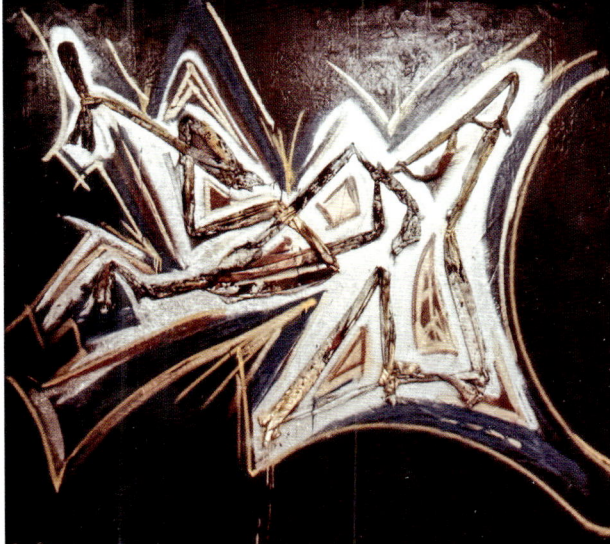

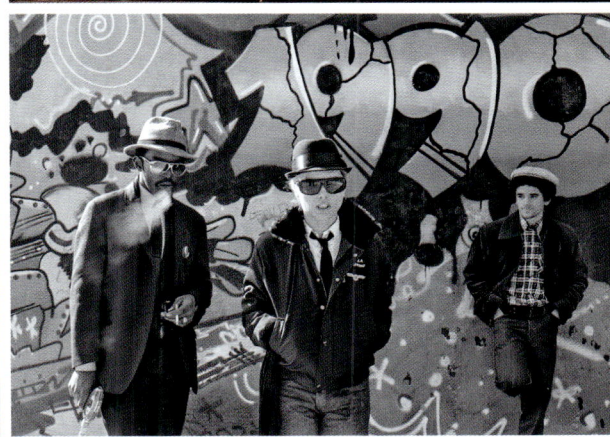

With Debbie and Lee in front of the *Graffiti 1990* mural on Cherry Street, 1980

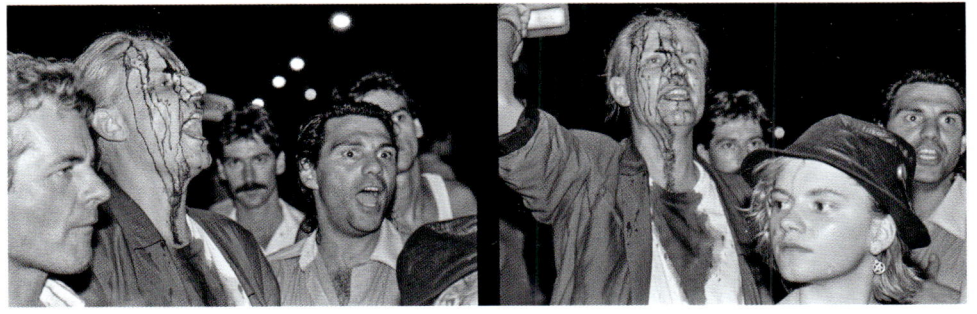

Rudolf Piper, an owner of Danceteria, after being brutally beaten by the NYPD at the Tompkins Square Park riot, shot by Ai Weiwei, August 1988

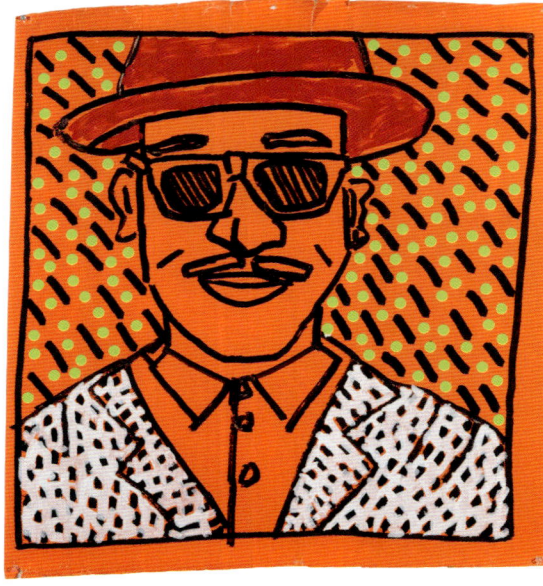

My Day-Glo portrait by Keith, 1981

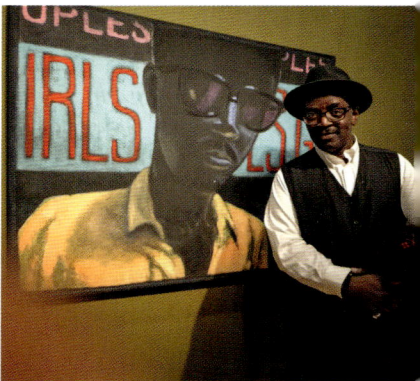

In front of Jane Dickson's portrait of me in the permanent collection of the Smithsonian's National Portrait Gallery, ca. 2017–2018

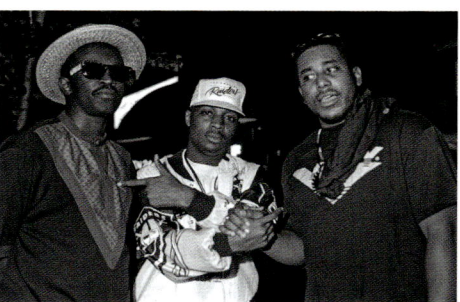

Hanging with Chuck D of Public Enemy and Tone Loc at a party to celebrate the release of *Lōc-ed After Dark*, 1989

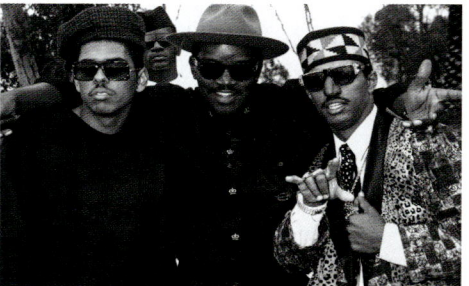

With one of my favorite hip-hop groups, Digital Underground, at a *Yo! MTV Raps* taping in Los Angeles, 1990

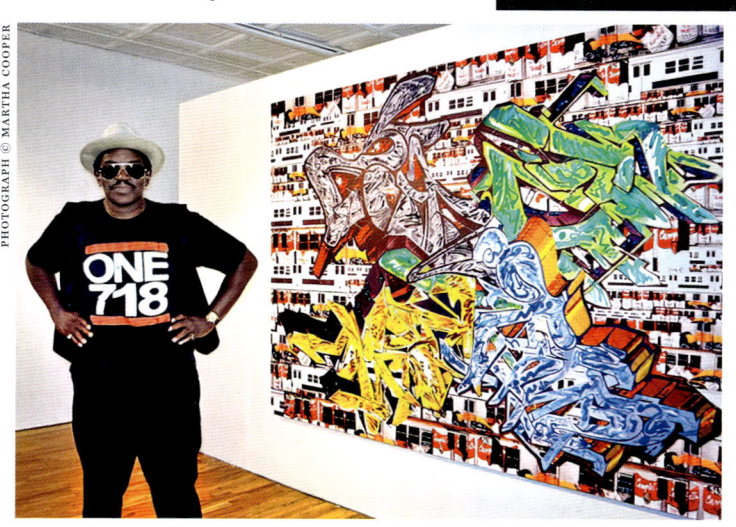

In front of *Metro Movement* from my New York: New Work exhibition, Gallery 151, New York, 2011

PHOTOGRAPH © MARTHA COOPER

This felt like real exposure—the kind we were looking for, an appreciation from a respected and known critic and personality. In the weed-smoker's bible, no less.

I had to show Jean. So I stopped by the *High Times* offices, grabbed a few copies, and made my way over to where he was staying with his off-and-on girlfriend, Alexis Adler. She had studied biology at Barnard and, in addition to being a total class act and great with Jean, also kept fantastic cannabis available for her friends. Alexis, in fact, was so consistent with her high-quality weed that I introduced her to my dad, who made occasional trips to the East Village to pick some up from her. Her pad was on the top floor of a walk-up on East Twelfth Street between A and B. There was no working doorbell—typical New York—so you had to yell up whenever you visited. So that day it was the usual drill. "Yo, Jean!" I called out from down below a couple of times. A second or two later, he stuck his head out the window and tossed the key down in a sock—*clang!*—right onto the sidewalk. I hiked up all those stairs, and he opened the door in his boxers. "Fred, what's up, man?"

The apartment was simple and raw, typical East Village. Jean's clothes were piled up in a big mound on the floor, and he picked around for a pair of jeans to slip into. In the kitchen, there was one of those old-school white fridges from the 1950s, and Jean had turned it into an art piece—he'd squeezed out the words "grape jelly" in purple acrylic, straight from the tube, onto the door. There was a smeared handprint too—probably his. The whole thing had that signature, haphazard Jean vibe, like a wild child unleashed.

I remember saying, "Jean, are you sure this is okay?" I was concerned that Alexis, who was cool, might not be so cool about this. I'd heard about Jean getting kicked out of other people's pads for doing that kind of thing. "*Dude, you painted on my wall—get the fuck out!*" He'd have to gather up his pile of clothes into a big ball and leave. But

Jean just waved it off. "Oh, yeah, Fred, it's okay. I just did it. Alexis doesn't mind."

He took the copy of *High Times* and looked at Mick Jagger on the cover. I told him Lee had done another big mural that could have made the cover, but Mick came through at the last minute, so obviously they had to go with him. "But check out the layout, man," I said, flipping through it, "and this big story by Glenn, and this fly picture of you..."

Jean quickly flipped through it and slid it across the table. "It's cool, but it's just one article, man."

In the years that followed, I often found myself thinking back to that moment at Alexis's apartment, because Jean was right—it was just one article. He knew there would be many, many more. His confidence and audacity—remarkable!

Another important article hit my radar. It was on the cover of *The Village Voice*, with the headline: "The First Radical Art Show of the '80s." It was about something called the Times Square Show, and it sounded incredible: a self-curated, no-rules, art free-for-all, billed as the summer art spectacular, and featuring every kind of artist from all over the scene. I ran into my friend Diego Cortez, the downtown curator and cofounder of the Mudd Club, and asked, "Yo, Diego, did you see *The Village Voice*?" He said, "Yeah, John Ahearn's on the cover, and his art group Colab are putting on that show."

Colab—short for Collaborative Projects Inc.—was a collective known for pulling off guerrilla-style pop-up art shows. The year before, they had done the Just Another Asshole Show at a shop on Bleecker

UPTOWN/DOWNTOWN

Street; there'd even been a benefit party for it at the Mudd Club. And earlier that year they'd staged the Real Estate Show, which had really turned heads. They had been trying for months to get the city to rent them an abandoned building on Delancey Street for a legit art space. But when that stalled, they just said "fuck it" and mounted the show there anyway. The theme was spot-on: shitty landlords and rising rents. Gentrification was on the minds of everyone downtown in 1980 but was yet to fully unfold. The Real Estate Show lasted one day before the city shut it down. But the blowback—protests, media coverage, and noise—kept it alive for weeks afterward.

The Times Square Show was set to run the entire month of June, with events happening every weekend night. I knew I had to be part of it somehow. Diego said, "There's something happening there in a couple of days. We'll go this week." And we did.

The venue was a former massage parlor/whorehouse at 201 West Forty-First Street, just west of Seventh Avenue, across from the old Nederlander Theatre. Outside, a sign promised "FOUR FLOORS OPEN TO THE PUBLIC."

Right when you walked in, you saw a life-size cardboard cutout of James Brown holding court in the lobby. Off to the right, there was a little shop selling things like "Love Canal Potatoes" by Becky Howland. It was something like Claes Oldenburg's famous East Village *Store* in the early sixties, reborn as a chaotic parody of museum gift shops. The four floors were chopped into themed zones, like the TV Lounge or the Money, Love, and Death Room. Here was just about every artist I was curious about and wanted to know, all under one roof, like a carnival. I was especially struck by John Ahearn's lifecast heads—realistic busts of mostly Black and Latin South Bronx residents—mounted all over the place. There was a voodoo shrine made of razor blades and broken glass. It was raw and real. Most of the artists involved didn't have galleries or representation—this was a new generation, the ones who'd missed the SoHo loft scene and were making their own space.

For me, the Times Square Show was like the famous Armory Show of 1913—a major turning point in art history. And I got to witness it. Even better, I got to be part of it.

On the third floor, in a space showing work by Kenny Scharf, Tom Otterness, Kiki Smith, and a bunch of other downtown artists, I spotted a poster I recognized. It was for a movie called *The Deadly Art of Survival*. I had encountered that poster a few times around Lee's hood and it always caught my eye. I pointed it out to Lee and said I was sure it was one of those underground, independent art films.

The poster showed a guy with a bloodied face in front of a chain-link fence; the image was a bold, three-color silkscreen job with that super-edgy, urban vibe I loved. Lee told me that the guy in the poster was a karate teacher named Nathan who lived in the Smith Projects. So it must be an urban kung-fu film! The genre was having a real moment.

So I turned to Diego and said, "That poster—who made it?" He said, "Oh, that's Charlie Ahearn, John's twin brother. He directed that movie." I told Diego that I needed to meet this cat. "Well," Diego said, pointing across the room, "that's Charlie right over there."

I went up to Charlie and said, "Man, I have been seeing your poster around, and I love it. How can I see the movie?" Then I gave him the rundown—graffiti, the Fabulous 5, the Rome show with Lee Quiñones. Charlie was like, "Wait—you work with *Lee*, the graffiti writer?" It turned out that Charlie had been trying to figure out how to do a film around Lee. Since a lot of *The Deadly Art of Survival* was shot right in Lee's neighborhood, Charlie, seeing Lee's work, had asked around about him and even met him once. But Lee, true to form, wasn't the easiest guy to pin down.

I couldn't believe it. Right away I hit Charlie with my idea for an art-house movie about graffiti, rap, and breakdancing: "Man, if you put *all* of that into a movie, it would be so dope." ("Dope" was the new slang term popping at uptown parties.)

Charlie said, "Fred, why don't you and Lee show up here tomorrow? I'll give you fifty dollars for some spray paint—you can do a piece outside on the building." So that's what we did. Lee put up a "FAB," and I followed with a "5." When Charlie came back to check it out, he stared for a second, turned to Lee, and said, "Fuck, this really is you."

We were then invited to install some work inside the show, which turned out to be a couple of my paintings—one was a classic "FRED," and the other was a backdrop of throw-up outlines spelling "FAB 5" over a multicolored abstract background. We hung them up with push pins on the third floor near Charlie's movie poster. *TV Party* photographer Bobby Grossman came by and snapped some shots of me sitting in front of the pieces after the installation. I'd scrawled a little message beside them in black marker: "EXCUSE ME WHILE I VANDALIZE!" In the shot, I'm rocking my bell-shaped Kangol and a pair of shades, parked on some random banquette—God knows where it came from.

Afterward, Lee and I were hanging out in that third-floor space when this white guy with glasses, who looked like he was barely out of high school, came bounding in. He stopped in front of the paintings, took a second to soak them in, and then turned to the room like he was giving a gallery tour. "Hey guys, I just heard Fred and Lee of the Fabulous 5 crew made these! They had a big graffiti show in Rome. Yeah, man, these guys are important—you really should know about their work!"

EVERYBODY'S FLY

Lee and I looked at each other like, "What the hell? Is this a joke?" Just then, John Ahearn passed through and called out, "Fred! Lee! All good? You cool with how the work's installed?"

The kid turned to me and Lee, his face flushed a deep red. "Oh my god," he said. "I feel so stupid. Let me pull my foot out of my mouth."

Then he stuck out a hand and introduced himself: "I'm Keith Haring."

9

Man, I thought you two were the po-po!

Years later, Hilton Als would write that the Times Square Show "combined the refined and the dissolute: how perfect was that, since New York was a disaster area then so why couldn't an exhibition be a disaster area, too?" It was inspired chaos, appropriately so. This was Times Square, after all, a place I had been obsessed with since I was a kid, coming there maybe a couple of times a year with my parents or an older relative to see a movie at one of the gigantic first-run theaters and gawking at all the hustlers, the peep-show parlors, the arcades.

Every once in a while, I'd take the A train up to Times Square and just soak up all the squalor, the vice, and the rattiness. The pure excitement of the place. To walk down Forty-Second Street between Eighth Avenue and Broadway, with every building on either side a movie theater and every marquee shouting the titles of kung-fu, Blaxploitation, action, and porno films, with a million lights blinking and flashing—that never got old. It was pure New York. At least, New York as it was then. That jagged edge.

All throughout June, I was hanging out at the Times Square Show. This wasn't the kind of show where people hit the opening and then forget about it. It was twenty-four seven. There was a crowd all day, every day. I was going several nights a week, and it felt as much like a club as an art exhibition.

As the month went on, it felt like more and more art was getting added in. Jean brought back his SAMO in one of the stairwells and contributed to the so-called Fashion Room. Kenny Scharf—a young artist with a graffiti vibe who turned out to be one of Keith Haring's closest friends—turned one of the building's air conditioners into something out of *Star Trek*. Charlie Ahearn showed his films *Twins* and *The Deadly Art of Survival*. There was a screening of *Nosferatu* and a documentary about the reggae/dub poet Linton Kwesi Johnson called *Dread Beat an' Blood*. The Raybeats, a post-punk version of the Ventures, played a show. Johnny Dynell from the Mudd Club spun records on the final night, which also featured a video piece that the great Colab artist Walter Robinson had made about one of my favorite punk bands, Suicide.

It was a wild month. It felt like so many barriers in the art world were coming down. There were Latin artists, Black artists, radical feminist artists—every kind of artist—at the Times Square Show. It was creative anarchy in the best way, with this overall feeling of just going for it—whoever you were, whatever you did, wherever you came from. The Times Square Show wasn't just an art event. It was the first pivotal art show of the new decade—the one that previewed everything that was about to come. For me, it meant positive exposure, both for my own work and for the idea that graffiti belonged in the contemporary art conversation.

A ton of friendships were born at the show. Keith and I became tight. I also became friends with his pal Kenny Scharf. Charlie and I clicked right away—Lee said we were "two peas in a pod." Charlie felt like our friendship was somehow preordained.

He totally got the idea of making a movie that would present graffiti, rap, and breakdancing as a new urban culture—a three-headed monster from the street. We started working on ideas for what would become *Wild Style* over pots of Bustelo at his funky loft apartment way downtown, near Wall Street. We both agreed that Lee would make the perfect central character: a vulnerable yet determined outsider graffiti writer named Zoro, trying to make it as an artist but insisting on doing it his own way. We basically wanted Lee to play himself—the greatest, most wanted, and most enigmatic of all graffiti artists.

Lee being Lee, it took some convincing to get him to commit. When it looked like he might back out, Charlie told him he understood—we'd just find somebody else to play the character inspired by him. We auditioned a great young actor from the Negro Ensemble Company named Giancarlo Esposito. We'd seen him in an off-Broadway play and loved his performance—he would've been great. But he was a SAG actor, which was a problem for our low-budget shoot. And besides, we were still holding out hope that Lee would say yes.

What finally did it was when Charlie reminded him there'd be a hot make-out scene between his character, Zoro, and his girl, who'd be played by his real-life girlfriend, the graffiti artist Lady Pink. That helped tip the scales. In fact, we wanted all our characters—the artists, dancers, DJs, and MCs—to play themselves. It was going to be a scripted movie with a cinema verité vibe. The idea of some actor making out with Lady Pink? That sealed the deal. Lee agreed to play Zoro. Crisis averted.

Charlie and I felt that our movie needed to document this new culture right at its source: the Bronx. My own experience in that borough was still pretty limited. I remember watching the Yankees in the 1977 World Series and seeing fires glowing in the distance on TV. That's what the Bronx was like then—it was literally burning down. Jimmy Carter went up there and couldn't believe what he saw. It was Fort Apache time.

Gangs ran entire sections of the Bronx in those days: the Savage Skulls, Black Spades, Ghetto Brothers, Seven Immortals. Some former Black Spades who called themselves the Casanova Crew worked security at Flash's parties. They were as tough as anybody who might think of starting trouble.

We had some gangs in Bed-Stuy too, and things could get ugly. Motherfuckers might step to you, like, "What's up? The hell you doing around here?" You might have to knuckle up, show off your fifty-two-block skills, and fight somebody for a few rounds, and then they'd let you go. It never got *that* ill. There were always kids playing skelly and Ringolevio in the streets, girls jumping rope and playing hopscotch, rows of townhouses that stood up straight. The Bronx was a whole different reality.

I admit it could go both ways. Charlie would say, "People in the Bronx don't dare go to Brooklyn! You've got a lot of gun-toting stickup kids out there! You can get shot in Brooklyn!"

I brought him out to Hancock Street to check out the vibe, and I'm pretty sure he changed his mind—at least about my part of Brooklyn. But Charlie was always down. He was ready to go anywhere, talk to anybody, up for anything. Just this unstoppable ball of energy from upstate New York.

In the Bronx, the rap scene was jumping off. You had Grandmaster Flash, Busy Bee Starski, Grand Wizzard Theodore and the Fantastic Five, the Treacherous Three, Doug E. Fresh (the Original Human Beat Box), Afrika Bambaataa and the Zulu Nation, Charlie

Chase, the Cold Crush Brothers... all the most influential and legendary cats. The real shit was going down.

Within a couple of weeks after we met, Charlie and I threw ourselves into it completely. These were missions where I'd just hope nothing bad would happen, nobody would try to test us: this little white dude from Manhattan and a tall, skinny Black guy from Brooklyn. But everything worked out. People just loved Charlie. He was 100 percent sincere, treated everyone with respect, and wanted to do the right thing. That came across instantly.

In the coming months, Charlie and I easily went to more than a dozen Bronx parties and jams—we couldn't get enough. The one I remember best was one of our first. It was way up in the north Bronx, at the end of the 5 line, at Haffen Park, which everyone called the Valley. Chief Rocker Busy Bee Starski was there, along with Rodney C and the Funky 4, DJ Breakout, and others. It was already getting dark by the time we showed up. When we walked into the park, James Brown was blasting from one direction and Jamaican dancehall from another.

I knew all about the Jamaican thing—after all, that was the focus of my old radio show. People have always assumed that rap and DJ culture came out of Jamaica because DJ Kool Herc, who helped set it all off in the Bronx in the early '70s, was born there. But Herc was twelve when he came to the Bronx, and it was awhile before he started spinning. He, like many others, was deeply influenced by the mobile DJs I'd grown up loving in Brooklyn—Pete DJ Jones, Flowers, and the like. What's really interesting is how dancehall reggae's toasting, New York City's mobile DJ scene, and rap developed almost simultaneously, mostly unaware of each other, and they were largely inspired by slick, jive-talking Black disc jockeys on the radio—the original DJs.

We decided to go the James Brown direction. To this day, Charlie jokes, "I wonder what would have happened with our movie if we'd gone over to the reggae side."

We followed the music to a little amphitheater with maybe seventy-five people hanging out. That's where we spotted Busy Bee Starski, holding a big lit joint. He looked nervous when we rolled up, eyeballing us.

"What's up?" he said.

Charlie, in his usual Charlie way, blurted out, "I'm Charlie Ahearn, this is Fred, and we're making a movie about the rap scene!"

Busy Bee was like, "Huh?" It took him a second to process what Charlie had just said. Then he cracked a huge smile, threw an arm around Charlie's shoulders, and hauled him up onto the stage.

He grabbed the mic and yelled out to the crowd, "Yo! This is my producer, Charlie Ahearn! We're making a movie about the rap scene!"

Everybody went crazy.

Later, Busy Bee explained why he'd looked so tense at first. "Man, I thought you two were the po-po—the POLICE!" To him, we looked like something out of a TV cop show, like the Mod Squad come to life.

Charlie and I dove deep into the mad energy of those Bronx parties. Everything felt exciting and new. I'd spent a lot of time explaining to Charlie the connections I saw between this scene and the raw, rebellious energy of punk and New Wave. He locked in right away.

A big part of our research involved taking a ton of photographs at those parties, which Charlie turned into an experimental project he called *Scratch Ecstasy*. He would take slide transparencies from the various events, grab a straight pin, and etch into them the names of rappers and the slogans they'd chant—stuff like "Rock the house" and "Yes yes, y'all." Then we'd bring a slide projector to Bronx party spots like the Ecstasy Garage and show Charlie's images on a bedsheet screen. The kids loved it. Party promoters started adding Charlie himself to the flyers as a featured attraction: Charlie Video!

We also filmed performances—on video and 16mm film—so we could study the nuances and learn the rhythms of what was happening. We knew this hot visual material would help us sell the movie to investors, who had no clue what was going on in the Bronx. After all, at that point, hardly anyone outside the scene had seen anything like it.

Everything was coming together—*Hey, we're in preproduction!* But every time we went up to the Bronx, I always had this thought in the back of my mind: *Man, I just hope no one steps to us.* As much as people embraced us, there was still a whiff of danger in the air. We might cross the wrong crew at the wrong time. I was down by law—official tissue, as it were—but that was in Bed-Stuy, where I was known. The Bronx was different. You could feel the predators out there, stickup kids on the prowl, always hunting for prey. I never tried to freak Charlie out—he was always ready to roll—but I kept my head on extra swivel every time we went up there. One of the things I'll never forget about those parties was the smell of angel dust—that funky, chemical reek, almost like a Magic Marker. It was everywhere. You'd catch it in the air along with sweat and weed, and sometimes the sharper, numbing scent of a "woola"—a joint laced with cocaine. (This was before crack took over.)

One night, at one of those jams, we did have a genuinely scary encounter. There was a guy who had clearly smoked mad dust. Slight resemblance to running back Jim Brown but taller and a few shades lighter. Shirt off, muscles flexed, eyes glazed, he looked like Frankenstein—no, Blackenstein—stalking through the crowd, his head rolling side to side. Everyone gave him a wide berth. I was keeping an eye on him all night, just hoping he wouldn't lock on to us.

EVERYBODY'S FLY

Then, from across the room, he locked in on Charlie. He started moving toward us. I was standing next to Charlie, thinking, *Fuck! Here we go.* My heart was pounding, adrenaline bubbling. I was sure this dude was about to beat the shit out of Charlie. But Charlie, being Charlie, just looked back with this big, happy smile on his face. I was scanning the area for a bottle, a chair—anything I could grab. I was ready to rumble, certain it was about... to go... DOWN!

The guy stepped right up to Charlie, who was just standing there with the camera around his neck. He held the camera up and said to me, "Fred! I think he wants me to take his picture!"

The muscle dude stared blankly, rolled his head around again, paused... and then, without a word, turned and slid off, disappearing back into the crowd. Charlie had disarmed him with nothing but his camera and those Howdy Doody good vibes. I swear, I didn't breathe for a full minute.

On my end, aside from soaking in the whole scene, I was making connections with the major players, piling up tapes, sketching out ideas for what our movie could be, and keeping my downtown comrades in the loop. I kept telling them how big this was going to be.

I arranged a trip to the Bronx for some of the *TV Party* crew—including Glenn, Chris, and Debbie—with help from the early rap promoter Ray Chandler. I'd first met Ray at a Grandmaster Flash jam at the Smith Houses, and we'd stayed in touch. Ray was this super-tall ex-cop who managed Flash and was organizing a big rap party at the Police Athletic League rec center at 183rd and Webster Avenue, the site of many a legendary jam.

I've got to confess: at first, Ray was a little skeptical of me. I was just a young Black kid with big ideas about making a film, who was allegedly tight with Blondie, one of the biggest bands out there. But I showed him some of the press I'd been getting, including the *High Times* piece. Once he saw I was serious, we were cool.

When we got to the door and were being led in, some of the kids who were jammed in the lobby started bugging out when they saw Ray escorting this crew of white folks. One kid looked at Debbie and said, "Yo, man, it's Patty Duke!" The Patty Duke was a popular dance back then, named after the old syndicated TV show that played as reruns late at night. Another kid checked out Glenn and said, "Yo, and he looks like *The Jerk!*"—a shoutout to the Steve Martin movie. Chris remembers somebody calling us Kool and the Gang. My fedora got a little attention too.

As I remember it, there were three or four groups on the bill that night—Cold Crush, the Fantastic Five, Rayvon & Johnny Wa (a beat-boxing, rapping, and singing duo), and the all-female Mercedes Ladies, three Black girls rapping and rocking cowboy hats. They made an impression on Debbie. She loved their vibe—we all did.

Sitting up in the balcony, watching this parade of DJs and MCs tear it up below, I could tell my downtown friends were blown away. Chris said it was a musical game changer for him. Debbie said rap felt like a new kind of folk music—honest, rooted in the lives of these young people, sprouting straight from the street with no commercial backing or recognition from the wider world. It was organic. It was real.

Back then, there was a car service called OJ—it was like Uber, decades before Uber. The OJ fleet was top-of-the-line luxury: four-door Cadillacs, Lincolns, and, best of all, Buick Electra 225s and Oldsmobile 98s, all for about twenty-five bucks an hour. OJ was fly shit in the fledgling rap scene. MCs were always dropping rhymes about riding around in OJs or having one "on hold," which meant you had the car and driver for an hour or more—just to go shopping, cruise around, hop in and out, and show off.

The most popular OJ drivers would blast Flash and Funky Four Plus One tapes during the ride. There was even an OJ reference in "Rapper's Delight." They were the upscale alternative to the "gypsy cabs" that worked outer-borough neighborhoods. Yellow cabs, those motherfuckers, mostly stuck to Manhattan and were notorious for refusing to pick up Black and brown folks—especially if you were headed back to the hood.

At the end of the night, Ray called a couple of OJs for us, and that's how me, Chris, Debbie, Glenn, and the crew rode back down to more familiar territory—riding the high of the PAL jam in these dope-ass OJ cars, in finest rap style, all the way home.

Claudio Bruni invited me and Lee to do a second gallery show in Italy, this time in Milan, scheduled for the end of the year. The Canal Zone situation hadn't worked out that great for us, and we needed a studio of our own. We didn't have any money for such a thing, so we improvised and made one in an abandoned seaport warehouse on Cherry Street at Mechanics Alley, right up next to the Manhattan Bridge. It was a couple of blocks from Lee's apartment and across the street from the *Graffiti 1979/1990* handball court. The place was a beat-up brick building, practically falling apart. Lee and I would sneak in and work, guerrilla style, whenever we could. It was basically a squat studio.

Getting into a derelict building was no big deal for either of us. Graffiti gets you into some weird places. Being in that warehouse took me back to my days of running around the old Rand Rubber factory in Bed-Stuy. It was our own private place, but it still felt a bit like hitting layups—we clearly were not supposed to be there. The main difference at Cherry Street was that we didn't have to worry as much about the cops, or third rails, or all the other logistical hassles that came with doing graff. For Lee, that was a huge plus. He liked doing his work without a bunch of other writers crowding him or trying to cop his style.

We still had the occasional visitor. I remember Charlie Ahearn checking it out, and Bobby Grossman coming by to snap a photo of me and Lee standing in front of a white wall I'd emblazoned with the words "CREATIVE VANDALISM by FABULOUS 5" in red spray paint.

So we had created this space for ourselves, sketchy as it was. The holes in the ceiling were so big you could actually look up and see the Manhattan Bridge. We'd do our work during the day and make sure to get out before sundown. We were experimenting—doing graff-style pieces on different surfaces: paper, canvas, whatever we could get our hands on. We'd staple the material to the wall, get to work, let the pieces dry (mostly), then take them down, roll them up, and stash them at Lee's apartment. It was no Canal Zone, but it was ours.

I was determined to make change via every and any available medium: art, film, television, music. Jean felt the same way: *by any means necessary*. We'd talk like generals plotting moves on a battlefield map, looking to invade new territory. In Keith Haring, we found another general.

Keith was enthralled by the graffiti scene. For a white kid from Pennsylvania studying at the School of Visual Arts, he knew a ton about it. He wanted to be part of it, but he didn't want to be some kid from basically the Amish Country exercising what we might later call "white privilege." When I started hanging with him, he was deep into wheat-pasting these wild collages all over the East Village. He would cut headlines from the *New York Post* and rearrange them into twisted, remixed configurations: "REAGAN SLAIN BY HERO COP," "RONALD REAGAN ACCUSED OF TV STAR SEX DEATH," "MOB FLEES AT POPE RALLY." They were jarring and hilarious; they put me in mind of Burroughs and his cut-ups. Keith told me that every now and then someone would get pissed and come at him or try to rip them down.

It was the season of the Carter-Reagan election, and so much seemed to be hanging in the balance. Nerves were on edge. Keith's tabloid collages were eerie warnings about the future. They hit something deep for all of us—mirrors held up to the moment. David Wojnarowicz's work was even more confrontational: He would stencil burning houses onto parked cars and buildings all over the East Village. Graffiti had always made statements too—perhaps not quite as literally, and not explicitly activist. But it was still about resistance, questioning authority, giving voice to the voiceless in a time of growing dread.

As the new decade began, it felt like the country and downtown New York were pulling in opposite directions. America was swinging hard to the right, trying to drag itself back to the 1950s. The Lower East Side was all edge, all experimentation, a revolution in motion. You could feel that tension in the art, in the music, and in the streets. That was the atmosphere I came up in. That's where I grew as an artist.

Keith and I would often walk the downtown streets together, talking about art and life, graffiti and rap, smoking joints, just wandering. We'd check out the tags and wall pieces by locals like LA2 and Chino. When something stood out—when the graffiti really hit—Keith might say, "Now, I could see *that* in MoMA or the Whitney," and I'd usually agree, appreciating how Keith saw the same aesthetic beauty and power I was seeing.

We'd duck into galleries and bookshops, and flip through magazines at Gem Spa, the cramped newsstand, soda fountain, and candy store at St. Mark's Place and Second Avenue. If we found ourselves on East Second Street, we'd remember that Oldenburg had done his famous *Store* there in the early 1960s. (Years later, Keith would open his own store, Pop Shop, down on Lafayette.)

I loved Keith's nonstop energy and the total respect he had for the culture, this guy who came from so far outside my frame of reference. Like, he'd even been a Deadhead! Not many of those in Bed-Stuy. But as we became friends, my feeling was simple: This cat is good people and cool. With me he's down by law.

Keith was part of the mix at Club 57, which had opened a couple of years earlier in the basement of a Polish church at 57 St. Mark's Place. I thought of it as the junior-varsity version of the Mudd Club. It drew a younger crowd and was less of a cool spot to be seen in—but to be honest, Club 57 was wilder, more avant-garde, more street.

Keith was always asking about the Mudd Club; you could tell it was a scene he wanted in on. He always had his feelers out for whatever was popping. He'd also had Jean on his radar for a while. Keith told me that, at SVA, he and Kenny Scharf would spot Jean hanging around their school from time to time, as Jean would occasionally make a few bucks posing for life-drawing classes there. With his distinctive, ever-shifting hairstyles and natural swagger, Jean made an impression on them. They were like, *Who the hell is that kid?* A couple of times, Keith would see Jean breeze through SVA—and not long after, discover a fresh SAMO tag. Over time, Keith and Kenny got friendly with Jean, so there was already a built-in connection between us.

Keith brought me over to SVA a couple of times, introducing me to his friends, including the outlandish John Sex. When we were getting ready to leave, I noticed Keith would kiss John and other guys on the cheek goodbye. That was new to me. It was my first inkling that Keith might be gay.

EVERYBODY'S FLY

He never brought it up until one day when we were walking around downtown, from the East Village over to West Village. At one point, a young couple passed us on the sidewalk, pushing a stroller. They looked straight out of the suburbs or the Midwest—or maybe even, like Keith himself, Pennsylvania. Just regular, straight-laced white folks. Keith watched them go by with this kind of wistful look, then turned to me and said, "Fred, that was supposed to be me." I asked him what he meant. He told me that if he hadn't figured out that he was gay—or that he was an artist, and that he needed to be in New York—he probably would have ended up just like that guy, pushing a stroller down a small-town street.

That moment hit me, as there was nothing outwardly "gay" about Keith, nothing stereotypically swish or feminine. He'd just told me matter-of-factly that he was gay, and that was that. Cool.

Keith told me he wanted to participate in graffiti, but he had to find a way that was authentic to him. I remember a day, not long after the Times Square Show, when he called me up, excited and breathless, saying he had something for me to check out at his studio, a Midtown walkup he shared with Kenny Scharf. What he showed me was a breakthrough: the first drawings of his "radiant baby," done in black ink on white paper. I loved it right away. It clearly came out of everything he'd been doing up to that point, but it was more refined, more iconic.

I told him I'd just seen one of those babies on the base of the streetlamp downstairs.

His face lit up. "Yes," he said, "that's the first one I did on the street!" There'd be many more to come.

Keith loved good music and had heard that this private West Village club called the Paradise Garage played the best dance music anywhere. I assured him it was true—and that I knew how to get us in. So one weekend night, we headed down there. I got a couple of members to bring us in, and the place blew Keith's mind.

UPTOWN/DOWNTOWN

The Garage wasn't at all what Keith imagined a disco would be—not some uptight, white Studio 54 kind of scene. It was a glorious mix: all types of people, including Latin and Black, gay, and (a little) straight. Keith said it reminded him of a Grateful Dead show—total freedom and nonstop dancing. But it wasn't a hippie scene. It was contemporary, urban, pure New York, with Larry Levan spinning and delivering the most incredible dance music through that massive sound system.

What I remember about Keith that first time at Paradise Garage is him whirling around and around, saying "Wow, wow, wow" all night long. It was a new kind of energy for him, and he wanted to lose himself in it.

I lost myself in it too, in more ways than one. I remember another night at the Garage when we'd both dropped acid and were dancing like mad—me, Keith, some folks we met, some girls I knew. It was a great time... until suddenly it wasn't. Something shifted. I was like, "Whoa, what the heck's happening?"

I said, "Yo, Keith, I feel a little weird." He came with me up to the club's roof deck to keep an eye on me while I got some air and tried to pull myself together.

It was a bad trip, no doubt. The fresh air helped, but the Garage's pummeling sound system was so powerful I could still feel that bass vibrating the whole building, vibrating my bones. The feeling came in waves. I couldn't tell if the waves matched what Larry was spinning or if my brain was stuck in overdrive, like a subwoofer had taken up residence in my skull.

We must've been up there for forty minutes. My brain was deep in the vortex. I got paranoid: *What if this feeling never stops? What if I spend the rest of my life with bass thumping in my head? What if I end up like one of those homeless bugged-out bag men who live on the streets, on the trains?*

I could see worry on Keith's face. "Fred," he said calmly, "let's get out of here. Let's go outside so you can walk it off."

We walked around downtown until the sun came up and eventually found a café. I still felt off, but I was coming back to earth. And Keith, he had been with me every step of the way, making sure I was good.

Keith kept returning to Paradise Garage and eventually got tight with the crew that ran the place. Before long, he painted a bunch of his signature characters in the club's entry lounge. You could see the influence the Garage had on him—dancing figures, pulsing with energy, began showing up in his work. He started hitting the subways with white chalk, drawing on the black paper that covered unsold ad panels. It was graffiti-inspired, but entirely his own.

Keith had found his voice—and he never looked back.

I hadn't seen Chris and Debbie in a while. They had been out in Los Angeles working on new music. Then one day they called me up and said they were back in town. They asked me to come by and listen to some things they'd been working on. So I went up to their place on Fifty-Eighth Street, and they played a cassette with a few of the new tracks. I was feeling it immediately. The songs were fresh, with a vibe that was still Blondie but looser, dancier. I remembered them saying they wanted to make music you could really move to.

Then Chris held up another cassette. "This one is something different," he said.

The moment it started playing, I could feel the beat in my chest. It had this massive, throbbing groove, kind of like Chic meets David Bowie. Debbie's vocals were so dreamy, hypnotic. I was loving it. And then... she started rapping.

UPTOWN/DOWNTOWN

What???

I couldn't believe it. And not just rapping—she was rapping about us. *"Fab Five Freddy told me everybody's fly..."* Then came the "man from Mars" line—a throwback to the rap I had done for her, and a perfect nod to Chris's obsession with old B movies. She was referencing *TV Party*, Flash being fast, all these details from our world, things I shared with her, layered into this wild, futuristic track.

To me, it sounded like something they'd put together as a goof while recording their new album: a fun one-off, just for me. Whatever it was, I loved it. I was floored, touched, flattered, blown away.

Not long after, around Thanksgiving, I met up with Richard Goldstein from *The Village Voice*. He was writing an extensive article about graffiti that featured me, Blade, Haze, the Soul Artists crew, and others. We talked about the Campbell's soup can train and my ideas about pushing graffiti into the art world.

"The paintings I do," I told him, "I want people to look at them as an art *based* on graffiti."

I spoke about reading *Artforum*, my obsession with Dada, and my love of rap. I wanted to keep the message as positive as possible. In the back of my mind, I was imagining some kid in a place like Bed-Stuy stumbling onto the article and thinking, *Damn, maybe this could be me.* "With a little time and paint," I said, "anything is possible."

A few days later, I flew to Milan for the show Claudio Bruni had set up for me and Lee. This time, Lee didn't make the trip, so I represented us solo at the Galleria Paolo Seno, showing pieces similar to what we'd exhibited the year before in Rome. It felt like a sequel—but unlike Rome, there wasn't much wild running around; it was all business. I even took on a few commissions from some friendly Milanese folks, graffiti-style versions of their names on canvas, like what I had on display.

But there was one exception. The B-52s were in town on their *Wild Planet* tour, playing Milan's big arena, the PalaLido, on November 29. Perfect. I was into those guys—loved their music—and had met them through *TV Party*. At the show, I somehow ended up meeting the tennis star Vitas Gerulaitis; this was the same year he lost the French Open final to Björn Borg. I remember the band kicking things off with "Planet Claire" while the Italians danced like maniacs. Vitas and I were having a blast, and when the show ended, he turned to me and said, "Fred, it's time to go backstage!"

When we rolled up, Fred Schneider and Kate Pierson from the group spotted me right away. "Oh my god . . . Fred! What are you doing here?" I told them about the gallery show. "We're going to be in Paris next week," Kate said. "You have to come hang out!" So that's what I did.

It was my first time in Paris. Rome and Milan were cool, but this was electrifying. Maybe even more so because it wasn't planned. I kept saying to myself, "I'm in Paris!"

I made a beeline to the Louvre, amazed at how much bigger it was than the Met. I took in as much as I could, thinking about how much art had flowed through this city. I paid a respectful hello to the *Mona Lisa*, but what really knocked me out were the movie-screen-size works by Delacroix. I had read his journals and loved how he talked about the struggle of the painter—good days and bad days. Any artist could relate. Some days you're standing in front of a canvas and it's just not happening. Or you screw up and have to scrape the paint off and start over. Even *this* guy experienced that. A revelation.

I'd been told the coolest clubs in Paris were Le Palace and Les Bains Douches. So I set a course for Le Palace, on Rue du Faubourg-Montmartre, and found a Studio 54–style velvet-rope situation waiting for me. But as soon as the guardian of the rope heard my American accent, he whisked me right in. Typical club scene.

UPTOWN/DOWNTOWN

When I linked up with the B-52s, I learned that Talking Heads were also touring Europe. The two bands were playing in Paris, two days apart, and they were all headed to a party thrown by Jean-François Bizot, the publisher of *Actuel* magazine—which I thought was the coolest magazine in the world. It was a big-format, *Life*-size, full-color magazine that had started as a jazz magazine in the 1960s and evolved into a bible for everything cool and countercultural.

At the party, I bumped into David Byrne. I'd met him a couple times at *TV Party*, but we didn't really know each other. We were chatting when Jean-François, our host, slid over. We said hello, and I figured he was about to start talking to David about "Psycho Killer" or something. But then David was suddenly all up in this guy's ear, telling him who *I* was, about the Campbell's soup can train, the graffiti scene, *TV Party*. "Fred is bringing this new culture to the scene—graffiti, rap," he said. "He's trying to make a movie. If you really want to know what's going on in New York right now, you have to talk to him."

Jean-François handed me his card and told me to swing by his office the next day—we should talk about doing something together for *Actuel*. Wow, okay.

I was buzzing when I left the party with Chris Frantz and Tina Weymouth—the husband-and-wife rhythm section of Talking Heads. We decided to grab a bite at La Coupole, so we jumped into a taxi and headed to Montparnasse. As soon as we got in the cab, I froze. A very familiar song was thumping from the car stereo—the same one Debbie and Chris had played for me back in New York only a few weeks earlier, the one with Debbie rapping. I was like, *What the fuck*? I must have been thinking out loud, because I said, "Wait—how did a French cab driver get his hands on this song?" Tina laughed. Chris said, "Oh yeah, I've heard this—it's from the new Blondie album. *Autoamerican*. It just came out."

That's when it hit me: The song wasn't just a fun one-off they'd made for me. It was real. It was on the new album. And it was about to be the next single.

The song was "Rapture."

I'm not sure I can describe how stunned I was to hear that song thousands of miles away from home, on another continent, in a taxi, with half of Talking Heads. I thought to myself: *Wait till I tell my moms about this!*

The next day, I rallied and met up with Jean-François at his office. The conversation we had set the wheels in motion for *Actuel* to run a piece on me and the New York scene I had only just begun to describe to him. I was bugging, thinking about how this could expose what we'd been doing to all of France—maybe even all of Europe.

I flew home to New York a couple of days later, exhausted but riding a total high. When I landed at JFK, I discovered that every newspaper had the same face on the front page: John Lennon's. The man I'd once tried to call on the phone when I was a kid in Bed-Stuy had been gunned down by a freakin' kook—right in my hometown, New York City. I felt sick. John Lennon was dead, and Ronald Reagan was about to be president. What was this new decade gonna be about?

10

A whole new art world ready to replace the old one

Like the snapshot of my first Campbell's soup can train, most photos of whole-car pieces back then were taken on pocket-size 110 Instamatics. Cheap little cameras with a pop-up flash cube—rinky-dink shit. But that's what a lot of graffiti writers had. Since the city was running so many cars through the buffer, mostly smearing the graffiti, it was the only way anyone could preserve their work—so many of those pieces vanished in a blur.

As the 1980s got into gear, two photographers, Martha Cooper and Henry Chalfant, began building real connections in the scene and started presenting what was happening in the layups to a broader world. It was another huge step in getting graffiti seen as art—bringing it into the consciousness of the wider public and giving the writers a kind of visual immortality. Kids around the world would study their photos like blueprints.

Their approaches were totally different. Henry—who was also a sculptor with a studio in SoHo and showed at OK Harris, the gallery known for its Photorealists—used auto-wind to shoot a train as it rolled into the station: *click, click, click, click, click*. Later, he'd collage the shots together to make a full panoramic view of the whole car, cropped tight with no background. (He first landed on this technique while photographing a Fabulous 5 piece that said "Merry Christmas.") It was like he was turning subway murals into flat, two-dimensional paintings on canvas. For the first time, people could really study every detail—every swoosh, every fade, every razor-sharp outline.

Martha shot trains in their environment, giving her photographs the feeling of landscape. You'd see these incredible cars by Dondi, Seen, or Blade cruising along elevated tracks, framed by the rugged backdrop of the Bronx—images that gave you a visceral feel for New York City. The trains were explosions of color and life streaking through a drab, burned-out, rundown cityscape—which is exactly how we in the graffiti community saw them.

Martha captured the New York that came after the city's near bankruptcy, after the infamous *Daily News* headline FORD TO CITY: DROP DEAD, after the blackout, after the Son of Sam. Her photographs found beauty and defiance in the ruins. Martha also helped put breakdancing on the map: The *New York Post* sent her to cover what they claimed was a riot in a Washington Heights subway station—it turned out to be a mild dispute over who had won a dance contest. There was no violence.

Both she and Henry were passionate about what they were doing. They were real artists, on a mission, as I was, to celebrate and elevate the movement. Together, they would create *Subway Art*, a landmark book and still the best visual document of the New York graff scene at that time. In a way, what they did on photo paper was what Charlie and I were looking to do on film.

As Henry and Martha got deeper into the scene, they gave their phone numbers to the writers, who would call whenever they finished a piece, leaving messages on their answering machines. *Yo, this*

UPTOWN/DOWNTOWN

is so-and-so. I just did a whole car on such-and-such a line, on such-and-such a side. If it was the side that caught the morning light, they might say, like Lee often did, "Sunny side up!" There was always pressure to get work documented, because no one ever knew when a train would be sent to the buff. Some ran a week. Some lasted three months. Others got scrubbed immediately. The windows usually got buffed first, so at least your piece wouldn't vanish entirely—but it would look like someone punched giant holes through it.

As soon as the calls came in, Henry and Martha would be off and running. Their photos ended up preserving an entire era of graffiti that might otherwise have vanished without a trace.

I was lucky they both shot the second Campbell's soup can train. Henry's photo is all about image: the car isolated, every detail crisp. Martha's shows the train rolling on an elevated line through the South Bronx, set against a backdrop of distressed brown brick. Without those two photos, there would be no evidence of that piece at all—just word of mouth, some press descriptions, and the ballpoint-pen sketches in my notebook.

Thanks to them, I know Lee and I painted car #7543 on the Lexington Avenue IRT. I've been told it was an R22 subway car, one of many that served as rolling canvases for graffiti writers. They were destined for the scrapyard in just a few years' time. Similar cars were dumped in the ocean to make artificial reefs.

In January 1981, Reagan was sworn in and Blondie released "Rapture" as a single. Soon, the song was everywhere. Lee, Jean, and I were invited to appear in the video. Lee and I showed up early at a soundstage uptown with some paint and got to work creating a graffiti backdrop—just like we had for the video for "The Hardest Part." Lee wrote his name and tucked in his trademark "Mom"; Jean added a few tags and SAMO slogans. I painted a piece that said "RAP," which was the whole point of the video: celebrating this new sound and culture.

Debbie lip-synced the lyrics as the rest of the band drifted through the set, and a wild cast of New York characters moved in and out of the frame, like she was wandering the streets of downtown. There were some *TV Party* folks there—Walter Steding, Lenny Ferraro, a few of the audience regulars. A random mix of Mudd Club people. A tall dancer named William Barnes in a white suit. Several Black women from a Haitian cultural dance troupe doing voodoo ceremony moves, also dressed all in white.

A gorgeous friend of mine, Janice "Chee Chee" Lawrence-Clarke, whom we considered the Grace Jones of Brooklyn, was styled in a tartan kilt like a Highland lass. There was even a goat named Mona, led on a leash by Marissa Stahovich, a Vidal Sassoon hairstylist.

As the cameras rolled, Lee and I pretended to spray-paint the pieces we'd already made so the fumes would be gone before shooting time. I showed Lee how to fake it—just mimic the gestures, keep it moving with the beat. Chris called the whole thing a "cartoon version of reality," and that was the vibe: gritty but surreal. As someone interested in film, I was fascinated by the director, a British guy who went by Keef, as he kept all the chaos flowing. This production felt like a miniature movie, except it was shot on video instead of film.

When Chris and Debbie were putting the video together, I called up Grandmaster Flash. "Yo, Flash," I said, "I'm friends with Blondie, and we're making a video for their new song, 'Rapture.' You have to come be in it. I hipped them to everything—you, me—and we both get shouted out in the song!" I gave him the address and the time to show up.

Chris and Debbie definitely wanted Flash there. And I had no doubt he'd come—and maybe even steal the whole show. But the day of the shoot, he didn't turn up. I figured he probably didn't believe me, didn't think I was really tight with these actual rock stars.

So I told Chris and Debbie, "Look, Jean can fill in for Flash. I'll just show him how to do some DJ moves." They were cool with it. I gave Jean a crash course at the turntables, just enough so he could fake it. But when the cameras rolled and Debbie strolled up to him, delivering the first line of the rap (*"Fab 5 Freddy told me..."*), Jean, instead of doing what I'd showed him, just stood there smiling, having no clue what to do with the turntables.

So that's what you see in the finished "Rapture" video. It might be my favorite moment in the whole thing—Jean being Jean, a little off script, full of charm, totally himself. (Not long after, he started DJing occasionally at downtown parties and clubs.)

Afterward, Flash told me why he didn't show: "Sylvia didn't want me to go."

He meant Sylvia Robinson, one of the founders of Sugar Hill Records, who had signed him and the Furious Five. Sylvia knew Flash and other key figures on the scene had connected with me—and about the moves I was making. Not good, from her perspective. Sylvia and her husband, Joe Robinson, were determined to control everything. They wanted to do big things, but only if they were calling the shots. Most of the rappers they signed were teenagers without strong lawyers or savvy managers. Flash and the Furious Five felt like they couldn't risk stepping out of line. It was old-school, exploitative music-industry shit, straight up.

It was a missed opportunity for Flash. "Rapture" went on to become the first number-one single to feature rapping—and the first rap hit to use original music, not just a beat lifted from an existing record. The video was also a first: the first time millions of people saw someone rapping on-screen.

Flash might've missed the shoot, but he was still gassed to get a shoutout in the song. It's something he's always been thankful for.

Soon Debbie—who was gearing up to make a solo album—got another big chance to put rap in front of a national audience. She'd been invited to host *Saturday Night Live* and perform a couple of songs. Even better, the show had asked her to pick a second musical guest. She and Chris hit me up.

"Freddy, for the second musical act, we want it to be a rap group. Who do you suggest?"

I told her that Flash and the Furious Five were obviously incredible, as were the Cold Crush Brothers and the Fantastic Five—all amazing showmen, at the very top of the heap. But I had another idea.

"The Funky Four Plus One," I said. "They've got four male MCs, fronted by a girl—Sha Rock—kind of like a rap Blondie. Sha's got an incredible voice and flow, and they've got a hot record out on Sugar Hill right now called "That's the Joint." Charlie and I are planning to feature them in our movie. They're a perfect fit."

In November, when I was in Europe, the Funky Four had performed at an event downtown at the Kitchen in SoHo called "Dubbed in Glamour." It was organized by Edit DeAk, the Hungarian-born critic and editor behind the brilliant underground zine *Art-Rite*. Edit—flaming red hair, the funkiest clothes imaginable—had been letting me use her SoHo loft on Wooster Street from time to time. (Decades later, murals I had done there with Jean and Futura would be rediscovered behind Sheetrock walls.)

Edit's loft was a major gathering spot for artists, critics, and curators of every stripe. That's where I first met Jeffrey Deitch—a suit-and-tie corporate art adviser at the time—who would go on to become a major gallerist and curator, not to mention a lifelong friend and ally. Jeffrey and Edit were early champions of what I was up to. I got them into rap too and helped bring the Funky Four into Edit's

UPTOWN/DOWNTOWN

Kitchen extravaganza, where Debbie, unable to be there in person, introduced the group by phone.

So when I recommended the Funky Four Plus One to Debbie and Chris for *SNL*, they were already well primed.

On Valentine's Day 1981, introduced by Debbie in person, the Funky Four Plus One hit the national stage. Keith Keith, K. K. Rockwell, Lil' Rodney C, Jazzy Jeff, and Sha Rock (who was pregnant at the time and wore a baggy pink shirt to hide the bump) became the first rap group to perform live on national television. They did "That's the Joint," an iconic record if there ever was one. I was at 30 Rock when it went down, and I remember being mesmerized by the Funky Four's performance, even though they did it to a canned track instead of a live DJ.

I was also struck by a young Black guy who had recently joined the cast: only twenty years old, from Brooklyn like me. His name was Eddie Murphy.

It was a little unusual that Debbie did *SNL* solo, especially with "Rapture" climbing the charts and headed for number one. But a few things were going on. For one, she had a solo album in the works, produced by Nile Rodgers and Bernard Edwards of Chic. For another, Blondie was feeling burned out. And Chris's health was shaky—he wasn't feeling great and nobody could figure out what was wrong. There was concern all around.

But for now, "Rapture" was everywhere, all the time. It was a major moment in the culture. I was proud to have helped light that fuse. And I loved the song.

Over the years, people have asked me tough questions about "Rapture"—about the fact that it was a white New Wave band doing rap. Did I feel ripped off by Blondie? Not at all. We were friends. They shouted me out. Chris and Debbie were genuine fans of this new music, just like I was.

To me, there was no doubt that "Rapture" was coming from the right place—and that it was going to be good for everybody. Sure, it wasn't coming straight from the culture. But it wasn't some cynical, contrived trash cooked up in a boardroom either. Blondie was picking up on the same street energy the rest of us were. They were doing their part to put this music in front of a bigger audience—busting it out of New York City and pushing it onto the airwaves from coast to coast.

My radio hero Frankie Crocker spun the hell out of it on WBLS. Guys like Grandmaster Flash and Afrika Bambaataa felt the same way I did about "Rapture": It was a gift, almost beyond description.

The day after *Saturday Night Live*, the landmark New York/New Wave show opened in Long Island City at the P.S. 1 Contemporary Art Center. It was curated by Diego Cortez—one of the Mudd Club insiders—and it felt like the next step beyond the Times Square Show.

The advertisement for the show in *Artforum* was a full-page Bobby Grossman photo of me, Debbie, and Lee in front of the *Graffiti 1990* mural on Cherry Street. All three of us were represented in a big way. Lee's main contribution was an enormous graffiti-style portrait of Debbie on aluminum panels—his way of paying her back for everything she'd done for the culture and for including him, and graffiti, in the "Rapture" video.

I had a couple of graffiti-style paintings in the show myself, including one of my largest works yet: the word "SEX," also on aluminum sheets. Charlie Ahearn snapped a photo of me standing in front of it. Another piece was more in line with what I'd shown in Rome and Milan—an attempt to use the gestures of tagging to create pure abstract forms. Diego mounted that piece high up on a wall that also had a couple of works by David Byrne—and, as a huge bonus, right next to Henry Chalfant's photograph of the second Campbell's soup can train.

The entire exhibition was like that—floor-to-ceiling, wall-to-wall, with so much to look at your head would spin. Almost instantly, there was a line down the block every day to see this thing Diego had put together—the first major institutional showcase of downtown and street culture.

The artists came from every corner of the cutting-edge map: more than fifteen hundred works by more than a hundred contributors. There were performance artists, avant-garde poets, punk rockers, No Wavers, and Diego made sure to include graff-related artists like Keith, Futura 2000, Crash, Daze, and Lady Pink. Claes Oldenburg even donated funds for their materials.

New York/New Wave was a breakout moment for Jean, whose work—dominating an entire wall of the exhibition space—got a ton of attention. During the packed opening, he hid under a table. Peter Schjeldahl gave him a major shoutout in *The Village Voice*, but the mainstream press seemed flummoxed by the whole thing. Glenn O'Brien came to the rescue in *Interview:* "Here's a whole new art world ready to replace the old one. Of course the old one is not going to just pack up and move to Chicago because of an art show in Long Island City. But I can tell they're scared. And why? I think because here is art based on life, not on art. The public might like it."

For me, it felt radical to be in the middle of that profusion of creativity.

Andy Warhol was included too—and he actually showed up, meeting me, Lee, and even Lee's father. I had run into Andy again around this time, when Chris and Debbie brought me to Regine's, the swanky nightclub at East Fifty-Ninth and Park Avenue, for an event. He didn't say much, but he acknowledged who I was and let me know he understood what the graffiti thing was about.

To me, it was another sign of Andy's genius—his ability to stay plugged in to whatever and wherever the newest cultural energy was coming from. That's how he kept himself charged up and evolving. Andy always had his eye on the scene, and in early 1981, he knew that the scene was bubbling at P.S. 1.

It was cool seeing Keith's work get some exposure at P.S. 1. He'd been hovering more and more at the edges of the Mudd Club. Steve Mass had hired him as a kind of cleanup guy. Steve knew that Keith and his Club 57 posse wanted to get into the mix at the Mudd Club, but he didn't think they were cool enough. So the custodial job was like a bone he tossed Keith's way.

I remember Keith telling me, "Steve treats me so bad. He treats me like shit. When I go to get paid, he just slips my money under the door. He won't even open it!" Keith would show up at Steve's place, hoping for a little face time, but Steve wouldn't give him the time of day.

That started to change pretty quickly when Steve began hearing all the buzz about Keith—about the wild stuff he was doing over at Club 57 and the cool gatherings he and Kenny were throwing at their Midtown apartment/studio. Kenny had turned one of the rooms into a little Day-Glo psychedelic fantasyland, where we'd all take mushrooms and groove to amazing music.

When Keith and Kenny organized a big blacklight art show at Club 57, they invited me to take part. By then, I was getting friendly with that whole crew—Debi Mazar, Ann Magnuson, Dan Friedman, Tseng Kwong Chi, John Sex—as more and more Mudd Club people were mingling with them. The blending of those two downtown worlds had probably been inevitable, so Steve finally relented and started welcoming the Club 57 crew into the Mudd Club fold. He came to understand that Keith was someone really special: *Wait a second, this kid is doing cool shit.*

Steve tapped Keith to curate shows in the Mudd Club's new fourth-floor art gallery, starting with his killer Lower Manhattan

UPTOWN/DOWNTOWN

Drawing Show, which featured work by me, Keith, Lee, Jean, Kenny, and many others. This feeling of a community among younger artists kept building, and Keith was a major animating force behind it.

I also found myself developing a crush on his and Kenny's roommate—an English girl who was smart, cool, and kind of posh. She was a talented artist too, with work in the Mudd Club show. Keith swore there was no way anything would ever happen between us. Then one night, he came home with his boyfriend after a long night of partying and was surprised to find the two of us fast asleep together. The romance was short-lived.

I had been introducing Keith to more artists emerging from the graff scene, including Futura 2000, who had absolutely incredible style. I first met Futura on the Upper West Side, where he grew up, at one of the regular meetings of the Soul Artists—the graffiti collective he founded with Ali. They had heard about what Lee and I had been doing in Italy and downtown, and they reached out. So I headed up to one of their meetings. The collective included some serious graffiti vets, all trying to figure out how to elevate their work the way Lee and I had been doing.

Right away, I could tell Futura was a sharp cat. Talent and intelligence just radiated from the guy, and his raging style was fresh and unique. I knew I could move with him, help plug him in. He was exactly the kind of artist I was hoping to bring into the fold—someone rooted in graffiti but ready to break through in the gallery world. Jean and I were always scheming on how to open doors for more artists of color, and Futura was part of that vision.

Jean and I would have these strategy sessions and joke about how careful we had to be about who we brought in. We knew how it could go. We didn't want stickup-kid, rob-and-steal energy creeping in and messing everything up, especially with the media always looking for a reason to cast us in a negative light. With Futura, there was never any worry. Same thing with Ali—brilliant, grounded, a natural leader.

He was also the mastermind behind a music collective called J. Walter Negro and the Loose Jointz. Their single "Shoot the Pump" was this wild rap/disco/rock mash-up that charted in England but should have blown up everywhere.

Futura and I got a studio together at Kenkeleba House, an alternative space down on East Second Street, past Avenue C, created to support Black artists. That part of Alphabet City was ultra edgy. Dope was being sold on the streets in broad daylight, like it was a farmer's market. Multiple drug-dealing squads—mostly Puerto Rican roughnecks—controlled the block, and people would be on line to cop heroin and coke. Getting to the studio was like navigating an obstacle course of dealers barking the brand names of their products—"Sudden Death!" "Presidential!" "Colt 45!" "Hot Sauce!"—and users nodding out on the sidewalk. Dealing was just part of the Lower East Side streetscape back then, more in-your-face than I'd ever seen anywhere in my life.

Futura still lived uptown but would crash some nights at his pal Gerb's place on St. Mark's, not far from Club 57. Gerb was the coolest—our official smoke man. He always had the best California bud, plus hash and mushrooms. His apartment became a natural gathering place for our crew. There was this long hallway he'd painted hot pink. One day, while we were hanging and puffing, Gerb said, "Yo, Fred, feel free to tag that hall." So I did. I wrote my name nice and big on Gerb's pristine pink wall.

Since Gerb knew so many graff writers, that hallway quickly became a monumental collaborative mural, with contributions from Futura, Keith, Jean, Dondi, Revolt, Zephyr—everybody. It was a graffiti wall of fame.

Keith said that Steve Mass wanted me to curate the next big art show at the Mudd Club. I tapped Futura to help. He was starting to get his feet wet in the scene, and this would get some eyeballs on him and his work. I wanted to showcase graffiti in a gallery setting—but also expand how people thought about it, pushing their expectations and possibilities. I called the show Beyond Words.

On the exhibition poster, which I designed myself with the help of John Sex, who laid it out for the printer, I described the work in the show with a subtitle: "graffiti based—rooted—inspired." I wanted it to be clear that we were not just trying to co-opt the outlaw cool of pure street graffiti. Instead, Beyond Words would explore a broader interpretation of what graffiti could be—how it might evolve, how it could function in a new context.

We brought in artists like Lee, Jean, Keith, Kenny, and Rammellzee—the mad-scientist Afro-Futurist who had called my house back when *The Village Voice* article came out. (I later wrote that Ramm was "part street physics professor, part trickster.") We had Lady Pink, Phase 2, Zephyr, Dondi, and Johnny "Crash" Matos, who'd curated the Graffiti Art Success for America show up in the Bronx at Fashion Moda, which Lee and I had also taken part in. (I'd pushed the owner of Fashion Moda, Stefan Eins, to give Crash, Daze, and Lady Pink a leg up.)

Thanks to a fantastic suggestion from Edit DeAk, Alan Vega of Suicide contributed work. So did Francesco Clemente and Iggy Pop. Henry and Martha and Charlie showed their photos. It was a celebration of culture straight from the street. Jean's piece, in fact, paid tribute to a sign right on Fourth Avenue in Brooklyn, near where he grew up, that read: FLATS FIX.

Beyond Words would be the biggest and most focused show yet to celebrate the evolving artistry and influence of graffiti.

Steve Mass was hyped about what we had up our sleeves and said, "How about bringing in some of those rap guys to perform at the opening?" He was right on target. It was the perfect occasion. Most of the graffiti artists I had invited to be in the show hadn't been introduced to the downtown scene yet. That was also true of the DJs and MCs who Charlie and I had been getting to know in the Bronx, as we kept moving forward with the preproduction and research phase for our movie, which we'd decided to call *Wild Style*—a term used to describe a bold, intricate, and yes, wild variety of graffiti.

So I thought, *Hell yeah, I'm gonna set this off right.*

I pulled together a lineup that would've lit up any Bronx jam: Grand Wizzard Theodore and the Fantastic Five, the Cold Crush Brothers, and Afrika Bambaataa. Busy Bee, the Chief Rocker himself, came through. It was a full-on rap revue—like a night at the P.A.L. on Webster Avenue—but this time it was happening at 77 White Street in Lower Manhattan. The Mudd Club crowd had no idea what was about to hit them. The opening night—April 9—was *on fire*. The fourth-floor gallery was jammed, and down on the dance floor, it was raging.

Beyond Words was the first time a big, mixed New York crowd got to experience graffiti and rap culture up close and in person. And a lot of them became fans right then and there. The show brought people together who wouldn't usually be in the same room. Like I've said, the downtown scene wasn't exactly filled with people of color hanging out. There was a small handful of us: me, Jean, Michael Holman, a couple of others. But that night, it was different. Latin and Black guys from the Bronx and Lower East Side were dancing and hanging out with white punk rock, New Wave, arty types. Everyone was checking out each other's moves and gear. You could feel the barriers coming down. It was electric.

That kind of moment didn't happen often. But when it did, to me, that was New York.

At Keith's request, I had hooked Afrika Bambaataa up with a night at Club 57 not long before. Bam loved it. I knew there was no better DJ on earth to preside over the opening festivities of Beyond Words.

Bam had earned the title "Master of Records" for a reason: nobody had a deeper, more unpredictable vinyl collection—or more adventurous, omnivorous taste. He'd toggle from "Dance to the Music" by Sly and the Family Stone to "Mary, Mary" by the Monkees, sliding into Kraftwerk and Captain Sky along the way, all while mixing live and layering like a mad scientist. He'd take the opening drum count from the "Sgt. Pepper Reprise" and loop the shit out of it. Then he'd drop "The Pink Panther Theme."

Bambaataa saw his mission as one of peace—bringing people together. And grooving hard.

Beyond Words sent ripples through the art world and the graff scene alike. Writers from all five boroughs flocked to White Street to soak up the energy and see their heroes' work on gallery walls. It felt momentous. A lot of these kids brought their piece books to get signed. Before long, tags began popping up all over the Mudd Club—from the fourth-floor gallery all the way down. For a few weeks, the place turned into a full-blown graffiti convention: a free-flowing street-art environment.

Not everyone was thrilled. Ross Bleckner, who owned the building, was alarmed by the explosion of tags. I got a memo that he was pissed, so I went over to smooth things out. Thankfully, he turned out to be pretty cool about it. There was also a minor flare-up when a few writers with old beef crossed paths—somebody had gone over somebody else's work. It wasn't a big deal, but to an outsider, it might have looked like heavy hood shit. I figured this kind of friction was inevitable when you started merging different worlds. I did a little damage control and everything was fine.

Beyond Words cemented the fact that I had become the visible link between different universes—New Wave and rap, the art world and the graffiti world. That spring, a new electric flavor was pulsing across the five boroughs—not just in Lower Manhattan or the Bronx—and the Mudd Club felt like its epicenter. The show helped give birth to the modern concept of street art.

It was also the last hurrah for that shining era of the Mudd Club.

EVERYBODY'S FLY

Keith had decided that Steve Mass was just an authority figure who still couldn't stop treating him like shit. By then, Keith was blowing up—he had a little money in his pocket and plenty of momentum. He told Steve to go fuck himself and walked away. And that was the end of Keith's wildly successful, wildly short stint organizing art shows at the Mudd Club.

Every once in a while, Jean and I would head to the Cedar Tavern on University Place, always imagining the days when Jackson Pollock, Willem de Kooning, Franz Kline, and the rest of the Abstract Expressionist crew were hanging out, drinking, getting into fistfights. We'd heard the story about Kerouac pissing in an ashtray and getting banned for life. The original tavern had been torn down, replaced almost two decades before Jean and I ever started going, but the air still felt haunted.

We never caused any trouble there ourselves, but Jean liked to keep people off balance. Glenn O'Brien once told me about bringing him to a fancy event. Somebody asked Jean, in that polite, vaguely condescending way, "And what do you do?" Jean deadpanned: "Oh, I manage a McDonald's."

Jean loved doing weird shit with his hair, like growing out six-inch dreads from the back of his head, with a dyed-blond mohawk in the front. Walking around with Jean, I'd see that other pedestrians, usually white women, would literally cross to the other side of the street in order to avoid us. He told me that sometimes when he got onto an elevator, people would step off. The opposite could also happen. Sometimes cute girls on the scene—usually white—would reach up and touch his hair like he was in a petting zoo. Jean didn't let that slide. He'd knock their hands away, putting them in deep check. I remember him humiliating one girl to the point of tears as she realized she was straight outta line.

Another of Jean's hairstyles was dreads sprouting out of the back and a clean, close crop in front—a look we called a Caesar. I once asked him why he wore it that way. "Oh," he said, "say I walk into a place to apply for a job. They see me from the front and think, 'Here's a nice, clean-cut, well-spoken young man. I'm going to hire him.' After I get the job I turn around to leave, they see the back of my head, freak out, and say, 'Oh my God, what have I done? You're fired!'"

Glenn had cast Jean in a movie called *New York Beat*, which was parallel, in many ways, to what Charlie and I were doing. While we were focused on the Bronx, Glenn—the writer and producer—was focused on downtown. We had Lee as our main character; Glenn had Jean. He brought in Edo Bertoglio from *TV Party* to direct and populated the cast with many of the hipsters we were seeing and hanging out with on a daily basis. Debbie, for instance, played a bag lady. Lee and I had our own cameos—there's a scene where we're spray-painting a storefront and a woman walks by. I say to her, "Hey, sexy, like it? It's art!" *True to life!* The film—an extended Lower East Side fairy tale—would end up being released decades later as *Downtown 81*.

After Beyond Words, I was included in a show at the Contemporary Art Center in Geneva. The Europe pipeline was flowing. Jean had a solo show in Italy, at Emilio Mazzoli's gallery in Modena, arranged by Diego Cortez. To me, that was the moment when Jean's rocket really began to blast off.

I ran into him one day on First Avenue, just after he got back.

"Hey, how'd it go in Italy?"

"Fred, it went well, man. I made some money. Look!"

He pulled a fat wad of bills out of his pocket.

"Here, man." He peeled off a couple of bills, folded them, and slipped them into my shirt pocket. I thanked him, assuming it was twenty bucks or whatever. But when I pulled the cash out to move it to my pants pocket, I was stunned to find two crisp $100 bills.

"Damn, Jean. Thanks, man. I got you for this."

"Nah, Fred. You know how we do. That's you, man."

We'd been used to stretching every penny—jumping turnstiles, scraping together change for food or a bag of weed. Now Jean was talking about throwing a post-Italy victory-lap dinner at John's, the old-school Italian joint on East Twelfth. Everybody was like, "Yo, what the hell is this? A dinner? A sit-down dinner?" I was thinking, *Wow, this is just so... classy.*

Jean had that way about him. He figured shit out fast—how to host a proper dinner, what wine to drink, how to assemble the perfect mix of people. Glenn, Keith, Diego, and Futura were there, along with Arto Lindsay and John Lurie from the Lounge Lizards. David Byrne showed up. Michael Holman was there, and so was Leisa Stroud, the bleached blonde Mudd Clubber. Jean's girlfriend at the time, Suzanne Mallouk too. I can't remember who else, but these were the people Jean dug and trusted—cool enough, in his eyes, to make the guest list.

So there we were, sitting around a long table lit by giant dripping candles, eating angel-hair pasta and shrimp Fra Diavolo, sipping Pinot Grigio and Barbera—all on Jean's dime. I kept thinking, *How much is this costing? And how does he even know how to do this?*

It was Jean making a statement, generous and elegant. And everyone at the table got the message loud and clear: Our host was poised to do big things, and we raised our glasses in salute.

That was also the first night I ever had prosciutto and melon. For Jean, that appetizer would become a minor obsession—a symbol of who we were and where we were headed. It turned into our thing, whenever we had money in our pockets and went out on the town together. It defined that whole era.

Prosciutto and melon!

11

It's about time we got some publicity for this goddam rap shit

Futura and I went to the St. Marks Cinema to check out *Underground U.S.A.*, a midnight movie that had been running for six months straight. It was a ramshackle, 16mm art film by Eric Mitchell about the downtown scene, kind of a *Sunset Boulevard* send-up. But instead of silent-era Hollywood, the ghosts it conjured were from the Warhol Factory days of the 1960s. I ended up running into the blonde bombshell star of *Underground U.S.A.*, Patti Astor, at a party the writer Duncan Smith hosted at his Bowery loft—held, for some reason, in honor of the nineteenth-century French poet Stéphane Mallarmé. The moment I saw Patti, I made a beeline for her.

"Patti Astor," I said, "you are my favorite movie star."

I was holding a paper plate and offered it to her: "May I have your autograph?"

Patti had starred in a number of underground films and was the Kim Novak—or the Mae West—of downtown. She had also appeared with Duncan in another of Eric's films, *Kidnapped*. Amos Poe had put her in his art flick *Unmade Beds*, a *Breathless*-style riff that starred Debbie and the *other* Duncan—Duncan Hannah, the painter. I later learned that Patti had been part of the student protests at Columbia in '68, when she was an undergrad. Patti had been down with the counterculture her whole life, it seemed. She looked me over.

"Why, of course," she said in that squeaky voice of hers. "You must be my new best friend!" She signed the plate with a flourish—and, on the spot, we *did* pretty much become best friends.

I was impressed that she already knew about the graffiti scene, so I blurted out, "You know, Patti, you should be an art dealer—because you look hotter than Mary Boone!" At the time, Mary Boone was showing the likes of Julian Schnabel and David Salle at her gallery on West Broadway in SoHo, and *New York* magazine was about to crown her the "New Queen of the Art Scene." She was attractive in a Marlo Thomas kind of way. Patti got a kick out of the suggestion, hooting with laughter. But I thought, *Actually, this could really be something.*

As Charlie and I were making moves with *Wild Style*, lining up DJs, MCs, graffiti artists, and members of the breakdancing Rock Steady Crew to appear in the film, we were pumped to see that a bunch of the people we hoped to feature were set to perform at the first-ever Sugarhill Rapper's Convention, held at the 369th Regiment Armory in Harlem, right on the Harlem River. The lineup was stacked: the Sugarhill Gang, Grandmaster Flash and the Furious Five, the Funky Four Plus One, Afrika Bambaataa, Grand Wizzard Theodore—the list went on and on. No question, this was the biggest rap event to date, in a space that held something like ten thousand people. A pivotal moment, for real.

Charlie and I went, with him snapping photos. Patti was there too—silver outfit, blond hair shining like a spotlight—along with Edit, Diego, Rene Ricard, and a few other Mudd Club types. There was basically no security, and there was Patti, in the middle of it all. Charlie and I were like, *Wow*. He took a few pictures.

I knew a bit about the 369th Regiment—the Harlem Hellfighters, the all-Black unit that fought in the First World War with extraordinary valor and saw more combat than any other American regiment. One of their members was the famous bandleader James Reese Europe, whose regimental band toured France in 1918, introducing jazz to the Continent. "We won France by playing music which was ours," Europe said, "and not a pale imitation of others." He meant that he played music that was unapologetically Black.

Now, more than sixty years later, at the Hellfighters' own armory in Harlem, the latest unapologetically Black music was taking center stage. Charlie and I stood there, watching the crowd and our friends onstage, both of us stunned at how big this rap scene was getting— and how much further it still could go.

For me, it confirmed what we already suspected: *Wild Style* was right on the money, and we needed to bust ass and get this film made while the pot was still getting hot. Grandmaster Flash and the Furious Five were fast ascending beyond the street level we wanted to capture. If we waited too long, the whole thing could pass us by.

The Fantastic Five were mid-set, doing their thing, when we heard what sounded like a firecracker go off. *Wait, was that a pistol?* Suddenly, it was stampede time. Classic old-school rap-party shit: Someone gets into a squabble or fires a shot into the air just to show off, and the whole crowd freaks out. Everybody scrambled for the exits. When we finally made it outside, there was Patti and her crew on the sidewalk. A bunch of us headed back downtown and ended up drinking late into the night.

Despite the abrupt ending, Patti was electrified by the First Annual Sugarhill Rapper's Convention. She knew Charlie and I were working on *Wild Style*, and as the reigning queen of downtown underground movies, she naturally started lobbying for one of the major roles not already spoken for—the downtown female reporter looking to write about the Bronx graffiti and rap scenes. It was just about the only part not meant to be played by someone playing themselves.

Turns out Patti had known Charlie since their childhood in upstate New York, but even so, we kept putting her off, thinking we needed someone mousier for the role. But then Charlie got his photos back from that night at the armory: Patti in her shiny silver outfit, platinum hair glowing under the lights. The images looked like movie stills. We looked at each other—it was so obvious. Patti got the part.

One afternoon that spring, Glenn O'Brien and I met up with Anya Phillips at a restaurant on Second Avenue. Anya wasn't just one of the founders of the Mudd Club and James Chance's girlfriend—she was a downtown muse, full stop. She held forth on *TV Party*, designed stage outfits for Debbie, and radiated a ferocious, punk-glam energy—a fashionista with an S&M edge. Anya had come to New York from Taipei, and the word was she also worked as a dominatrix. That didn't surprise me; a few other downtown-scene women also worked in that lane, under the mistress Terence Sellers.

Glenn and I were meeting with Anya to help plan a benefit event for her as she had recently been diagnosed with cancer. Glenn would toss out names of performers to see if she approved, and she'd be like, "Oh, *that* motherfucker. He will *definitely* be there. He would show up for the opening of a jar of piss."

Wow, I thought, *what a character, I mean, she's terminal and the clock is ticking.*

"That motherfucker" would be there, for sure. But would Anya?

UPTOWN/DOWNTOWN

She must have known she had very little time left. But she handled the whole thing like ice-cold business—organizing, in effect, her own memorial.

Anya died in June, at age twenty-six, barely a month after the benefit for her at Bonds, a former clothing store turned massive disco in Times Square. She was iceberg cold to the bitter end.

Summer 1981. Keith Haring and I were walking near Avenue D and Houston Street just after midnight on a humid, sticky night when I caught a faint whiff of spray paint. Like a bloodhound, I tracked it, leading us across the street and around the corner until we stumbled upon an invitational graffiti project under way in the courtyard of P.S. 22.

A half-dozen local writers were busy doing pieces, while a bunch of kids ran around, just being kids. The school had commissioned a collaborative mural. Keith was delighted. He'd brought along a handful of the little buttons he'd made of the "radiant baby" he'd been tagging all over the place and passed these out to all the kids, who got excited when they recognized the image. The next day, Keith returned to P.S. 22 and painted a frieze, hundreds of feet long, maybe fifteen inches tall, running along the top of the wall above all the other graffiti. He filled it with his ever-growing cast of characters. It was a stunning piece.

Rap programs had started creeping onto FM radio—still at odd hours, but I was making tapes whenever I could. *Wild Style* was simmering. With funding coming through, thanks to the German network ZDF and Channel 4 in the UK, we could finally get moving. Everything felt like it was bubbling. The Specials at the Ritz—me, Chris, and Debbie there, along with none other than David Bowie at a show for the ages. *Wow.* A breakdance battle between the Rock Steady Crew and the Dynamic Rockers at a roller rink in Queens, followed by a second showdown at Lincoln Center—the first time anything rap-related ever hit a place like that, a shrine of high culture.

There was a brand-new cable channel, though almost no one I knew had cable—except for Debbie and Chris, who had outright predicted it: MTV. Nothing but music videos, all day, every day.

Then there was a chilling article in *The New York Times*, reporting on a deadly new form of cancer seen in "homosexuals."

And at Bonds, an initial slate of eight shows by my favorite British band, the Clash, ballooned into a seventeen-show marathon. The city came down on them and the club for overselling, so the band added extra nights to make good.

The Clash were curious and looking to explore rap and graffiti. They loved what Blondie had done with me on "Rapture," and through various channels, they got in touch with Futura. They commissioned him to paint a giant banner for the opening night to drape from the roof of Bonds. They also decided to tap rap artists to open for them.

I was there that first night when Grandmaster Flash and the Furious Five kicked things off. What was supposed to be a barrier-breaking night turned ugly fast. The mostly white crowd booed the group off the stage. I was just glad that Bonds sold beer in cups, not bottles—because those cups started flying. It was painful to watch. Joe Strummer and Mick Jones were furious. They chewed out the crowd; then later gave public props to Flash, the Funky Four, the Treacherous Three, and other rap groups in their interviews—making it clear they stood with the music.

The New York media covered the Clash's Bonds residency like it was a weeks-long riot in the heart of the city. It helped the band reach a bigger audience—and, perversely, probably helped rap too in the long run. That moment exposed more people to the music, even if the crowd didn't know what to do with it yet.

Not that Black music fans weren't already tuned in to the Clash. Frankie Crocker had been spinning "The Magnificent Seven" on WBLS all the time. He dropped in a sample of one of Clint Eastwood's lines from the movie *Dirty Harry*, talking about his .44-Magnum, and the song blew up. Joe Strummer was amazed. "These four white guys from London on BLS," he said. "It was fantastic." Larry Levan would start spinning that remix at the Paradise Garage.

Futura got tight with the Clash during their Bonds run, and they invited him to join their Radio Clash tour in England. At every stop, he'd come out onstage and paint a live backdrop. He even started rapping during the shows. I'd made him copies of some of my rap-party tapes—he learned all the lyrics, and he got pretty good and wrote his own rap about graffiti. Between shows, he'd sneak off and bring NYC-style graff to the UK streets.

I remember the day he got back from touring with the Clash. I was hanging with Zephyr at Gerb's crib on St. Marks, awaiting his return, ready to hear all about it. Futura rolled in wearing a hardcore leather motorcycle jacket, his hair piled high and slicked back like a full-on English teddy-boy rocker. I thought he'd gone and joined the Clash for real! He was feeling the punk vibes, for sure, and he'd nailed the look.

The appreciation was mutual. The Clash were getting all the way into it: graffiti, rap, the New York scene. They came down to Second Street to visit our studio and even checked out the amphitheater where we were staging the climactic *Wild Style* jam, emblazoned with Lee's murals.

One afternoon, Dondi and I went with Futura to Electric Lady Studios on Eighth Street, where he rapped over an instrumental track the Clash had recorded. The song was called "The Escapades of Futura 2000"—"*Graffiti is rockin' and on the go!*" He name-checked me, Jean, Keith, Taki, even the graff writer called LSD. It was a little manifesto for what we were up to.

The Clash also had him rap on a number called "Overpowered by Funk": "*This is a message from Futura...*"—which became, no surprise, one of my favorite cuts on *Combat Rock*. That album came out the next year and launched the Clash into the Top 40.

And then there was the afternoon at Charlie's place at Forty-Third Street and Eighth Avenue in Times Square, a dusty old seventh-floor walk-up filled with low-level show-biz managers and voice coaches. He lived there with his wife, the great artist Jane Dickson. Patti came by to talk with us about her role in *Wild Style*. We were deep in conversation when she suddenly shifted gears.

"Fred, listen," she said. "We've got this little space in the East Village, on Eleventh Street, and we're going to turn it into a gallery. We want to show the work of our friends." I was like, *Wow, she actually went out and did it.* Which was so Patti. *You really are hotter than Mary Boone!*

Patti had recently thrown a party that started with Futura painting a mural in her apartment on East Third Street and morphed into a barbecue out back—this funky little yard behind a shop at Second Avenue and Second Street. A bunch of cool artists and Mudd Club–types showed up, drinking beer and eating burgers and ribs. Watching Patti in the midst of this, I could already see it: her as curator, gallerist, host. Just like Charlie and I had seen Patti at the Harlem armory and knew she had to play the reporter in *Wild Style*—she had the energy.

Turns out, her friend Bill Stelling had a tiny storefront he'd been using as a textile studio. Since Patti knew so many artists, they figured they could get something going—a gallery with street sensibility, a downtown vibe, something to contrast with SoHo's blue-chip slickness. And of course, a great excuse to gather the crew and drink cocktails and cheap jug wine.

They were planning a soft launch with a show by Patti's husband, Steven Kramer, an artist and musician who played with the Contortions. They were separated but still close. The first *real* show would be Kenny Scharf, his first solo exhibition. Kenny had just "customized" a bunch of appliances in Patti's apartment. Would I like to do the second show?

I was like, "Sure."

Patti told me that she and Bill had the idea that the artists themselves should name the gallery, and that with every new show it would have a new name. "Kenny decided to call it *Fun*," Patti told me. "So what do you want to call it for your show?"

"Well, Kenny's thing is fun—his work is inspired by *The Jetsons* and *The Flintstones* and all that Hanna-Barbera stuff. So I'll call mine the Serious Gallery, just so we can have some contrast. You know, change it up."

Patti loved it. But by the time Steve's and Kenny's shows had come and gone, the name Fun Gallery had started to stick—at least in our little downtown world. So when Patti and I sat down to plan my October show, she was like, "Fred, I'm sorry, but do you mind if we keep the name Fun Gallery? We just don't have the money to print new stationery"—which probably meant like a hundred bucks.

She had cut the word *fun* out of a comic book and pasted it onto some paper, and that became the gallery's permanent logo. Honestly, it was kind of perfect. So the soon-to-be famous Fun Gallery stayed Fun.

And fun was exactly what it was about. The place was so tiny, it felt like you were in a friend's extra-small studio apartment. But from the start, you could tell something special was happening. No art gallery in the world had that kind of energy. The Fun Gallery was an *experience*.

EVERYBODY'S FLY

As Patti put it—contrasting the Fun Gallery to what, say, Mary Boone was doing in SoHo: "White walls, white wine, white people, and overblown paintings you had to have gone to art school to even pretend to understand. Snooze. *Our* gallery was going to be an artists' gallery, as opposed to the moneyed enclaves to the south." And that's exactly what it became.

Right away, the Fun Gallery was a thing, a multiracial, very cool, very *fun* thing that felt fresh and new. People came out of the woodwork just to be in the mix: Jean, Keith, Kenny, Futura, Dondi, Zephyr, and Revolt, a member of the famous graffiti crew Rolling Thunder Writers. Lee sprayed "Mom" on the front window, and as Bill put it, that immediately gave the Fun Gallery cred with the street kids in the neighborhood.

He and Patti didn't want some stiff gallery for boring, art-school-trained artists. They wanted it to be a party with all their friends, kind of like how the Times Square Show had been. They also wanted to connect to the energy up at Fashion Moda, the graffiti-focused art space in the Bronx. The Fun Gallery brought all these currents together right in the heart of the East Village: graffiti kids, punk rockers, English hipsters, underground filmmakers, Mudd Clubbers. Hot DJs spinning dance music. It was a straight-up phenomenon.

At my opening, I was floored when a limo rolled up and parked right in front of the gallery. We all stared as the Swiss art dealer Bruno Bischofberger—one of the biggest contemporary dealers in the world—stepped out and walked into the Fun Gallery. *What the hell...?*

He ended up buying one of my pieces. That bugged everybody out. We were just trying to put on a show for our cool-ass friends—and now Bruno Bischofberger had us on his radar. Which meant that, suddenly, so did everyone else. Word flew through the downtown scene: *What the hell is going on over there?*

UPTOWN/DOWNTOWN

Patti, with her squeaky laugh, thanked me for helping bring the Fun Gallery into the "big time."

The Fun Gallery became something more consequential than any of us had imagined. Suddenly, the East Village had its own gallery movement. Within no time, a dozen commercial galleries had popped up in the neighborhood—and over the next few years, there would be dozens more. I started thinking of Patti as a kind of latter-day Baroness Pannonica de Koenigswarter, the jazz patron my father and his buddies talked about when I was a kid—a powerful, style-forward woman who championed work made by people on the fringes, especially artists of color.

And it wasn't just Patti. I realized I was surrounded by women who played that kind of role while also making creative statements of their own, such as Debbie and Edit. I felt lucky to know them.

Wild Style was shaping up. Charlie and I were on a mission to make a lightly fictionalized version of what was actually going on in the streets—the rap parties in the Bronx, whole subway cars being painted in the layups, breakdancing crews throwing down furious moves. It would all build to a packed-to-the-hilt jam at the East River Park amphitheater, near where Lee had grown up in the Smith Houses.

Charlie and I were going to the movies together a lot back then, always discussing what we saw. I remember a double-feature at a revival house: *The Harder They Come*, the Jamaican crime classic starring Jimmy Cliff, with its raw look at Rastafari life and the reggae scene, and *Black Orpheus*, a retelling of an ancient Greek myth set in a Rio favela during Carnaval, full of gorgeous bossa nova music. We talked about how we wanted *Wild Style* to have a similar vibe—

authentic, honest, street-level, and also poetic and super colorful, all with a killer soundtrack.

To keep things as real as possible, we cast graffiti artists, DJs, MCs, and B-boys as themselves. We landed some of the very best: artists like Lee, Lady Pink, Dondi, Crash, Daze, Zephyr, and Rammellzee—many of whom had been in the Beyond Words show. On the music side, we had Busy Bee Starski, Grandmaster Flash, the Funky Four, the Cold Crush Brothers, Grand Mixer D.ST, the Fantastic Five, and Grand Wizzard Theodore. And for breakdancers, we had the Rock Steady Crew, the best in the game.

Having provided the initial concept, and finding in Charlie the ideal collaborator, I settled into the roles of coproducer and music director, and Charlie wrote, directed, and produced. My role meant having a heavy hand in just about every part of the film while also staging the performances and composing the original music.

Charlie argued early on that it we couldn't have the DJs use actual records in the movie—we'd run into massive copyright trouble. No "Funky Drummer" by James Brown, no "Apache" by the Incredible Bongo Band, no "Seven Minutes of Funk" by the Whole Darn Family. I pushed back: "Come on, Charlie, let's just use those records"— because that's what DJs actually used. And we were trying to document the real thing. But Charlie stuck to his guns, and he was right. Who knew what kind of lawsuits might have come at us?

So I said, "Okay, Charlie, this will be my job."

The solution I came up with was to head into the studio and create about a dozen original, one-minute-long drum break-style cuts— tracks that felt just like the break beats DJs used to scratch and cut in the parks and clubs. Our DJs would use those recordings during the film's rap performances.

Since I had practically zero experience in a recording studio, I brought in Chris Stein. We called up Lenny Ferraro from the TV

Party Orchestra. On the show, Lenny played a fake magician named the Great Luigi Ciccolini—but in real life, he was a fierce R&B drummer who'd played with Jerry Butler and Aretha Franklin.

I told Lenny what we were looking for: absolutely killer beats. He said, "Sure thing, Freddy. Just give me eight bars of the breakbeats the DJs love, and I'll take it from there." I played him a few examples, and he promised we'd get the drums down in no time. He nailed it, as I knew he would. Then David Harper, a funky bass player from Philly, laid down his parts over Lenny's beats. Chris added his magic—guitar riffs and pedal-driven atmospherics to give the tracks some different flavors. I tossed in a few sound effects, and on one especially hot cut I called "Down by Law," I even dropped a few lyrics. And that's how I built the foundation music for *Wild Style*.

We pressed about a hundred twelve-inch copies of the tracks at 45 RPM and handed them out to the DJs in the movie, who used them during filming. Over time, those ultra-rare 45s—"Down by Law," "Subway Theme," and others—became highly sought after, especially once DJs started going on deep vinyl dives to uncover every groove ever sampled on a rap record. For years afterward, one of the big mysteries on the DJ circuit was: *Yo, what were those records they sampled from in* Wild Style?

On the casting front, we had filled every role except one—Phade, a character inspired by the great Phase 2. Phase was a legend from the early days of graffiti, and we'd learned he was designing flyers for rap jams at spots like the Ecstasy Garage in the Bronx. He would even get on the mic and drop rhymes from time to time under the name Lonnie Wood. He was a real-deal, living link between graffiti and rap. We loved what he stood for and thought he'd be perfect to play this character.

Charlie and I kept trying to get him to come down to the Times Square office to talk about the movie, but he'd never show. Time was running out. We were in the eleventh hour of preproduction. Phase was going to keep us dangling forever. So finally, we were like, *fuck it*, and started auditioning other people for the role of Phade. But none of them had that... thing.

Then one day in the office, I noticed Charlie giving me a funny look.

"Charlie," I said, "why are you staring at me like that?"

"Fred, I think *you* could be the Phade character."

"Charlie, no freakin' way."

I didn't want anything to do with acting or being on-screen. I was happy staying behind the scenes. It was fun going in front of the camera for *TV Party*, but that was just a bunch of us goofing around. This was a movie. But Charlie being Charlie, he kept at it. And kept at it. And eventually, he talked me into it.

So, at the very last minute, I ended up with a lead role in *Wild Style*.

With the extra three hundred bucks a week—that was the deciding factor for me—I could finally afford my own apartment. I found a spot at 42 Clinton Street on the Lower East Side. Rent was $350 a month, and the place was basically a cold-water flat since the boiler was busted and nobody seemed to give a shit about fixing it. But I didn't care. At least I wouldn't have to make any more late-night treks to Utica Avenue on the A train.

Phade, in some ways, was a lot like me. A guy with a few things going, plugged into the scene, trying to help push rap and graffiti and breakdancing into the wider world. I had a decent gift of gab, but I modeled Phade after a couple of real fast-talking cats I knew from around: Kase 2—the legendary one-armed graffiti innovator, whose way with words impressed me almost as much as his artwork; and DJ AJ, who worked with Busy Bee and promoted MC battles where, somehow, Busy Bee always walked away with the win.

Putting that character together got me thinking about how Black folks have always used language—twisting it, flipping it, turning it inside out. Everything a remix, like the music we were documenting in the Bronx. It went all the way back to slavery, when it was illegal to teach enslaved people to read or write, and so the English language got reworked into something different, something new. I thought about my father and his jazz friends, how they had their own way of talking, a certain slang that came from their era, which always fascinated me. They might say, "Man, that was *dynamite*!" And now here was a new kind of slang for a new kind of world. (Years later, a word like *bling* would come out of hip-hop and quickly land in the pages of *Webster's*—it sometimes made my head spin how fast that happened.)

Phade is the guy in *Wild Style* who is always hyping people up, making connections and power moves while framing what was happening as *culture*. He preps the artists to meet Patti's character, Virginia—a downtown reporter who rolls up in the South Bronx behind the wheel of a 1970s jalopy, Blondie's "Pretty Baby" blasting from the speakers. (Her character was loosely based on a real writer we knew, who wrote one of the first stories on breakdancing and, let's just say, got close to a couple of members of the Rock Steady Crew.)

If there's one moment that sums up Phade, it's the scene where Zephyr's character, Z-Roc, is saying maybe it's better if this all stays underground, so it won't get ruined by going pop. And Phade goes: "*You serious?* Hey man, it's about time we got some publicity for this goddam rap shit."

There's a similar moment where Phade tries to convince Lee's character—Zoro, the mysterious but revered graffiti writer—to meet with the reporter. Zoro wants nothing to do with it. Like the real Lee, he was cautious and paranoid about being exposed to the cops. Phade tells him that getting publicity means getting paid. "You're gonna have money like Barry White, man!" he says. "You can do all kinds of crazy shit you wanna do when you get that bread!" (Years later, I heard that the Zoro character was an inspiration for the British street artist Banksy's decision to work anonymously, on the down-low.)

That tension—wanting to make it but feeling suspicious and exposed—radiates from Zoro, who is trying to succeed on his own terms. His story mirrored what a lot of us were feeling at that time. We were coming up from a scene that most of the world hated or ignored, trying to push our art into the culture while feeling like total outsiders. Zoro has to choose: Stay an anonymous outlaw, or team up with fancy uptown collectors. It was like what happened with Lee and me and Claudio Bruni.

In one scene, a collector played by the Elizabeth Taylor–gorgeous Niva Kislac literally wants to hook up with Zoro. (In real life, Niva was an art collector known to have had a thing for some of the artists she collected.)

Lee was still uneasy about appearing in *Wild Style*—and not just because he and his co-star-slash-love-interest Lady Pink were on-again, off-again in real life. He still feared arrest. He kept his head on swivel, always in stealth mode. This was around the time Mayor Koch boasted about putting six German shepherd attack dogs in a Queens layup. The antigraffiti squeeze was on. But Lee's paranoia ended up feeding the Zoro character perfectly. Charlie liked to say we were creating an "iconic version" of Lee—not the real Lee, but a kind of archetype. This was *Wild Style* in a nutshell: part street-level cinema verité, part colorful comic book. Loose and raw, but mythic.

As we structured the story, we'd sometimes get stuck. What got us unstuck was just looking around—at our friends, at the scene. We'd spot something going down and say, "That's it." The story of *Wild Style* was always right in front of us.

Then there were all the MCs and DJs we filmed, often at the Dixie, this banging club up the street from the Black Door, a funky old storefront that used to be another early Bronx rap spot. It bears repeating: So much of early rap evolved in unlikely venues—parks, the P.A.L., gyms, broken-down discos that had peaked in the 1970s, when disco was the hot-shit thing. Beside the Dixie and the Black Door, there was the Hevalo, the T-Connection, the Ecstasy Garage, and—most famous of all—Disco Fever, which was like a *real* club and part of the culture.

Charlie and I fell in love with places like that and the people who brought them to life. Rap promoters knew those joints were on life support, and the owners were happy to see something new take root.

There was often no real lighting in those places, especially the gymnasium-type dance halls or the P.A.L. Sometimes the only light came from something jerry-rigged at the DJ table—a rinky-dink strobe light amid a jumble of wires, a red light, or a bare bulb for ambience, or just something with enough glow so the DJ could see what he was doing. That kind of darkness—the shadows, the makeshift setups—felt totally unique to those parties up in the Bronx.

Busy Bee steals the show in so many scenes. The guy was electric—funny, magnetic, impossible to ignore. He, DJ Hollywood, and maybe a few other MCs used to rap about a place called "the Alps." You'd be at a jam, and somebody on mic would shout, "Where's that place we work it out?" and the crowd would holler back, "At the Alps we work it out!"

Charlie and I would be like, "What the hell is that? The actual Alps?" We cracked up every time. We laughed even harder when someone finally told us that the Alps was the name of a busted old motel in the Bronx—a "hot sheet" joint for by-the-hour hookups. Vice was probably raiding it all the time. But since a lot of the Bronx rap kids were still living with their parents, they'd sneak off to the Alps to handle their romantic business.

There were rivalries among the MCs and the crews up there—real ones. We learned that the Cold Crush Brothers and the Fantastic Romantic Five had all been friends growing up, but by the time Charlie and I showed up, they were at each other like it was show-biz Wrestle-Mania. The famous "throwdown" scene we shot outside on the basketball court captured the vibe between them perfectly. (In the late 1990s, that *Wild Style* basketball scene was recreated in a Sprite commercial with some of those same rappers—plus NBA stars Kobe Bryant and Tim Duncan.)

The incredible MC Rodney C of the Funky Four lived right up the street from the Dixie, and we were in and out of his house all the time, meeting his family and his then-lady, the singer and former Sequence rapper Angie B, aka Angie Stone. That kind of familial vibe was everywhere during the making of *Wild Style*. But there was also tension—especially with the Funky Four.

A few weeks before we started shooting, Rodney came to me, upset. "Yo, Fred, man—Sugar Hill is ripping us off. We're getting robbed!" I said, "What do you mean?" And he was like, "I'm looking at the numbers. We've got a hit record and the money math... it ain't *mathing* right." He was talking about "That's the Joint," the song the Funky Four had performed on *Saturday Night Live*.

Rodney was not happy and asked me to help. I felt so bad for the Funky Four. These were kids from the hood, and suddenly they were in the thick of the music business—a notoriously exploitative industry—with nobody really looking out for them. I didn't know much about recording contracts or what their particular deal looked like, so I turned to Chris and Debbie. They said to bring the Funky Four Plus One over to their apartment and we'd all talk it through.

So I got the whole crew together—including Sha Rock—and we sat down with Debbie and Chris. The Funky Four laid everything out. Debbie listened carefully and said, "Listen, guys, we're going to let you use our lawyer, okay? But one thing you must do to make this work: You have to stay together."

She was emphatic. Debbie and Chris knew the industry was ruthless and fickle—success could be here today, gone tomorrow. And they understood that for these young artists, this might be their one shot to make real money. The Funky Four had come as far as any rap group had at that point—and they had so much further to go. If Blondie was going to go to bat for them, they had to keep doing what they were doing and stick together.

Whenever they were ready, I told them, I would connect them with Blondie's attorney. The Funky Four left the apartment elated, sincerely thanking me—and knowing that Debbie and Chris had their backs. Everything looked good.

A couple of weeks later, we were on set in the Bronx when Rodney came up to me and said, "Yo, I need to talk to you."

"What's up, Rodney?"

"Listen, man. The Funky Four—it's over."

"Rodney, what? What are you talking about?"

"Man, Sylvia broke up the group!"

He told me that when they left Chris and Debbie's place, everybody had been in sync. They all agreed: stand strong, ten toes down, united. They had a meeting with Sylvia, and Rodney spoke up, saying they weren't happy, the money was funny, and that they'd hired a lawyer to renegotiate. Sylvia turned around and convinced Sha Rock, Jazzy, and Keith that they needed to stay on the label. K. K. Rockwell stuck with Rodney. The two of them would form a duo.

"Can you believe this shit, Fred? It's officially over. I hear the label is auditioning replacements for me and K. K. next week."

I was stunned. Charlie and I had been fired up to feature the Funky Four Plus One in *Wild Style*. This was a huge loss.

So... what about the movie? I was thinking, when Rodney looked at me and said, "Listen, man, I wrote this rhyme, and I want you to hear it."

A tear slid from the corner of my eye as Rodney delivered his rhyme—*"Here's a little story that must be told / about two cool brothers that were put on hold..."* Bar after bar, bittersweet and defiant, all about being held back, having your ego stepped on, your pride wounded, sticking by your true-blue brother, battling on.

Sugar Hill could have been the greatest thing in Black music ever, a label that could have made billions while launching rap to the top of the charts. But its owners could not evolve beyond the predatory playbook they had learned as industry veterans coming up in the bare-knuckled, mobbed-up music business of the early 1960s. Sugar Hill made history by breaking some of rap's first big hits, but all that bad karma came back around. The label folded just a few years later, run into the ground by greed.

After the premature end of the Funky Four Plus One, Rodney C and K. K. Rockwell reemerged as Double Trouble, performing "Stoop Rap," that savage rhyme about their troubles with Sugar Hill, in *Wild Style*, sitting side by side on a stoop—one of my favorite musical sequences in the film.

Finally, on a Saturday afternoon in October, we shot our big finale—the amphitheater jam. I designed the flyer by hand and printed a couple thousand copies to spread around: "ALL FLY GUYS + GALS FREE." The lineup was insane—maybe even better than the Harlem Armory jam. We had Grandmaster Flash and the Furious Five, Grand Wizzard Theodore and the Fantastic Five, the Cold Crush Brothers, and the scene-stealing Busy Bee Starski. Lee painted an epic mural across the back of the amphitheater, and the energy was sky high.

I remember being blown away by Cowboy of the Furious Five—one of the greatest rappers to ever live. It felt like we had captured these artists at their fullest moment of glory, right as the scene was peaking in the streets—just before it would blast off and go global.

When Charlie and I sat down at the Moviola editing machine to review the footage and listen to the sound, it was like—*uh oh*. The picture was amazing, but the sound was a disaster. After some investigating with the tech crew, we learned that the stereo Nagra recording deck we'd used hadn't been set up properly to handle the volume of the show. The audio was blown out, distorted beyond repair. The only solution was to reshoot it.

It had taken everything we had just to pull off the amphitheater jam, our most expensive shoot day. We'd even risked arrest, since we'd tried—but failed—to get a permit. So how could we possibly do another one? Well, we had to.

Then we looked at the footage from the Dixie. Same problem. The sound was totally screwed. You know: *totally fucked!*

We'd have to reshoot everything.

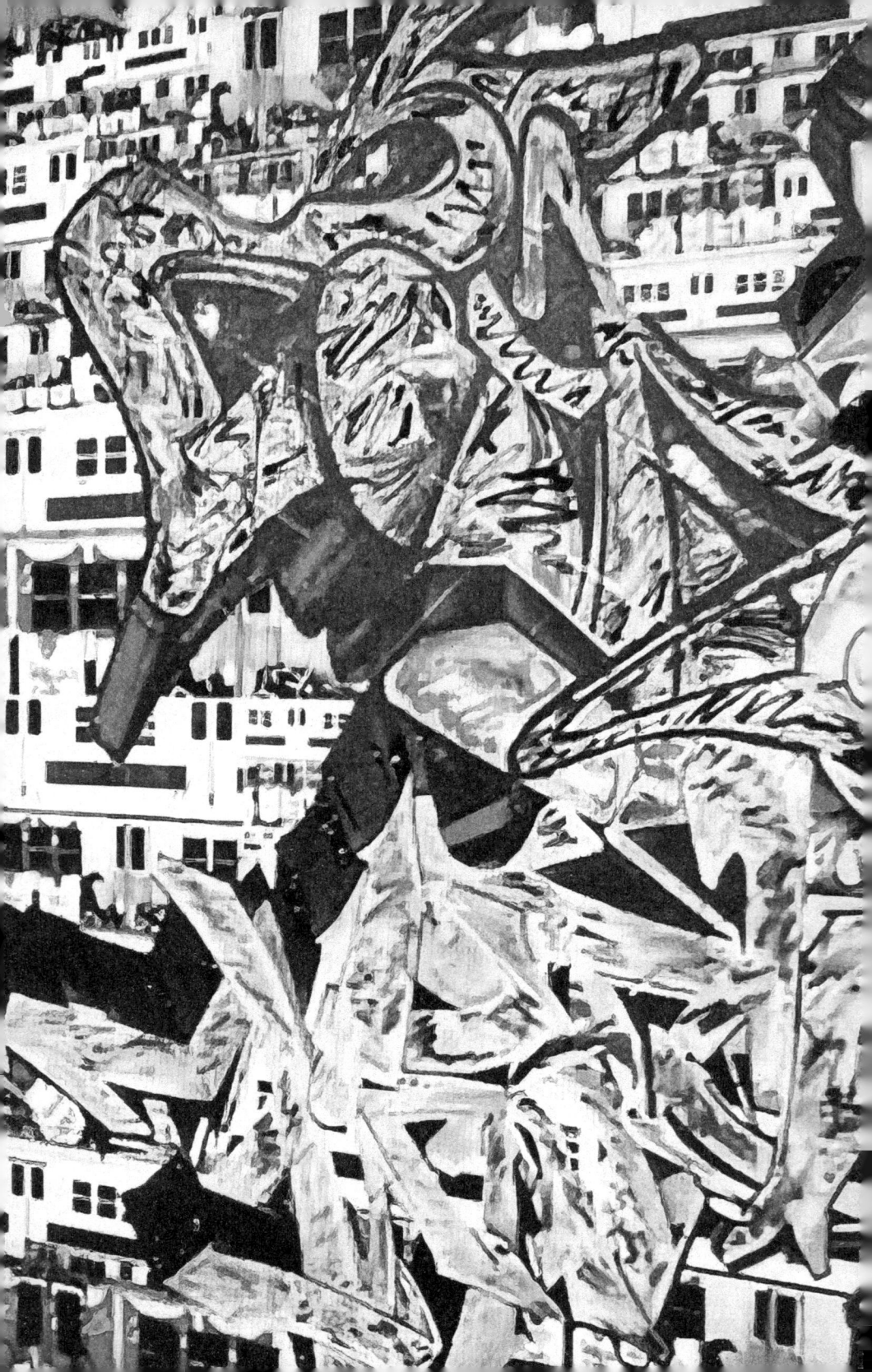

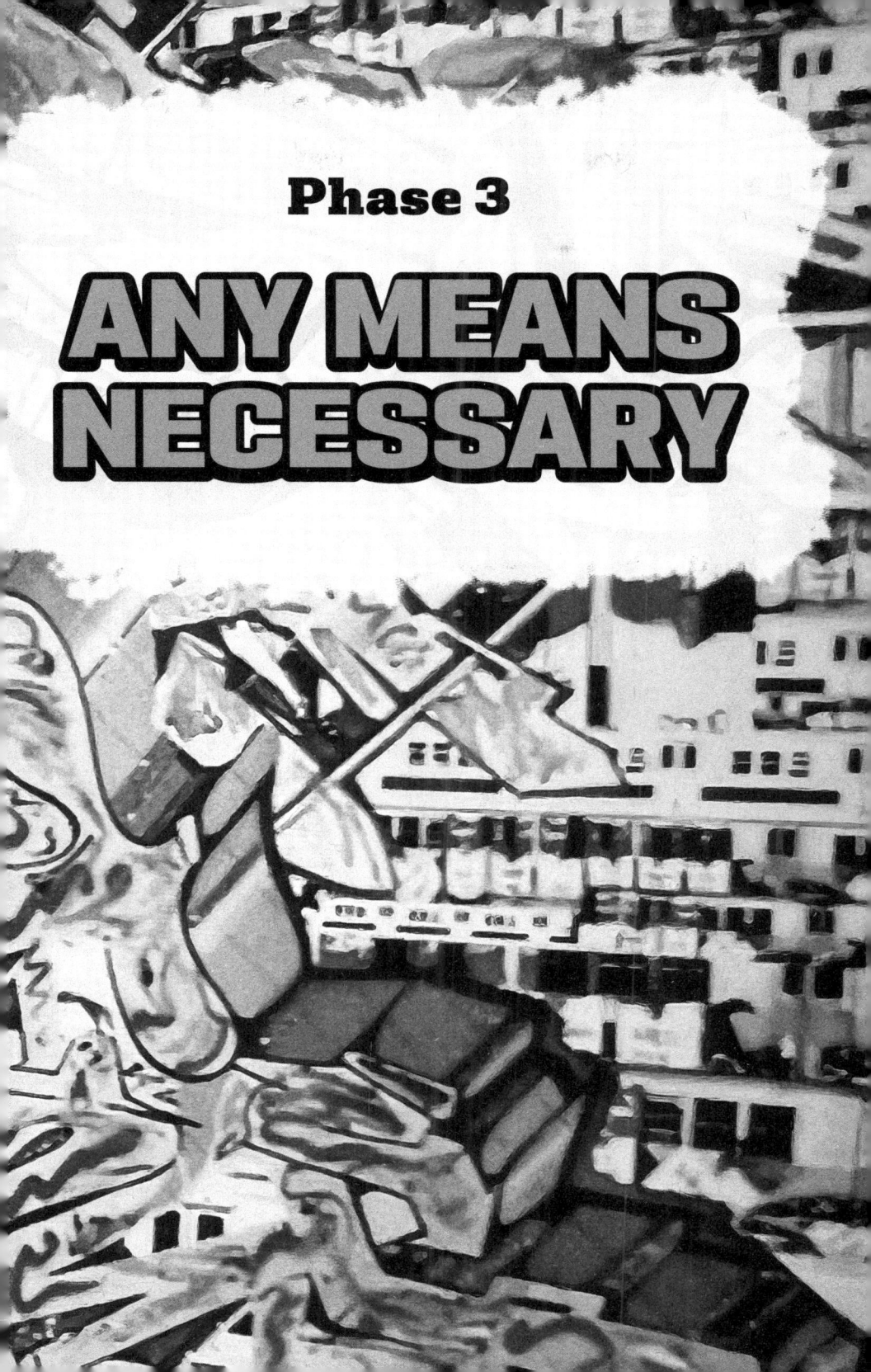

12

This stuff is really fresh!

As we were making *Wild Style*, one big question kept bouncing around in my head: What should we call this new culture of rap, graffiti, and breakdancing?

The origins of the term "hip-hop" are hard to pin down. When I hosted a show at the Kitchen—featuring the Rock Steady Crew breakdancing, subway mural projections from our *Wild Style* artists (taken from photographs by Henry Chalfant and Martha Cooper), me rapping, and my old Hancock Street pal DJ Spy on the turntables—we called it Graffiti Rock. (An earlier version of Graffiti Rock, organized by Henry, had been slated for a SoHo space called Common Ground but got canceled.) In other words, as 1981 turned the corner into 1982, there wasn't any consensus on what to name this thing.

"Hip-hop" was a familiar phrase—most rappers used it. Who said it first? Hard to say. Lovebug Starski is often credited with popularizing it, along with others, including DJ Hollywood. I'd always heard that Cowboy, from the Furious Five, was also among the first. The story goes that he started rapping "hip, hop, hip, hop" to tease his boy Kokomo, who had joined the army and was about to ship out. Cowboy was imitating a drill sergeant—"left, right, left, right"—and it stuck. It's sometimes said that Lovebug and Cowboy riffed on it together. Grandmaster Flash told me that it was actually Anna Monroe, his girlfriend at the time, who got it going. It was *her brother* who had just joined the army. She hopped on the mic with her "hip, hop, hip, hop" thing, teasing her brother one night at a party, then Cowboy grabbed on to it, and the two of *them* even did it in tandem. One way or another, it caught on. It became a part of the rap vocabulary, typically used by MCs in between raps to keep the party pumping—like a filler, a refrain.

I remember that at some point, when you'd be telling someone about a party you'd just been to, you'd find yourself saying, "It was one of them *hibbedy-hop* jams—you know, where they talk on the mic, saying, '*Hibbedy-hop and you don't stop.*'" That kind of thing. The phrase had definitely been floating around long before the Sugarhill Gang used it in "Rapper's Delight." Bit by bit, "hip-hop" started to seep into the language of this new culture—this thing that still didn't have a name. Even then, though, and up to that point, you never saw the term on a flyer for a rap jam.

As Charlie and I got closer to postproduction on *Wild Style*, that phrase—*hip-hop*—kept rolling around my brain. Finally, I was like, "You know, Charlie, I think we should call all of this 'hip-hop,' because that's what the rappers say—it captures the energy and spirit of what we're doing, all of it."

Up until then, we'd mostly called it "rap," a term that would stick around forever. But "rap" only described one piece of a larger urban culture our film focused on—the MCs and DJs—and didn't capture graffiti or breakdancing. And honestly, I'd gotten into the scene because of the DJs. They were the foundation, the stars back when I started going to jams—before the MCs took center stage. At that point, there were still a lot of hot DJs who didn't even work with rappers.

So Charlie and I made a conscious decision: We'd start using "hip-hop" to describe the whole thing. I began to mention this to people in the scene, like Afrika Bambaataa. When he agreed it was the perfect phrase to represent it all, that was all the confirmation I needed. From that point forward, Charlie and I began pushing "hip-hop" in every conversation about our film.

I also thought back to conversations I'd had as a kid with my godfather, Max Roach, about how he and his peers honestly never cared for the term "jazz." It came out of whorehouses in the Tenderloin District of New Orleans—Storyville—as slang for sex. They felt it demeaned their music and stripped them of control over their music. Max had even planned to call his autobiography *Jazz Is a Four-Letter Word*, because no jazz musician ever got a say in what their art was called. Thinking about that made me realize how important it was that the name for the culture I was championing should come from inside that culture—not from the outside looking in.

And I liked the poetry of it. "Hip-hop" had a ring to it—just like "bebop," the form of jazz Max had helped pioneer. The "op" was the ring that made 'em both swing!

The first time the term "hip-hop" appeared in print as a label for this new, growing culture was in the January 1982 issue of the *East Village Eye*—a landmark edition devoted entirely to rap, graffiti, and breakdancing. It was the first time any publication had done anything like it. The honor of putting "hip-hop" into print went to none other than my old Canal Zone friend, Michael Holman, who used it in an interview with Bambaataa.

Not long before that issue dropped, I'd been talking with Michael, telling him that *Wild Style* was getting close to completion and that Charlie and I had decided to use "hip-hop" as the umbrella term in promoting the film. Michael immediately got it. He was becoming a key player—an articulate spokesperson, a documentarian, and the manager of the New York City Breakers crew. In 1984, he would go on to launch *Graffiti Rock*, a pioneering syndicated hip-hop TV show whose title was inspired by our event at the Kitchen. It only lasted one episode. Maybe Michael wasn't the ideal host, but mainly the show was ahead of the curve—too far ahead, especially for the cornball suits he had to deal with, who were generally clueless.

To me, that issue of the *East Village Eye* is the "birth certificate" of hip-hop—and the first published glimpse at what hip-hop journalism might look like. It included a write-up on *Wild Style*, an interview with me, a photo spread by Futura, a fashion piece, and a Lisa Kahane photo portfolio of the Rock Steady Crew and Dynamic Rockers at Lincoln Center. Lee's artwork was splashed across the front cover. The whole thing felt *major*.

As quickly as we could, Charlie and I moved to reshoot the amphitheater show and the performances at the Dixie. But the Furious Five couldn't make it this time around—they were blowing up, moving beyond the street scene we were capturing in *Wild Style*. They were about to go on tour opening for Rick James, hitting big venues across the country. It hurt to know we'd filmed Grandmaster Flash and the Furious Five in their full glory... and had to scrap it. Cold Crush had scheduling issues, too, though thankfully we still had them in other scenes.

But the second amphitheater jam—the one that ultimately made it into the movie—was maybe even wilder than the first. Among the cavalcade of DJs, MCs, and dancers, my outlandish protégé Rammellzee delivered an apex performance, a full-blown crescendo for the film. He rapped in an improvised style he called "gangster duck," waving a toy shotgun while Grand Mixer D.ST was furiously cutting and scratching and the Rock Steady Crew were throwing down their fiercest, most mind-boggling moves. I was zipping around backstage during his performance, but seeing the footage later was incredible. (And this time, the sound was *perfecto*!) Al Diaz, Jean's old SAMO partner, once compared Ramm to Sun Ra—a true visionary, carving his own path in both art and music. Years later, Cypress Hill would take their name from a phrase Ramm used during his *Wild Style* performance, shouting out a tough housing project in East New York.

Grandmaster Caz said that *Wild Style* was the validation he and other Bronx rap artists had been waiting for. They'd gotten used to people saying that rap wasn't going to amount to anything—and suddenly here came folks from the outside saying, "Hell, yeah! This is cool enough to freeze hot water!" As for the graffiti side of it, *Wild Style* deepened my connection with so many artists I knew were ready to move into other rooms, other spaces—with the potential of becoming something bigger. A *movement*. And that was the thing for me: I always wanted to have, and be part of, a movement. *Wild Style* was the engine for that.

Above all, Charlie and I were proud that we'd celebrated a group of young, diverse, creative people whose world was usually portrayed like something out of *Fort Apache, The Bronx*: all melodrama and mean streets, basically ghetto porn, thugs and delinquents running wild like heartless savages. *Hell no!* We were showing how *regular* these young people were, how they dealt with insecurities and problems, and how ecstatic they were to have a creative outlet—whether their medium was beats, breaking, or aerosol paint.

We made *Wild Style* for the same kids who loved going to Times Square to check out the kung fu flicks, Blaxploitation films, adventure films, and B movies playing twenty-four seven. They needed action, and they needed laughs. Sure, we were making an underground art film—but we wanted these kids to see themselves onscreen. And we wanted it to have pop appeal.

From the moment we got into editing, we knew we were onto something. Our genius editor, Steve Brown, brought strong ideas to the table and had a killer sense of humor. He rolled with the rough-and-ready nature of our production and had a laser eye for pulling out the funny bits and framing them just right. We were holed up with Steve for weeks—at the Film Center Building on Ninth Avenue near Times Square, and to our surprise, our neighbors across the hall were none other than the Clash. They were cutting footage from their Bonds residency for a documentary to be called *The Clash on Broadway* before heading out on tour again. We were in and out of one another's editing rooms, looking over one another's shoulders.

I got tight with Don Letts, the Clash's videographer and collaborator, an English-Jamaican guy with dreads who had turned the British punks on to reggae and dub. By night, Futura and I (and whoever else from our crew) would hang with Don, bouncing from clubs to gigs downtown, going until the wee hours. The next day, around noon, Don and I would be back at the Film Center, pulling together our films, burning spliffs on the fire escape during work breaks, and finding all kinds of common ground.

One afternoon, Don popped over from across the hall. But instead of offering me a joint, he looked totally out of it. I was like, "Yo, Don, what's up?"

"Man, I don't even know where to start. You're not going to believe this, Freddy, but the Clash just broke up."

"What?!"

"Yeah, man, the Clash is no more."

Some kind of beef had gone down among the band members, and they had decided to call it quits. We didn't know it at the time, but thankfully that would not be the end of the story for the Clash. Still, there was a shake-up coming—Topper Headon, their drummer, would be replaced that spring. It was the beginning of a slow unraveling, right as the band was on the verge of a new commercial peak.

As Charlie and I were putting the finishing touches on *Wild Style* and our time at the Film Center Building was winding down, a brand-new song landed like an alien spacecraft in the middle of the hip-hop conversation: Afrika Bambaataa's "Planet Rock."

Bam had been inspired by spinning for the mixed crowds at the Mudd Club and Club 57—the spiky-haired punks, the Bronx B-boys, the two-tone ska heads, and everyone in between. "Planet Rock" carried themes of futurism, diversity, and unity. It borrowed riffs from Captain Sky's "Super Sporm" and Kraftwerk's "Trans-Europe Express," and it hit like a transmission from another galaxy. To me, it completely revolutionized electronic dance music—an Afrofuturistic, funked-up hip-hop masterpiece riding the Mothership.

"Planet Rock" became one of rap's biggest breakthrough singles. It established electro beat as a genre and pushed hip-hop into a new place in the cultural game. Melle Mel said it "ripped everything into a different dimension." This was a new level of ambition, a new level of artistic expression.

Next came the song I had been waiting years for—a rap single that was explicitly *about* something, that had something real to say about the urban experience: frustration, ambition, trying to hold it all together. It wasn't just another party invitation to wave your hands in the air like you just don't care. This was social commentary, the kind you'd expect from Marvin Gaye, Sly Stone, James Brown, or Gil Scott-Heron. It was Grandmaster Flash and the Furious Five's "The Message."

From the first bars, it hit like a live wire. Duke Bootee's and Melle Mel's verses rolled out in an unstoppable cascade of piercing hooks.

EVERYBODY'S FLY

Melle's flow was downright pyroclastic—on the level of Marvin Gaye's "What's Going On" or Stevie Wonder's "Living for the City." This was pure, undeniable ghetto truth in vivid, cinematic color, with a cast of stickup kids, smugglers, pickpockets, panhandlers, gamblers, and dropouts. And always, it came back around to Duke's unforgettable refrain: *"Don't push me 'cause I'm close to the edge / I'm trying not to lose my head."*

Hearing that single—a gripping rap about nitty-gritty real-deal life in any Black ghetto, which truly *was* like a jungle sometimes—validated my belief that this new art form had the potential to keep growing and growing in explosive ways. I had no doubt that this music—*hip-hop*—was going to speak loudly to a lot of people.

One day early in the year, I ran into a friend on the street who said how excited she was to check out the big rap party I was hosting that week. I was like, *Huh?* She whipped out a flyer—designed by Phase 2—and there was my name, right on it. I was supposed to be "master of ceremonies." It was happening at Negril, a one-flight-down reggae club on Second Avenue between Eleventh and Twelfth in the East Village. News to me.

Michael Holman was involved, along with somebody named Ruza Blue. I hit Michael up, asking what the heck was going on—and who *was* this Ruza Blue person? He apologized for jumping the gun and broke it all down for me: Calls had been made, but apparently my answering machine was full. Soon after, I met up with Michael and Blue.

I dug Blue's energy right away. Her vibe was sweet, cool, and unflappable. She was an English girl who'd heard "Rapture," with Debbie rapping about me and Flash, and wanted to be in the place where all these characters came from. So she rolled into town and started making things happen. She got into the mix from day one, meeting Michael, who brought her into the fold and schooled her on the who's who and what's what.

With Michael in her ear, Blue decided to try her hand at promoting a rap night at Negril. She pleaded with me to join the party—and how could I refuse?

So I did. And it was slamming.

I started doing weekly shows at Negril, with Afrika Bambaataa and DJ Jazzy Jay spinning, the Rock Steady Crew and the Floor Masters throwing down breakdance duels, and me—*Freddy B'Roc'Shockin'U'All*—as your host. Those were some sweaty nights. A ton of fun for five bucks a pop.

One night, I brought Blue up to Disco Fever in the Bronx so she could get a taste of the real deal. Grandmaster Flash was spinning and holding court. She bugged out and tried to convince Flash to come down to Negril to DJ, but he wasn't feeling that scene. In time, though, Blue ended up managing Flash.

Negril became a major hangout—one of those key places where the mix of people was electric—white and Black, downtown and uptown, gay and straight, fashionistas, No Wavers, and B-boys all vibing together. And Blue? She ran the show without a shred of drama. She was the right person at the right time—a dynamo who could make shit happen. And she did. I started calling her Kool Lady Blue, and the name stuck.

She had big plans, and tiny Negril wasn't going to hold them much longer. One afternoon, she brought me across town to the Roxy—the massive roller-disco on West Eighteenth Street off Tenth Avenue that could hold four thousand people. The roller-disco craze had cooled from its late-'70s boom, and the Roxy's attendance was slipping.

Blue wanted my take on the space. She was thinking of moving the Negril rap night over there. It was a big step. The Negril parties packed the house, but the place could barely hold two hundred people. A crowd that size inside the Roxy wouldn't cut it.

But Blue had a vision. She unrolled it right there: She'd drape a giant canvas backdrop floor to ceiling across the space and bring in graff writers to do wild pieces on it. She'd set up a DJ station against the center of the backdrop, and as the crowds got bigger, she'd pull the canvas back and open up more of the room. She had it all mapped out.

Sure enough, Blue turned the Roxy into one of New York's most popular spots—a major staging ground for the expansion of hip-hop culture beyond the Bronx. She wanted it to be what she called "a mash-up club, a cross-cultural experience for all tribes to share," and she kicked things off on a Friday summer night with a "Wheels of Steel" hip-hop party. I hosted, Afrika Bambaataa was on the decks, and we had a lineup of DJs, breakers, and even the NYC champion Double Dutch girls jumping two twirling ropes and hitting acrobatic tricks—a crowd-pleasing New York street tradition that Blue folded into the mix.

A few weeks later, Blue put the Roxy on the map in an explosive way. She was tight with Malcolm McLaren, the former manager of the Sex Pistols, and got her hands on a screening copy of *The Great Rock 'n' Roll Swindle,* the much-written-about, rarely seen documentary that Julien Temple had made about the band. It had never been screened in New York.

Blue put the movie up on a giant screen and followed it with one of the signature Roxy hip-hop dance parties, featuring Grand Mixer D.ST. The joint was *jumping off.* The film was brilliant, and for me it was a chance to finally get a closer look at the Sex Pistols, the band I had been reading about since first flipping through punk zines at that newsstand in Bed-Stuy.

A ton of punk and New Wave types showed up that night—zany,

high-rise hair, wild threads, the whole nine. Up until then, the Roxy crowd had mostly been fly girls and guys from the Chelsea projects, the Lower East Side, Harlem, and the Bronx—a tight Black and Latin mix, the usual hip-hop heads. I'd loved seeing these crowds mix at places like the Mudd Club, but given the size of the Roxy, this felt next level. I was worried some shit might go down.

But after the screening, it turned into a full-on admiration fest. The B-boys and girls were digging the way-out punk gear, and the punks were vibing hard on the uptown urban wear. Everybody got along beautifully. It was the first time I'd seen such a wide-ranging crowd in a big dance club without any drama. Two scenes appreciating each other, having fun—just a year after the Grandmaster Flash fiasco with the Clash at Bonds. That night elevated the Roxy and locked in Blue's legacy.

Month after month, the Roxy's hip-hop nights kept building, pulling in bigger crowds as Blue kept sliding that backdrop farther back. *Life* magazine sent their photographer Wayne Sorce to the Roxy to document the moment. He took a landmark photo: me and Phase 2 on the mic, Rock Steady busting moves on the floor, and Futura spraying a sheet of glass—every element of hip-hop right there in a single frame.

Another night at the Roxy, I lined up two DJs to spin in tandem—Master D and DJ High Priest (Nick Taylor, who played with Jean and Michael in Gray)—and brought along some *Wild Style* slides to project during the show. As I was getting ready to hop on the mic, I noticed Madonna hanging out with some of our crew. She'd recently started showing up on the scene.

I'd met her not long before, at Danceteria. Mark Kamins, a great DJ there who had produced music for David Byrne and others, introduced us. He was like, "Fred, I want you to meet this girl, Madonna. She's new in town, and I'm working on some music for her. Her debut track is about to drop." She was cute, no question. Her look had that cool-girl vibe you were seeing with all the sharp female bands coming out of the UK. The single Mark mentioned was "Everybody," and it would come out later that year on Sire Records.

When he previewed it for me, I thought it sounded like what would soon be called Latin hip-hop. It had echoes of the Phil Spector girl-group sound—streetwise and catchy, like the Ronettes back in the day—but with its own spin. Honestly, the track didn't blow me away, but it was kind of unique. Later, I was walking past a housing project on the Lower East Side one day and heard it pumping from a little boom box. A bunch of cute Puerto Rican girls were outside, dancing and singing along. I was like, *Whoa, that's Madonna's record!* They were totally feeling it.

That night at the Roxy, I was struck by how Madonna's style had evolved. She still had that British girl-group thing, like Bananarama, but now it was layered with Puerto Rican street-girl flair.

"Yo, Madonna!"

"Hi, Freddy!"

"Would you come up with me as a backup dancer?"

Madonna could definitely shake that body; she was also nice with the Webo too—the sexy, dry-humping dance that was big at the time. She was always down to dance and said she'd join me onstage. Maripol was there too—the funky French photographer whose Polaroids had been featured in the New York/New Wave show. She'd also produced Glenn's unreleased film *New York Beat* (later *Downtown 81*), starring Jean.

I asked Maripol if she'd dance too, and she was into it. Madonna was like, "Hey, let's both take our shirts off!" The two of them had incredible attitude and style, and no surprise, they were wearing super-cool bras. They both had that wild downtown confidence. The two of them wound up dancing behind me in their bras while I laid down my raps and Charlie Ahearn projected *Wild Style* slides on a screen behind us.

That was the night Madonna first met Maripol—the woman who'd go on to style her early look when she blew up as a full-on pop star—that sexy street-urchin look, with those rubber bracelets and crucifixes, the ones Maripol designed and first popularized downtown.

Having connected with *Actuel* when I was in Paris in 1980, I now found myself the focus of their editorial attention. Jean-François Bizot sent over ten reporters for a whirlwind thirty-six-hour mission to cover the New York scene. One of them got assigned to me. She called herself Élizabeth D. I showed Élizabeth around the East Village and brought her to the Fun Gallery, walking her through how we graffiti people were starting to show our work in actual art spaces. One night, I took her to a party at Keith and Kenny's pad. In the stairwell, we ran into this big, arty-looking white guy who appeared to be covered in fake blood. *Crazy NYC performance art!* But no—it turned out the dude was tripping on acid and had actually been stabbed, once in the kidney, once in the stomach. Before we knew what was up, fifteen cops came bursting in.

That gave Élizabeth something to write about. Welcome to New York!

I showed her around Bed-Stuy and up to the Bronx for a hip-hop party at the T-Connection, where Bambaataa was spinning and Busy Bee rocked the mic, along with others. The piece Élizabeth ended up writing for *Actuel* was a big one; it officially marked the beginning of the hip-hop French Connection.

I became friendly with the magazine's New York rep, Bernard Zekri. He had a giant apartment on Second Avenue that was a hub

EVERYBODY'S FLY

for people visiting from France, including *Actuel* editors, photographers, and writers—whoever was rolling through. Futura and I were there all the time. Out of those hangouts came a plan: a full-on *Actuel* spotlight on New York hip-hop, a multipage spread set for the fall issue, with another piece by Élizabeth. Since there would be built-in exposure from the magazine story, Bernard, who'd been hanging out at the Roxy and knew *Life* magazine was sniffing around, also came up with the idea that I should cut a rap single for the French market—*in French*.

He was insistent about it: *"Fred, let's make zis record!"*

The idea was that I would rap as a French version of Philip Marlowe—the hardboiled *détective privé* from Raymond Chandler's noir novels, the kind Humphrey Bogart played in the black-and-white flicks I loved watching on *Million Dollar Movie*. At first, I wasn't super into it. But eventually I thought, *Well, what the heck—nobody over here is going to hear this anyway*. Plus, the prospect of getting a few grand in my pocket didn't hurt either. I needed rent money. And really, how hard could this shit be? Bernard convinced this character named Jean Karakos—who owned a small French label called Celluloid Records—to finance the record and put it out.

We mapped out a song: "Change the Beat." Bernard's girlfriend, Ann Boyle, acted as my French tutor, helping me learn the lyrics phonetically. Once I got Bernard's words down, I'd practice rapping them with proper rhythm and energy. Then Ann would mimic my delivery, I'd record *her*, and I'd use the tape to fine-tune my pronunciation.

Ann had a great voice and I loved the sound of her French rapping. We headed out to Brooklyn to record the track at Martin Bisi's studio—with Bill Laswell from Material on eight-string bass, basically running the session, the rhythm inspired by a break beat I'd recorded from the Supreme Team radio show. I had an idea. "Yo," I said, "let's get Ann to rap the lyrics on the B-side!" At that point, rap B-sides were usually instrumental or remixed versions of the A-side. But Bill was into it. We laid Ann's vocals down and she sounded great, as I knew she would. She was psyched too, and said, "Well, now I need a cool rap name!" We tossed some names around, and I said, "How about *Beside*, since you're on the B-side?" She loved it, and so "Change the Beat" became a double-sided twelve-inch single: Fab Five Freddy/Beside. After laying down my French rap, we realized it only took up roughly three minutes. We needed a little more, so I dropped some of the rhymes in my repertoire, including my "man from Mars" rap. Ann—now Beside—rapped my lyrics in French on the flip.

A day or so later, when I heard the rough mix of the B-side version, Bill had added a strange robotic sound that had been run through a vocoder at the end of the song. I initially thought it was me, but I later learned it was the voice of Roger Trilling, Bill's manager, who was goofing around, saying, *"Ahhh, this stuff is really fresh!"* Liking what I heard, I said, "Why not, let's keep it," so we did. It's turned out to be one of the most sampled and scratched sounds in all of hip-hop!

The record dropped in France later that year. As the first French rap single, it helped to create a hip-hop audience in France, which today has the second-biggest hip-hop scene in the world after the United States.

But then something funny happened: The record boomeranged back to New York. Copies started popping up all over the city. I was *mortified* when "Change the Beat" started circulating as an import. But to my surprise, the hip-hop community was feeling it. Club DJs, like Grand Mixer D.ST, started spinning it, and WBLS even gave it some airplay.

Before I knew it, I was getting pulled up to perform "Change the Beat" at the Roxy and other joints around town.

EVERYBODY'S FLY

Not long after "Change the Beat" came out, Bill ended up producing an album for the jazz keyboardist Herbie Hancock. He tried steering Herbie toward hip-hop and even brought him down to the Roxy one night to soak up the scene. Bill and his crew worked up an instrumental track for Herbie to riff over, and they asked my man D.ST to add some scratching. D.ST brought his copy of the "Change the Beat" twelve-inch to the session.

The scratching you hear on Herbie Hancock's mega-hit "Rockit" is Grand Mixer D.ST cutting up the *"fresh"* bit from "Change the Beat."

"Rockit" became the first Grammy-winning track to feature scratching—and its massive success helped push "Change the Beat" into the history books. Last I checked, it's the third-most sampled song in the history of recorded music. It's been used in close to three thousand songs so far.

Bernard remembers that "Change the Beat" got off to a bit of a rocky start in France. After being declared "Single of the Week" and getting airplay, radio stations were flooded with angry phone calls. Apparently, a bunch of French listeners thought that when Ann and I were saying "change the beat," we were actually saying *"change de bite"*—French for "change the dick." It probably didn't help that the song's subtitle was "Une Sale Histoire"—a dirty story.

It was the season of performance.

That summer, as the Roxy was heating up, I stepped aboard the Staten Island Ferry to kick off the first performance of The Kitchen U.S.A. Touring—a traveling road show meant to carry the wild spirit of that SoHo art space to the country at large. Nearly a month of being on the road with an eclectic crew: avant-garde musicians Glenn Branca and David van Tieghem, actor and monologist Eric Bogosian, dancer Lisa Fox, and jazz-funk saxophonist Oliver Lake with his band, Jump Up. My segment was billed as "Fab Five Freddy and Friends," which meant I brought along DJ Spy on the turntables and Crazy Legs and Frosty Freeze from Rock Steady to dance.

We hit Baltimore, Washington, Pittsburgh, Madison, Minneapolis, Iowa City, Chicago, Detroit/Ann Arbor, Buffalo, and Toronto, crammed into a tour bus that had been previously used by Motörhead. In D.C., we performed at the legendary 9:30 Club; in Minneapolis, at both the Walker Art Center and at First Avenue, the club owned by Prince, who actually showed up for our show. We didn't get to hang with him, but there he was, up in the balcony, taking it all in.

After our show in Chicago, we went out to a club called the Warehouse and danced to a sound none of us had ever heard before—hypnotic, futuristic, heavy on the drum machine. It wasn't until later that I realized we had experienced house music in its infancy. The DJ was likely the house pioneer Frankie Knuckles—who, as it turns out, was from Brooklyn and had been tight with Larry Levan.

The Kitchen tour was my first real trip through the vast middle of America. From the bus windows, along those endless interstates, everything just looked... flat. Especially Iowa, with miles and miles of cornfields stretching out in every direction. It felt like we were in a ship crossing an ocean. Anytime we pulled over—whether for snacks, gas, or bathroom breaks—we got the heaviest double takes from the locals. Like, *Who the fuck are these people?* To them, we must have looked like space aliens.

At the shows, I'd get up and rock the mic, then bring out the dancers, who would tear it up, flying across the stage. DJ Spy would mix, cut, and scratch—basically giving a masterclass in turntablism. It was just as thrilling for me as it was for the audience.

I had already brought this culture downtown, to the art world, to the clubs, but it was clear it hadn't yet traveled far outside of New

York. Sure, a few rap singles—"Rapper's Delight," "Rapture," "The Message"—had made noise, but hearing something on the radio and *seeing* it come alive in front of you are two very different things. Most folks in the heartland had no idea that there was a whole cultural movement behind this rap thing. I knew they'd be blown away—and they were.

Set amid the minimalist, conceptual, No Wave context of the Kitchen tour, the appeal of our hip-hop segment was raw and direct, and totally electric. A critic from the Toronto *Globe and Mail* nailed it: "While all of these performances are undoubtedly 'interesting,' rapper Fab Five Freddy and his breakers proved that there's nothing like a beat to get a crowd going. That's the thing, finally. Found art makes it. Fab Five Freddy and his deejay have got the kind of street energy which is raw, which doesn't require any kind of mental fiddling." (The Toronto alt-weekly, *Now*, surprisingly had my face on the cover when we rolled into town.)

Back in New York, Chris and Debbie invited me to join them onstage at the Brendan Byrne Arena in the Meadowlands to guest on "Rapture," along with Nile Rodgers. Suddenly, I was rapping in front of twenty thousand Blondie fans, with Duran Duran opening the show. Robert Palmer wrote up the concert in *The New York Times* and called out my performance as a moment of "joyous un-self-conscious fun."

My father, who rarely missed an edition of the newspaper, saw the review and was impressed. And, I think, proud. He wasn't as outwardly expressive as my mom when it came to supporting my exploits, but seeing my name in the paper of record definitely brightened his day.

At times, his days needed brightening. Over the years, my father went through ups and downs—stretches where he'd slip into a dark place. Maybe it wasn't so surprising, given how deeply attuned he was to the ongoing struggle of Black people in this country. The fight for equality never seemed to end, especially during the Reaganite 1980s, with all that racist rhetoric about "welfare queens," when it felt like the dreams of Martin Luther King and Malcolm X were fading away.

As the summer heat rolled in, my father could become erratic, agitated, and angry, often up for days with little sleep. My mother would call me to let me know he was going through one of his bouts, and we'd give him wide berth during those phases when it seemed like he was close to the edge. Anything we could do to keep him from going under.

13

Who the hell is on this plane?

Jean was moving into a new studio on Crosby Street after a stint working in the basement beneath Annina Nosei's gallery on Prince Street. Annina had taken Jean under her wing, put him in a couple of shows, and set him up with a place to paint—a setup that quickly became notorious. The optics weren't great: a young Black artist tucked away in a white gallerist's cellar. Rumors ricocheted around about this wild painter shut up in a basement, creating in a frenzy. The noble savage mythology was sprouting up around Jean, and I told him, "You have to get out of there, man. This doesn't look right."

He agreed. It wasn't that Annina's basement was a hellhole, the way everybody imagined it—Jean going crazy down there, destroying canvases in fits of creative frustration. As I remember it, the place actually had a big skylight. It wasn't the subterranean dungeon that biographers and journalists later made it out to be. Annina had good intentions, but the narrative was problematic, to say the least.

Jean, like me, was always focused on the narrative. He wanted to control his story the way I wanted to control mine. He had a sense of history and understood that certain gestures would be remembered. That was part of his motivation for slashing his paintings at Annina's. But another part—one that people downplay—was simpler: He just wasn't happy with some of the work he was producing there.

The night it happened, when he famously destroyed a batch of paintings in Annina's basement, I met up with Jean and his then-assistant, Steve Torton, at one of our East Village hangs, Red Bar on First Avenue. We ordered cognacs.

"I went and slashed all those paintings," Jean said. "I'm out of there, man."

He never wanted to be trapped, and he knew how to use whatever power he had. He understood the value of his work, the commodification of it, and the racial dynamics that were always in play—and always in our faces. I remember Jean and me standing outside the Marlborough Gallery on Fifty-Seventh Street after the opening of a great group show that Diego Cortez had curated. Pat Griffin, a razor-sharp, attractive, dreadlocked Black architect and Harvard grad, was with us, and cab after cab sailed by, refusing to pick the three of us up. An empty limo with a Black driver spotted us and saw what was going on. He pulled over and Jean handed the brother a crisp fifty to drive us downtown like we were in our own private OJ.

The white folks downtown were always cool with me and Jean. They could be clueless or insensitive at times, but you didn't encounter overt racism. It was a creative scene, with a rebellious, bohemian attitude—like, *Hey, we're* all *outcasts down here.* We were living in a nice little bubble where skin color didn't mean a lot, even though the scene was primarily white. Sometimes, though, Jean and I talked about how we wished there were more cute Black girls on the scene.

Most of the time, we ended up going out with white girls, because those were the ones who were around.

Another thing Jean and I talked about, as we were getting exposed to more dealers and buyers and the spotlight was getting brighter, was how few Black collectors were dialed into what we were doing. One day, we sat down and made a list of possible Black collectors to cultivate—brainstorming top athletes and entertainers, like Reggie Jackson and Bill Cosby. We were convinced it would happen organically as the scene grew and developed, but we wanted to hurry it up. (It did eventually happen.)

Occasionally, Jean and I would talk about how everything could just go *poof* in an instant. He was doing well, I was doing well—but it was precarious, which was par for the course for most of us. That's just how it was. Patti Astor lived across the street from a big men's shelter in the East Village, and whenever I visited, I'd see all these indigent guys coming and going, hanging out on the street. A lot of them were Black. My age. Probably from the hood. Filthy, ragged, totally down and out. I'd wonder how it had happened to them—and if it could, sooner or later, happen to me.

One day on the subway, I recognized a guy I'd grown up with in Bed-Stuy. He was clearly living on the street—spaced out, unwashed, not all there. He noticed me looking over, so I walked down the car to say hello. I think he was shocked I wasn't moving away from him like everybody else. I was like, "What's up, man?" And his vibe was basically, *Well, I'm out here. You know.* When the train pulled into my stop, I reached into my pocket and handed him whatever I had—maybe thirty-four bucks.

Later, I told Jean about it. I said, "Yo man, you ever look at guys like that and wonder what happened?" He just stared back at me for what felt like a full minute without saying a word. I knew it was because he was haunted by those thoughts too. What if the bottom fell out? There was no safety net for guys like us. We were driven, focused, determined to make it—but it was such an untraveled road, with us being two young Black guys trying to stay in the mix.

Jean and I were always talking about pushing forward—strategizing, plotting our next moves on the cultural chessboard, getting our messages across... *by any means necessary*. By cutting up his paintings, Jean was severing ties with Annina, speeding along to whatever came next. That night at Red Bar, we toasted the whole shit and drank up. Then we puffed a fat spliff of sticky green.

Jean's next move was meeting Andy Warhol for real. There'd been a night at Club 57 with me, Jean, John Sex, and a few others joking around about staging a performance based on the Factory scene. "Who's gonna play Andy?" somebody called out. "I will," Jean said. Now Bruno Bischofberger arranged an actual hang between Andy and Jean. After the meeting, Jean went straight back to his studio and dashed off a piece called *Dos Cabezas*—a double portrait of him and Andy. Maybe two hours later, he was back at the Factory, handing it to Andy in person. That gesture is what sparked their friendship and kicked off the collaborations between them that followed.

That November, Jean showed new work at the Fun Gallery, which had moved into a roomier space at 254 East Tenth Street. He jammed the joint to the ceiling with paintings—some of his best work yet. At the opening, Jean brought a date for the occasion: Madonna, who had been with Futura for a hot minute.

A week later, I was meeting with Patti at the Fun Gallery when Jean jumped out of a cab with Diego Cortez. He excitedly showed me a stack of black-and-white Polaroids of himself wearing a suit, barefoot, with a Siamese cat on his lap.

"Yo, James Van Der Zee just took my portrait! These are the test shots!"

"Wow, Jean, these are incredible!"

Diego had recently met Van Der Zee and his wife, and he told us the legendary Harlem Renaissance photographer—who had once shot my grandfather—was still working, still using his classic, old-school camera. I couldn't believe it. In the actual portraits, Van Der Zee—ninety-six years old, with only about six months left to live—gave Jean a stunning, vintage look, like something pulled out of another era.

"Brilliant move," I told Jean. "I guess now I'll have to get Gordon Parks to shoot me!"

Blondie announced their breakup the same week as Jean's show. They had been hobbling along for a while, momentum broken by all kinds of issues—mostly Chris's health. He looked out of it, just completely wiped. There was real fear among our circle that he had AIDS, the name newly given to what people had been calling "gay cancer." It was terrifying. Chris ended up at Lenox Hill Hospital, where doctors eventually diagnosed him with an autoimmune disease called pemphigus. He was able to manage it with medication, but the recovery was long and complicated. As the 1980s kicked into high gear, Blondie faded into the background. To me, they left a huge void.

I didn't have time to sit with it. Almost immediately, I was flying back to Europe, this time with the New York City Rap Tour, the first international hip-hop road show. It had been put together by Bernard Zekri, who convinced Jean Karakos to rush out four more rap singles on his Celluloid label to accompany "Change the Beat" and capitalize on the moment. There was a version of Futura's "The Escapades of Futura 2000" (with music by the Clash), Phase 2's "The

Roxy," a track by Grand Mixer D.ST and the Infinity Rappers called "The Grand Mixer Cuts It Up," and the Smurfs' dance number, "Smurf for What It's Worth," featuring Bernard Fowler. It was a five-record set with back-cover art by Futura. Put the singles together and they made a complete art piece.

We called it the Roxy Tour, since the idea was to take the electric energy of Kool Lady Blue's nights at the Roxy and bring it to venues all over France, plus a couple of stops in London. The lineup was deep: me, Afrika Bambaataa, Grand Mixer D.ST with his Infinity Rappers, the Rock Steady Crew, Futura, Phase 2, Dondi, the Double Dutch jump-rope champs, Rammellzee... a full-on hip-hop variety show, with a cast and crew almost thirty people strong. We traveled like rock stars on a tour bus, just like we did on the Kitchen tour. But this time, it was straight-up wall-to-wall hip-hop culture—every piece of it.

We were in a bit of a quandary when it came to stagecraft. The question I was asking was: "How do we present this new thing?" We weren't a jazz ensemble with a horn player blowing at center stage, or a rock band with a guy taking a guitar solo. Audiences knew what to expect when it came to live music, no matter the genre. But this wasn't that.

And these venues weren't the Police Athletic League or the Roxy—places where the vibe was already built in and the heads knew what was up. In the early days of hip-hop, there was no blueprint for how to present it to a concert audience. So we had to make the shit up as we went.

We all gathered at the Roxy before heading to the airport for the tour. I pulled the crew together and said, "Let's just be our natural, cool selves onstage and rock the house the way we do at the Roxy. Let's just be who we are—*fly*. Rapping, breakdancing, the DJs cutting and mixing, we'll tag up the backdrop, just be cool as can be. It'll look like theater to the audience. We own this—so go and do your thing!"

We figured giving the crowd a kind of three-ring circus—a DJ here, an MC over there, Futura, Dondi, and Phase 2 painting in the back—might just do the trick.

When we got over to France, though, the audiences didn't know what the hell to make of us at first. But once we started rolling, they got into it. The French were already hip to jazz, soul, reggae, funk—Black music and style had always been on the radar over there. And so, in November 1982, with the New York City Rap Tour, the seeds of live hip-hop were officially planted in Europe.

It was basically Hip-Hop Awareness Month in France. The new spread had just dropped in *Actuel*—full-page shots of us and a big write-up. I was cast as the mouthpiece of the hip-hop movement, a role I was happy enough to play.

David Hershkovits, a writer and editor who would later cofound *Paper* magazine, came along for the ride to cover the tour for the *New York Daily News*. He interviewed me on the tour bus, and I laid out how I saw rap as connected to the Beats—Kerouac, Ginsberg, Burroughs. The way they used language was sparked by the rhythms of Charlie Parker and Dizzy Gillespie—the bebop giants whose music was always playing in my house when I was growing up.

When jazz turned into bebop, it broke free of the big-band orchestras and their formal arrangements. It was radical, improvisational, free-form. At the same time, New York painting leaped into Abstract Expressionism, pushing past representational imagery into something more raw, more immediate. The Beats came out of all that—they were the poetic offspring of the bebop revolution.

I traced that thread forward: from the Beats, to Bob Dylan and Lou Reed in the '60s, and on to the rap MCs of the '70s and '80s. It was all about rhythm, all about the beat. "It is the beat," I told David. "Rap is on the beat: *To the beat, y'all!* That's a weird thing, because I'm saying 'the beat,' and it's on the beat, and I *am* the beat. Those cats"—the Beats—"could have just said, *'The beat, y'all!'* That's the premise."

With hip-hop, the beat had become the message. It wasn't just the rhythm—it was the meaning.

I remember hitting all these small French towns—places like Belfort—and seeing that whoever was promoting the AC/DC tour kept plastering over our posters with their own. David started tearing their posters down. There were two, sometimes three AC/DC posters slapped on top of every one of ours.

I started thinking: *Who the hell are those guys, anyway?* They're not down with the culture. They're disconnected from the street, disconnected from anything real. Maybe once upon a time they were plugged into something raw—but how long ago was that? Now they were corporate rock. Muzak rock. The opposite of everything we stood for.

Maybe I could feel the revolution coming. I remember telling David about the time the Clash invited me to see them at Shea Stadium, opening for the Who. The Clash's energy blew me away. It was wild to witness that kind of stadium-concert madness up close. I'll never forget the roar when the Who's Roger Daltrey walked out onstage—pure godlike rock-star shit. My jaw dropped. I was standing in the wings, feeling the stadium erupt. The whole place was shaking.

But as I looked out at this aging, suburban white crowd, I was also thinking, *This is over.* A sea of people wishing it could be Woodstock all over again—and that just wasn't going to happen. No offense, but it was time for something new.

And I thought: *Maybe one day, hip-hop will generate that same kind of electricity.*

When the tour wrapped, Dondi and I decided to kick it in Paris for a few days before heading back to New York. We were rock stars in our own minds—just hanging out, soaking it in, having big fun.

I ran into a girl I knew from downtown, a model who'd gone out with Jean for five seconds. Normally, I wouldn't go near someone a buddy of mine had been with. But Betty Carson and I naturally gravitated toward each other. Or at least, she gravitated toward me.

She invited me to tag along on a shoot she was doing for Italian *Vogue* with a big-name fashion photographer. I was hyped to check out a high-end set. And Betty was a vision: cool, sophisticated, and drop-dead gorgeous. She was also obviously high as hell on something—maybe dope, maybe quaaludes. I remember thinking, *These people know she's high, right?* But I guess that was the look they were going for.

I could never get on the dope train. My father and his jazz crew had drilled that into me from early on—all the brilliant talent that went down the drain because of heroin. Charlie Parker, for one.

Back in Bed-Stuy, I'd grown up seeing guys nodding off on street corners. I remember one junkie, a little older than me, saying, "Man, when I get paid, I'm-a be so high, I'm-a be sucking my own dick." That was a common dope-fiend expression—meant to describe how high they wanted to be.

By the time I got to the East Village, dope was everywhere. There was a big-time romance around it downtown. A lot of folks dabbled—including Jean, from time to time. I knew I had to be careful.

A day or two after the shoot, I was settling into my seat for the flight to JFK. I looked up—and who did I see? Betty, slipping on board just before they closed the door. She knew I was flying home and, lo and behold, had bought herself a ticket.

I was like, "Oh, hey... what are you doing on this plane?"

She said, "I just wanted to be with you. I'm going back to New York too!"

It was a little weird, but also kind of sweet.

After we landed at JFK, we headed to my place on Clinton Street. When we walked in, it looked like the place had been ransacked. I thought I'd been robbed. *Life on the Lower East Side!* It took me a minute to realize what had happened: I'd left a window cracked for ventilation while I was gone, and during some kind of construction in the airshaft, a shit-ton of dust had blown in and coated everything in the apartment. There was no way we were sleeping in there.

Betty was like, "Let's go to the Chelsea."

So we went up to Twenty-Third Street and checked into the Chelsea Hotel. The lobby was incredible—lined with artwork, including one of Larry Rivers's *Dutch Masters* pieces—but the room was no better than what we were used to downtown. Grungy as hell. I looked around and thought, *This is the famous Chelsea Hotel? The place where Warhol shot* Chelsea Girls? *The supposed home of legendary artists, writers, musicians*? At least we had a bed.

I was ready to crash, but Betty was clearly not okay. She was curled up in a ball on the bed, moaning. I asked if it was something she ate on the flight. All she could say was, *"Ugggghhhh."*

Eventually, she told me what was really going on. She was dope sick—heroin withdrawal. Agonizing cramps, full-body pain. She was completely debilitated.

What a nightmare.

I knew what she needed. and I ended up schlepping over to the far East Village to get her a couple of bags. There was no other option—she needed help. But man, I felt like a piece of dirt having to score for her, knowing everything I did about dope.

That was the end of our brief romance.

Clinton Street was done too—completely uninhabitable. I left behind a bunch of shit, including some paintings, at least a couple of which ended up with Martin Wong, the artist who would go on to build a remarkable collection of graffiti-inspired art.

I had no clue where I was going to live next. Maybe back to Hancock Street. But all that could wait.

I was already on my way back to JFK.

Around New Year's, Charlie asked if I could go to Spain to represent *Wild Style* at the third annual Festival Internacional de Cine de Sevilla. He'd already screened a cut in Montreal and had been lining up more of these events to build buzz. It felt like we'd been waiting forever for *Wild Style* to get out in the world. These screenings and festivals were our best shot at finding a distributor.

I hopped on the old Train to the Plane—the one that ran on the A line, the cheap way to get to the airport. It was a long-ass ride, all the way through Brooklyn and into Queens. The car I was in was empty except for one guy way down at the other end. We kept glancing at each other. I felt like I knew him but couldn't quite place the face.

As the train pulled into the Howard Beach–JFK stop, he walked over to me and said: "Hey, are you Freddy? I'm Jim Jarmusch."

He was on his way to Seville too, bringing an early version of what would become his classic *Stranger Than Paradise*. We chatted on the flight, and when we landed in Seville, both of us were stunned to see a full-on media corps waiting on the tarmac—cameras, microphones, the works. We were like, *Who the heck is on this plane—Burt Reynolds?*

But when we stepped off the stairs, the press rushed in our direction. It was *us* they were there for. We were like, *Yo!* Clearly the festival had its media game together. Our minds were blown. And that was the kickoff to a wild week in Spain. The dictator Francisco Franco had recently died, and the Spanish were eager to dive back into culture, which had been stifled under his rule.

The 1983 Seville festival showcased a selection of New York underground films, so Amos Poe, who had been screening his work in Berlin, flew in too. The three of us had magical, ultra-fun days in that beautiful place... and some very late nights.

Someone wrote an article marveling at how these crazy downtown New Yorkers could be out until all hours and still show up bright and early, ready for panels, screenings, and meet-and-greets. We were living it up and holding it down.

At one of the events, a young Spanish guy came over, clearly eager to meet Amos—definitely a fan. He turned out to be Pedro Almodóvar.

One night, we were partying in some local hole in the wall when this gorgeous Spanish girl got up and started dancing flamenco around the room, swirling to the driving rhythms of two cats on guitars—very Gypsy Kings style. She made her way over to me and, God knows what got into me, but I got up and started throwing around flamenco moves of my own. The whole place erupted.

After one of our screenings, we met another stunning Spanish girl (were they *all* gorgeous?) who invited us to dinner at her family home. As we sat at the table, we started noticing bullfighting photos, figurines, and paintings of bulls everywhere. She explained that her father owned a renowned bull-breeding farm—he raised champion bulls destined for the ring.

Then there was the group of beautiful Spanish girls who sold us hash. They told us they'd take the ferry to Morocco, buy the shit, stuff it into balloons, swallow the balloons, ferry back, and wait for them to pass. Jim, Amos, and I had a laugh about smoking some "good ass"—and I have to admit, it was very good shit.

And on the complete opposite end of the spectrum, we found ourselves one afternoon in the middle of Seville's annual Three Kings procession—the city's massive celebration marking the end of the Christmas season. Just thousands of people lining the streets, watching a surreal parade of ornate floats as the kings tossed candy into the crowd.

The audience at the *Wild Style* screening was full of nerdy film types, clearly taking notes on this new culture from New York they'd only had the vaguest idea about. It felt like mission accomplished: more hip-hop seeds planted abroad.

Mostly, the festival was a schmooze fest, and I was doing my best to get *Wild Style*—and hip-hop—some real attention. That's how I struck up a conversation with the German filmmakers behind *Decoder*, one of the other films at the festival. A guy named Muscha was the director, and Trini Trimpop was the producer. Both were hip to the punk and New Wave scenes and knew all about Amos's work.

Trini and I hit it off right away. He turned out to be the drummer for Die Toten Hosen ("Dead Pants"), a German punk band that was basically their version of the Sex Pistols. They were on the verge of blowing up and had just signed to EMI Records.

Trini invited me to Düsseldorf to work with the band, and I took him up on it not long after the Spain trip. I crashed at his place and spent nights drinking at a local joint called Checker's, where one evening, to my amazement, Trini introduced me to Ralf Hütter from Kraftwerk. Ralf had no idea who I was, but I did my best to explain the massive influence Kraftwerk—especially "Trans-Europe Express"—had on the New York DJ scene in the late '70s. He was genuinely happy to hear it.

Trini, meanwhile, turned me on to a metal band I instantly fell in love with: Motörhead.

I was in and out of the studio with Die Toten Hosen for a couple of weeks. They'd already recorded a punk version of an old German drinking song called "Eisgekühlter Bommerlunder" (Ice-cold Bommerlunder), which was freaky enough—and even freakier that it actually became a hit.

As part of their new EMI deal, Trini told me, they were being asked to record a fresh version of "Eisgekühlter Bommerlunder." But as true punks, the band didn't want to repeat themselves or do anything close to the original. So Trini pitched them on a wild idea: *What if Freddy produced a funky version and rapped on it?*

We hit the studio and had a blast. I threw down a handful of rhymes: *"You ready? I came across the ocean on the subway line, invited to a wild party by some friends of mine."* The concept was simple: I had come over from New York to teach these German dudes how to rap—but the joke was, they couldn't rap at all. We had a lot of laughs and finished the track. They called it "Hip Hop Bommi Bop," and I was credited as "Freddy Love."

Some weeks later, I was back in New York when Trini got in touch.

"Hallo, Freddy, guess what? We're going to release the record as a single—and we want to bring you back for a promo tour across Germany."

I was like, *Sure, what the hell?* A few more dollars in the pocket.

Next thing I knew, we were performing "Hip Hop Bommi Bop" on the German version of *Top of the Pops*. This song was actually gaining traction. For this TV appearance they shot a totally insane video for the song. Let me give you a few key words: *Jungle. Tribal. Blackface. Cannibals. Cauldron. Me getting boiled in oil.* The intention was not racist per se—it was just meant to be a loud, in-your-face, goofy punk thing. But when people I knew back home started seeing the video online years later, they were like, *Yo.*

And I was like, *Oh shit... I hadn't even thought of it like that.*

No excuses. I mean, I was the guy lecturing Jean about the bad optics of making art in a white woman's basement—and here I was, participating in *this*. Still, the song caught on. People loved it, and more seeds were planted.

One other thing worth noting: "Hip Hop Bommi Bop" came out a few years before Run DMC and Aerosmith's "Walk This Way." So, in a way, it was one of the first real rock/hip-hop collaborations to break through, maybe the first.

At some point during my travels with Die Toten Hosen, something incredible happened at the Köln train station. I was walking through the massive outdoor area when a burst of movement in the distance caught my eye. *Can that be what I think it is?* I walked closer and saw a group of German kids—probably German-Turkish—wearing tracksuits... *breakdancing.*

One of them busted a move that stopped me in my tracks: It was an exact replica of a move that Crazy Legs had done in *Wild Style*—a move I had only ever seen *him* do.

I was like, *Wow, how can this be happening?*

I rushed to a pay phone, pumped in a bunch of coins, and called Charlie.

"You are not going to be believe what I just saw..."

Charlie, thousands of miles away, listened patiently. Then he said, "Fred, that's exciting to hear, but the film aired on German television a couple of months ago! It was on ZDF!"

These German kids had watched *Wild Style* on TV, taped it on their VCRs, and studied the Rock Steady moves until they had them down cold. For me, it was the first vivid indication that the culture we'd captured in *Wild Style* was ready to travel the world.

In September I found still more vindication, this time in London. I did a gig at the Albany Empire with a local popping-and-locking dance crew called Sidewalk, and we screened *Wild Style* at the Institute of Contemporary Arts, right on the Mall, overlooking St. James's Park. You could see Buckingham Palace down the street.

For the screening, we were joined by the phenomenal Black DJs who called themselves Mastermind Roadshow—true pioneers in the rise of hip-hop in Britain. The Mastermind guys, Herbie, Dave, and Max, were ecstatic that we'd brought *Wild Style* to their shores. Even more than that, they were pumped to be performing right on the Mall.

It meant everything to them, descendants of those Caribbean people from former British colonies who immigrated to England from the '40s through the '70s and became known as the Windrush generation. As young people of color in the UK, to showcase their talent in the literal heart of British power was a massive achievement. And it hit me too—the symbolism was unreal. Mastermind rocked the joint so hard, the Queen's windows were probably rattling. *To the beat, y'all!*

After a couple more screenings in New York and LA, the plans were finally laid for *Wild Style*'s official global premiere—not in New York, but in Japan.

We were flying a full-on hip-hop army overseas: me, Busy Bee, Bambaataa, Cold Crush, Double Trouble, the Rock Steady Crew, Grand Mixer D.ST, and Afrika Islam. Also along for the ride: Futura, Dondi, Lady Pink, Patti Astor, and of course, Charlie. And Fran Rubel Kuzui and Kaz Kuzui, the visionary couple, who were key to making it happen.

Add a few roadies and crew, and we were two dozen deep. Most of the crew had barely been out of New York City, let alone across the world. (Lee, unfortunately, couldn't make it.) It was a blitz: two weeks of screenings, performances, events, and television appearances across Tokyo, Osaka, Kyoto, and beyond—all of it organized by Dalai, the big Japanese distributor.

Charlie and I flew over in early October to get the ball rolling. About a week later, we headed out to the Tokyo airport to meet the rest of the crew when they touched down. We got an unholy earful about the fourteen-hour flight.

At JFK, with per diems in hand, a bunch of folks had made a beeline for the duty free, stocking up on Champagne. On the flight, corks were popping, boom boxes blasting, people crowding into the restrooms to use up whatever drugs they had left. Japan had a strict reputation—this was only a few years after Paul McCartney got locked up for bringing pot into the country.

We were staying in top hotels, doing television—Japan's version of *The Tonight Show*—and we premiered *Wild Style* at Shinjuku Toei Hall in Tokyo. That city was wild, like Times Square on steroids. I'd seen *Blade Runner* and loved it; I could totally see that Tokyo was the inspiration.

One afternoon, walking around the Shinjuku district, I came to a huge intersection. Hundreds of people were standing still on the corner, waiting for the signal. It was weird—there were no cars coming. So, like any self-respecting New Yorker, I stepped into the street to cross. Everyone was staring at me, some were even giggling, so I stopped halfway and started walking backward toward the curb. Then the light changed, the crowd began to move, and I had to start walking forward again.

Bang. A major dose of culture shock! I was so rattled I went back to the hotel, closed the shades, and went to bed.

For the live shows, we were booked into massive venues. And just like in France on the New York City Rap Tour, the crowds didn't know what the hell was happening at first, but once we got going, they started digging it. I was the master of ceremonies—hyping the crowd, performing "Change the Beat" and a few other raps, sauntering around the stage in my trench coat, à la Philip Marlowe.

It was surreal to look out and see these Japanese kids getting down—especially since there had been no setup whatsoever, no context. We were just dropped in from the sky. A British newspaper covering the tour put it best: Over the course of two weeks, "Japan, or at least Tokyo, had been transformed into a seeming extension of the South Bronx." Hip-hop had officially arrived in Asia. More seeds planted!

Osaka was a highlight for two reasons. First, when we arrived there, we hit a club and did a little show—the DJs cut and mixed, Rock Steady performed, we dropped a few raps. We went over to Kyoto for a night, and when we returned to Osaka, we headed straight back to that club, since the vibe was so right.

We were just chilling when somebody at our table was like, "Yo, do you hear that? Who's on the turntables?" It sounded dope. We figured one of our guys must have jumped in. We craned our necks, and looked over, only to discover that it was a couple of Japanese guys spinning. *Holy shit!*

It was like that moment in Köln with the German breakdancers. These kids had seen our show only two nights earlier, studied it, and were already throwing down on the wheels of steel—cutting and mixing, all on beat. It was wild.

The second Osaka highlight was a little less inspirational. Kay Gee from Cold Crush and I were hanging out in a hotel room with two Japanese girls making sign language, hoping to get it going. The vibe was chill, and we were just kicking it—when, out of nowhere, somebody started banging on the door. We looked at each other like, *What the hell?* The banging got louder. Someone was yelling in Japanese. Kay Gee was in his boxer shorts, and the whole thing turned awkward fast. The girls looked nervous, and the energy in the room dropped.

We finally opened the door—and standing there were a couple of Yakuza heavies, not looking friendly at all.

They shoved their way in, still shouting, as the girls bolted into the bathroom. Kay Gee and I didn't wait around to find out what was going on. We bolted out of the room and ran furiously down the hallway, Kay Gee barefoot and in his boxers, until one of our guys opened his door and let us dive into his room. We were scared shitless.

Later, we pieced it together: One of the Yakuza dudes had heard that his sister was at the hotel with the *Wild Style* crew. While searching the halls, they heard English and Japanese voices behind our door and figured that was it. Turns out that a couple of the Rock Steady guys had been partying with the sister and her friends—and somehow managed to sneak them out in the middle of all the chaos. That comedic tale became a huge highlight that has echoed until today.

We were taken to Yoyogi Park in Tokyo, where every Sunday a horde of Japanese rockabilly guys and gals dressed up in fifties attire, doing their leather-greaser thing—dancing to Jerry Lee Lewis and Chuck Berry or whatever on their portable tape decks. We rolled up in our hip-hop regalia with our boom boxes and New York swagger for a fun photo op, and Rock Steady tried to get a dance battle going. Except there was no contest.

No doubt, some of those rockabillies ditched their leather jackets soon after and got themselves into tracksuits. Hip-hop had that kind of pull.

14

His wig will glow and then people will know it's a wig

Back in NYC, the talk was all about Michael Stewart. Michael was a peripheral character on the downtown scene, a handsome young Black guy I first met one night at the Roxy, where he was hanging out with Suzanne Mallouk, Jean's ex. In the dark club lighting, I actually thought Michael *was* Jean at first. They had a similar build, similar hair, but Jean had just left for Tokyo—his first trip there—so it couldn't have been him.

I remember Suzanne registering my confusion as I approached, realizing this cat wasn't Jean at all. Maybe I was projecting, but I could swear she had a little smile on her face, like, *See? I got me a replacement.*

One night that fall, close to three in the morning, Michael was waiting for the L train at the First Avenue subway station—heading home to Brooklyn after a night at the Pyramid Club—when he was attacked by NYPD officers.

The cops claimed that Michael had been writing graffiti. As far as I'm concerned, they lied.

Michael was never a graffiti writer. He was a young guy trying to find his way into the scene, still figuring shit out. He probably had no idea how savage some of those cops could be. Maybe he didn't respond the way they expected when they rolled up on him. Maybe he challenged them. Whatever it was, they got hot and bothered and the savagery commenced. Michael probably resisted the uncalled-for aggression, and the whole thing spiraled out of control.

In the press, he became a "graffiti artist"—based solely on the cops' story. Suddenly he was being framed as another subway vandal. But I never saw convincing evidence of him tagging that station, or heard from anyone who actually knew Michael that he was into tagging. Jean, Keith, Futura, and I had been getting regular media for graffiti, so it was easy—and convenient—for the press to slap that label on him. *Look, here's another Black youth caught in the act of vandalizing a subway wall!* Naturally, the media sensationalized the story to the hilt.

Michael never recovered from his injuries. He went into a coma and died a couple of weeks later. He was twenty-five years old, murdered by the police.

Even if he had been tagging, Michael didn't deserve to die at the hands of those animals.

His death shook everybody I knew to the core. I remember Jean and I just looking at each other, shaking our heads. All the markers were there: young, Black, male, subway, Brooklynite, downtown...

"That could have been one of us," I said.

"That could have been one of us," Jean said.

Jean was at Keith's studio in the Cable Building on Broadway when he painted a tribute piece right onto the drywall—one that eventually became known as *Defacement (The Death of Michael Stewart)*. It was raw and haphazard—you could feel the emotion in it—and showed two cops clubbing Michael. When Keith later moved to another Broadway studio, he cut the whole thing out of the wall and took it with him.

Michael's death triggered a wave of anger and activism—the kind that would continue for decades, right through to the Black Lives Matter movement. The downtown press covered it heavily. *One of ours was murdered by the police.* Madonna headlined a benefit for Michael at Danceteria. Black leaders protested in front of the Criminal Court Building. Keith followed Jean's lead and painted another tribute.

Michael's death reverberated throughout the decade. Years later, in 1989, Spike Lee would dedicate *Do the Right Thing* to Michael and his family. Michael lived with his family in Fort Greene, the same Brooklyn neighborhood where Spike also lived. The police chokehold scene in the film was directly inspired by what happened to him. A grand jury—perhaps needless to say—refused to indict a single officer for Michael's murder.

There was a feeling, around the time of the Michael Stewart tragedy, of some corners being turned, pages flipped. Club 57 had closed. The Mudd Club was done. *TV Party* was off the air. Kool Lady Blue's "Wheels of Steel" hip-hop nights at the Roxy were winding down. Another election year was on the horizon.

But for me, the end of 1983 was also a whirlwind of creative expression and opportunity across multiple fronts. *By any means necessary.*

When I got back from Japan, I moved into a new pad on Ludlow Street and immediately started scrambling to get work together for another Fun Gallery show, set to open November 8. I made a series of paintings I called *Still Lifes in Space*—sci-fi-inflected compositions with subjects floating against black backgrounds.

At the show, I could feel the shift right away: The buyers were different now. Art advisers from the corporate world were all over the

Fun Gallery. I ended up selling one piece to the European-American Bank and another to Chase Manhattan.

Keith threw an afterparty for me in a two-story space on Houston Street off Broadway that Andy Warhol either owned or was renting. Keith set up black lights downstairs and turned the entire floor into a Day-Glo party zone. Andy showed up, and I remember thinking: *Holy shit—Andy's here, and it's* my *party.*

Everyone was having a great time, but then Andy disappeared.

I asked Keith, "Yo, what happened to Andy?"

He said, "Andy went upstairs. I think he's nervous about coming back down."

"Why?"

"Because his hair will glow and then people will know it's a wig."

For Andy, the combination of his synthetic white wig and the black lights was apparently a no-go. Maybe he was afraid of being photographed with glowing fake hair.

So I went upstairs, found him, and thanked him for coming to my party.

"Oh my God, Fred," he said. "You're so famous. You're so famous…"

A couple of days later, I rolled up to the Kitchen in SoHo for a two-night performance—a collab between me and my godfather, Max Roach.

A few years earlier, my dad had hipped Max to the fact that I was into the rap thing. I was nervous when I heard that. Max was one of the most important musical—and intellectual—inspirations in my life and a giant in American music. My dad told Max that I had been experimenting in this new genre with DJ Spy, my old friend from across the street. Max said he wanted to come by and check it out.

ANY MEANS NECESSARY

At that point, DJ Spy and I were just messing around. I wasn't sure I even considered rap to be music, strictly speaking. I mean, I certainly didn't see myself or Spy as *musicians*. My boy had a nice equipment setup and the right vinyl. I'd written some rhymes so I could hop on the mic at a park jam or block party, just to rock the house a lil' bit and let the ladies check me out. Nevertheless, we set a day and time for us to give Max a rap demonstration.

It hit me, even back then, that early rap and bebop had something in common: They were both based in improvisation. Spy and I had a rough idea of what would go down when he spun and I rapped, but there was no real structure. That would come later as the form evolved.

So Max came over to Hancock Street and we did our private performance over at Spy's house. Spy was cutting up hot break beats, mixing and scratching, and I laid down a handful of raps.

Afterward, as I was walking Max back to my house, he said, "Man, Freddy, what you and your man were laying down was amazing. I'm seriously talking as revolutionary as anything Dizzy, Bird, and I did back then."

I was like, *Yeah, really, Max?* Okay, my godfather is humoring me.

He must have read my skepticism, because he launched into a little lecture. Western music, he said, had always revolved around three elements: melody, harmony, and rhythm. You could combine them in interesting ways, adding here, subtracting there. But in the history of Black music, he explained, you could trace an increasing emphasis on rhythm.

"And what you and your friends are doing," Max said, "that's *all* rhythm." He saw it as the next step in the continuum of Black musical expression. "It's definitely going to be huge."

Max was clearly fascinated by rap, and he had the kind of mind that could draw a straight line from jazz to hip-hop. Like early jazz back in New Orleans, this new music came from poor Black communities. It shared a philosophy of making something grand and expressive out of very little—a trumpet part, a bass line, some drums, a record on a turntable. You took a simple element and stretched it into something brand new.

Max told me that whenever Charlie Parker heard a major shift in sound—something new hitting the scene that shook up the culture—he had a phrase. Like when the Cuban percussionist Chano Pozo hit the scene in the 1940s, or when the Nigerian drummer Babatunde Olatunji showed up in the late '50s. Bird would say, "There's some new pussy in town, gents—and it's time to check it out!" Now the "new pussy" was hip-hop.

For two packed nights at the Kitchen, DJ Spy and another DJ pal, Nick Taylor (aka DJ High Priest), were joined by Max on drums, along with the New York City Breakers, managed by Michael Holman. It was surreal—an improvisational collision of hip-hop and jazz.

Jon Pareles gave it a great write-up in *The New York Times*, calling it "an evening of pure, kinetic rhythm." Max seemed pleased.

In an interview we did together, he said, "Hip-hop lives in the world of sound—not the world of music—and that's why it's so revolutionary. What we as black people have always done is show that the world of sound is bigger than white people think." So Max was officially down with hip-hop.

But the biggest payoff? My father came to the Kitchen—and he dug it.

"Hey, *Fab 5 Freddy*," he said with a big grin, "that was *amazing*."

Wild Style was set to premiere for real: in Times Square, the perfect place. Charlie and I had first met at the Times Square Show, which got this whole ball rolling. We'd been inspired by the kung fu movies that played there twenty-four seven, and we'd spent endless hours working on the film at Charlie's spot nearby, editing at the Film Center Building. Charlie's wife, Jane Dickson, even painted a portrait of me bathed in the neon glow of a Times Square peep show. That piece is now in the permanent collection of the National Portrait Gallery, in Washington, D.C.

I had once been one of those kids who came to Times Square from all over the city to watch movies and drop change in the arcades. Now, Jean and Keith were the friends I'd come with to watch great films. The theaters on Forty-Second Street between Eighth and Broadway were as grimy and slimy as ever—but they still had the best deals: three films and air-conditioning for three bucks. Back then you were allowed to smoke in the theaters. Plenty of folks lit up cigarettes, but for me and my friends, weed was mandatory. You didn't go to Times Square or any movie house without pooling your money, buying a nickel bag, rolling up in Bambú papers, and putting that smoke in the air. Those light-blue clouds hanging in front of the screen were an essential part of the moviegoing experience for me. Watching the projector beam cut through the haze added to the magic. When they banned smoking in theaters, it felt like they'd banned popcorn.

Times Square was notoriously grungy and would stay that way for another decade or so. You could get your pockets picked in those funky movie houses if you weren't heads-up. A lot of guys hustling in Times Square didn't have rooms to go to, so they'd just crash in the cheap theaters on the Deuce, the nickname for Forty-Second Street. Among them, you had what were known as "creep thieves"—because they would creep up on you. Talk about sordid. Late at night, these guys would watch for someone dozing off during the movie, then sneak up next to them, lightly tapping pockets to feel for that telltale crunch of cash or a wallet. If they hit pay dirt, they'd slice the pocket open with a razor blade and ease the contents out. If the person woke up, it would for sure get ugly.

The floors of those theaters were sticky from soda and piss. That old urine stench could be unreal. But I dug Times Square almost as much as Coney Island: the lights and the excitement, the street people, the edge, the sex, and the danger.

Wild Style opened November 23, 1983, at the Embassy on Broadway, between Forty-Sixth and Forty-Seventh, a grand old movie house from the 1920s. Our distributor, First Run Pictures (where Spike Lee worked after he'd graduated from NYU), came up with the idea of handing out hundreds of flyers in clubs, schools, and theaters around the city—wherever young people were likely to be hanging. We were trying to reach the same kids who came to Times Square for kung fu flicks and action movies, the folks from the hood who were hip to the rap subculture, and the downtown film and art crowd. That was our dream—and we pulled it off.

The premiere was a total jam. From the opening shot of the *Graffiti 1990* mural and Zephyr and Revolt's animated opening credits, the crowd was locked in. You could hear kids shouting from every corner of the theater, "Yo, there's so-and-so!" "There's my man!" "That's that train we painted!" "That's Dondi!" "Check out Busy Bee!" When the Chief Rocker dropped his famous call-and-response—"Somebody say 'Ho!'"—the whole theater screamed back "Ho!" They were losing it. It was like, *Wow, they made a movie, and they actually put the real people on the screen, finally!* It felt huge.

Charlie said it didn't matter what the reviews said. This was the real verdict: *Wild Style* connected, viscerally, with the world it depicted. Grandmaster Flash called it "the most accurate movie about hip-hop culture." The judgment still stands: The film caught the culture at its source and touched a nerve.

We knew we weren't contending for an Oscar with our edgy, low-budget film. But we were amazed when *Wild Style* instantly became the second highest-grossing movie in New York City. (*Terms of Endearment* was number one that week.) As the Embassy run continued, kids from the Bronx and Harlem—and soon, from every corner of the city—kept coming, kept spreading the word. The movie was a reflection of who they were and how they felt. They saw themselves.

Charlie put it best: "They didn't feel like they were being made into some kind of 'other' people." That was everything. Movies had too often portrayed us in negative, stereotypical ways. We showed there was way more going on.

And another thing that felt so right: In 1983, when most people thought of rap, they still thought of "Rapper's Delight." *Wild Style* showed them what this new culture really looked like—and where it actually came from.

After three weeks, *Wild Style* was the highest-grossing release in the Embassy's ten-year run as a modern cinema. Soon we were opening in cities around the country—Boston, Chicago, Los Angeles. The *Times* started writing about me and Charlie, tracing the origins of this new thing called hip-hop. They even ran features about the soundtrack album, which Chris Stein released on his own label, Animal Records, a subsidiary of Chrysalis. Not bad for a little movie that PBS had refused to fund—slamming the door in our faces, incredulous that anyone would ever think of making a movie about such cultural "garbage."

It didn't take long for Hollywood to come sniffing around, thinking they knew better. Suddenly there was a wave of cheap, exploitative knockoffs, including a few from the production company Golan-Globus, known for cranking out schlock: *Rappin'*, *Breakin'*, *Breakin' 2*, and the like. Even Harry Belafonte got involved, producing a more polished *Wild Style* copycat called *Beat Street*. That movie had some cool people involved, and it was much better than the rest of them, but *Wild Style* will always be the first and best hip-hop movie, because it came from within the culture. It wasn't a projection—it was the real thing. It codified the three pillars I had been preaching about for years: rap music, graffiti art, and breakdancing. That was the foundation. We brought hip-hop out of the Bronx, out of New York City, and sent it out into the world with strength, love, honesty, and positivity. That's why *Wild Style* still resonates as a cultural touchstone. The roots were real and ran deep.

Or, as I like to say: *It could never be realer, the way we did it.*

Between *Wild Style* and the rap tours and the art shows, I started getting called "Hip-Hop's Renaissance Man." That meant a ton to me, as I had read—and loved—Giorgio Vasari's *Lives of the Artists*, first published in 1550, an incredible compendium of mini biographies of all the great Italian Renaissance painters and sculptors. Vasari, one of my favorites, like a kindred spirit, was *the* ultimate Renaissance man, one of my all-time heroes: not only a writer and historian but a painter and an architect who helped design the Uffizi in Florence. Vasari was even the guy who put the term "Renaissance" on the map.

I was honored and flattered beyond belief that anyone would refer to me as a modern-day Renaissance man.

Then it was 1984. Joe Strummer—touring with a new version of the Clash, minus Mick Jones—asked me to open for them at the Brixton Academy, in London. I brought along the Mastermind Roadshow DJ crew along to rock with me.

I had another gallery show in Italy. When UPI interviewed me, they asked if I thought moving graffiti into the art world was a form of selling out. I told them, channeling a bit of Phade from *Wild Style*,

"Selling out is my *objective*.... We have been given the opportunity to preserve our work and get paid for it."

Calvin Tomkins, one of my favorite art writers, did a *New Yorker* piece about me and other artists who had come out of the graffiti world—Lee, Jean, Keith, Futura, Zephyr, and Lady Pink. Big-gallery time had arrived. Jean was with Mary Boone, Lee was with Barbara Gladstone, Keith and Futura were with Tony Shafrazi, and I was in talks with Holly Solomon. Everything was leveling up.

Chase Manhattan Bank threw an art gala at their Wall Street headquarters, and I got an invite—along with Jean, Patti, and pretty much everyone else making big moves in the contemporary art world. It was black tie. *Uh oh.* I didn't own a tux, so I hit a thrift shop at Bowery and Houston, dropped twenty bucks, and threw together a look. I topped it off with a blue silk scarf I tied around my neck like a cravat. And I have to say—I was definitely looking good. Take that, Beau Brummell!

At the party, they handed us color-coded badges to indicate our "art person" status—I guess so we wouldn't be mistaken for Chase executives or random rich people. At some point, I was introduced to David Rockefeller, the head of Chase. He said he'd seen the Tomkins piece in *The New Yorker*, and we had a nice little back-and-forth.

In that moment, the crazy beauty of being an artist in New York hit me—the wild mix of people you end up crossing paths with. I was a twentysomething artist living in bohemian squalor on the Lower East Side. *Wild Style* wasn't ever going to make me rich. And yet there I was, talking to David freakin' Rockefeller. In a twenty-dollar tux, a feeling money couldn't buy.

Jean was flourishing in the art world. He was getting paid in full—and, like that line from *The Mack*, his pockets looked like they had the mumps. I remember when he came back from a show at

Bruno Bischofberger's gallery in Zurich. It felt so big-time. He pulled out a one-pound tin of Beluga caviar he'd picked up along the way. I was like, *Yo, what the hell? This is crazy!*

We were at his new studio and apartment, a Great Jones Street carriage house he was renting from Andy Warhol. He insisted we eat the caviar right then and there. He didn't have any crackers, so we spread it on slices of Wonder Bread, like two kids eating PB&Js. It was the next step beyond prosciutto and melon.

Just as I had hipped him to rap, I also turned Jean on to bebop. He'd heard some jazz growing in Brooklyn, though his father, Gerard, mostly favored the classical repertoire. I played him the records I loved, starting with *Jazz at Massey Hall*, and broke it down the same way my dad and his friends—who happened to be at that 1953 gig in Toronto—had broken it down for me: that Charlie Parker and Dizzy Gillespie had been beefing. That Diz was pissed Bird had pawned his sax to cover a heroin debt, then showed up for the gig with a cheap-ass Grafton plastic horn. That they settled it onstage with their instruments.

You can hear it on the classic tune "Salt Peanuts"—Diz and Bird dueling at the speed of light, trying to take each other out. (It's also one of the few times you hear Charlie Parker's voice on record—he introduces the song as "composed by my worthy constituent, Mr. Dizzy Gillespie.") I explained to Jean the concept of "cutting"—how jazz players would go at each other in battle, just like DJs and MCs were doing uptown.

Jean loved that story, loved the idea that hip-hop was part of a long tradition. He went out and bought a stack of jazz albums for the killer stereo he'd bought. After that, Charlie Parker, Dizzy Gillespie, John Coltrane, and Max Roach started to populate his paintings.

We'd often hang out at his place on Great Jones, light up some killer weed, throw on records, and talk about everything—music, art, life. We were also crazy for movies. We'd hit up theaters all the time, not just up in Times Square; two movies we especially loved were *Reds* and *Diva*. In those early days of VHS, Jean had stockpiled a sick collection of tapes. He'd play them on his big-screen television through a VCR setup that felt practically space-age at the time.

He got deep into art-house cinema—French New Wave stuff by Godard, surrealist films by Luis Buñuel, who I think Andy had hipped him to. One day he showed me Buñuel's *Un Chien Andalou*—the film with that infamous scene where a razor blade slices an eyeball, still one of the most indelible moments in the history of movies. We'd binge those VHS tapes all day, totally absorbed. Then Jean would be like, "Fred, come back tomorrow—we gotta watch more movies!"

If Jean ever had one of something, it seemed like he needed five more. That impulse extended to mood-altering substances too. There was no doubt that Jean enjoyed not only good weed but also dope and cocaine. You needed serious cash to keep up with those habits, and Jean, more and more, had it.

Coke was the drug of the era. At first, it felt like a special-occasion thing. Then the rich started burning it in glass pipes, freebasing like Richard Pryor, who famously set himself on fire. Not long after, the so-called "champagne of drugs" got cheaper and flooded the streets. Suddenly, it was crack—basically freebasing for the masses—and it hit like the plague. Crackheads stealing car radios and shit. I'd go back to Brooklyn to visit and be like, "Yo, where did everybody go?" You hardly saw kids outside anymore—no stickball, no Ringolevio. Concerned parents were keeping their kids indoors, afraid of all the crime and gunplay crack brought with it.

Cue the War on Drugs. New York City got hit extra hard. The hype turned political fast, and people started getting locked up left and right. Worse, sentencing was wildly unequal—way more time for tiny amounts of crack than for larger stashes of powdered cocaine. Essentially the same drug, different treatment. I'm talking football numbers.

It's not like I didn't indulge, but the fact that I was still stretching every paycheck that ever came my way thankfully put a hard cap on how much I could get into that life. I didn't have the budget to buy piles of coke for myself and my friends, even if I'd wanted to. What really saved me from sliding down that slippery mid-'80s slope, though, was Kat.

Kat was a gorgeous and smart artist from California, and she had a place way uptown, on 101st Street on the Upper West Side—a neighborhood I had rarely even been to. We hit it off, and before long, I moved in with her. A real girlfriend. I still spent most of my time downtown, and all my people were still there, but now I had somewhere to escape to, a place to sketch and think and make plans. A place where I could catch my breath and enjoy my first grown-up relationship. So long, Casanova days!

That fall, Jean and I had one of our most memorable museum-club outings. With Diego Cortez in tow, we made our way to MoMA to check out the "Primitivism" in 20th Century Art exhibition, which had just opened in September. The show featured works by the likes of Picasso, Gauguin, Modigliani, and Brancusi, along with so-called tribal objects from around the world. The juxtapositions between the pieces made by Indigenous people of color next to those of modern European artists—like the African masks that inspired Picasso's *Les Demoiselles d'Avignon*—was riveting. The three of us were bugging out: This was the "primitive" art that had detonated the Western canon, blowing apart centuries of rigid, representational form and clearing space for an entirely new way of seeing—the birth of modern art. (I also saw clear parallels to the Afro influence on the evolution of popular music.)

The Primitivism show was raked over the coals in *Artforum* for its Eurocentric point of view, and it felt like the entire city was talking about it. But the exhibition forced a deeper reckoning over the way colonial powers had plundered lands—from Polynesia to Africa—to build their museum collections of masks, figurines, and other incredible objects. For me, Jean, and Diego, it reshaped how we thought about our own work too—we were part of a long, complicated lineage.

Soon after, a museum show called The East Village Scene opened in Philly and traveled to Miami, featuring work by me, Jean, Futura, Keith, Kenny, and others—broadcasting our fringy downtown world to new audiences. It was clear that the creative energy of the East Village and Lower East Side was beginning to shape the culture at large.

That neighborhood was so vital to us—a magnet for outsiders drawn by cheap rent, cool bars, hole-in-the-wall galleries, and a constant influx of artists, punks, and other creative types. As I've said, we knew we were living in a kind of bubble. There was a strong us-against-them vibe, a rebellious current that had flowed through the East Village for generations—from the punk era back to the 1960s counterculture—whose ethos was still raging under the uptight surface of the Reagan 1980s.

Being in the East Village then meant you'd still see actual hippies—and even Yippies—roaming the streets. Abbie Hoffman sightings weren't uncommon. Aron Kay, the legendary "pie guy" who would accost bigwigs and throw pies in their faces, was a regular presence. You'd see this hairy, chubby dude with a thick mustache walking around and everybody would be like, "Yo! There goes the pie guy!"

The Yippies still had their headquarters over on Bleecker Street, just off the Bowery.

The neighborhood's radical spirit went all the way back to the turn of the century, when socialism and labor-union movements were synonymous with the area. The tenements photographed by Jacob Riis—those filthy and teeming places—were now our apartments, sometimes without hot water, sometimes with a bathtub doubling as the kitchen sink. Riis's images had helped spark a movement for basic human dignity. The protests that followed the infamous 1911 Triangle Shirtwaist Factory fire happened right in Tompkins Square Park, which for us was just the local hangout on a sunny day, with a joint and a forty of beer. There was so much of this radical history around us. And given my background, I was on that tip and aware from day one.

The vibe was anything goes. Everything revolved around creativity and staying close to the street—even as some of us were getting tapped by blue-chip galleries. I remember Keith and I talking about the need to find a balance: how to move into the art world without losing our downtown roots, without turning into out-of-touch elitists. Keith was serious about making work that connected with regular people and stayed affordable. The idea would lead him to open the Pop Shop on Lafayette Street, inspired by Claes Oldenburg's *The Store*, which had once popped up right here in the East Village.

We were aware that Pop artists and Abstract Expressionists had once walked these same streets. As we made our way to the Fun Gallery or CBGB, the Pyramid or the Red Bar, that history was so palpable. We bonded over the fact that we were living and working right where the action had always been—the newest wave in a tradition that stretched way back.

There was a super-hardcore notion of integrity and authenticity in the air. How far would you go to uphold it? For some, that meant going to wild extremes. We often talked about Lenny Ferraro's old roommate, the artist Henry "Banger" Benvenuti, a *TV Party* audience regular, who walked into the offices of the *SoHo Weekly News* one day and asked to speak with the art editor. When the receptionist told him the editor wasn't available, Banger said he'd like to leave a message. He then pulled a hatchet from his briefcase and chopped off two of his own fingers. "I'm doing this in the name of art," he said.

The East Village art scene was hitting new peaks. Pat Hearn had just opened a new version of her gallery way east, on Ninth between C and D—a new frontier. I remember thinking, *Man, that's edgy!* It was dope-fiend city over there, with syringes and empty dope bags scattered along the sidewalks. But month after month, people trekked those extra blocks for art openings. There was a popular saying at the time: "Avenue A, you're all right; Avenue B, be careful; Avenue C, you're crazy; Avenue D you're DEAD!" That summed it up. But when you started seeing limos parked outside Pat Hearn's shows, the real estate people took notice. It was *game on*.

The Christodora—a tall, funky old apartment building on Avenue B, near the northeast corner of Tompkins Square Park—had been a dilapidated shell for more than a decade. Now it was being transformed into expensive co-ops. It became the most visible symbol of the gentrification that was beginning to rage, gobbling up chunks of the East Village and Lower East Side, places where artists, musicians, and writers—people like us—had been the cutting edge. In fact, Charlie Parker's last home was just a couple of doors down from the Christodora, at 151 Avenue B. Jean and I always acknowledged it when we walked past.

Realizing that the Fun Gallery had been the first East Village gallery, it was like—*Wow, look what we started!* Then, in 1985, the Fun Gallery closed, a victim of its own success. Patti had always been amazing to us artists; she was officially down by law. But she didn't have the drive—or maybe the desire—to take the gallery further and keep it afloat. What Patti really wanted was to be back on the silver screen, ready for her next close-up.

And honestly, no one could compete with the wave of new galleries flooding the neighborhood, backed by owners and investors willing to pump half a million dollars into renovations. As Patti put it, "When the St. Marks Cinema turned into the Gap, I knew it was time to go."

Around the corner from the Christodora, on East Ninth Street, was El Bohio, a former public school that had become a Puerto Rican community center, home to squats and artist studios. I got myself a new studio there, in what used to be a classroom. That's where I hunkered down to work on new pieces for Holly Solomon's gallery, while watching the East Village transform all around me, day by day. I felt like I was in the eye of a storm I never imagined coming.

Around the time the Fun Gallery shut down, Madonna played a sold-out show at Madison Square Garden—capping her *Like a Virgin* tour with an exclamation point. At her invitation, I was there with Keith. What I remember most, aside from Madonna's electric performance, was hanging out backstage with JFK Jr. The other striking thing was the sea of young girls in full Madonna style—the look that Maripol had helped create: skinny black bracelets, lace gloves, and crucifix necklaces.

Madonna, the former Webo girl at the Roxy, was now an international pop icon, a real-deal superstar. It hit me, and probably a lot of our friends, that she had been paying close attention all along, taking notes on everything cool downtown and executing her pop takeover with surgical precision. It was all brilliantly plotted. I felt that Madonna stepped into the void Blondie had left behind. As Debbie had once been, Madonna was now the embodiment of the Marilyn Monroe archetype that American pop culture seemed to crave.

She was all over MTV, the twenty-four-seven music channel—which, by then, rarely played Blondie videos since there weren't any new ones to run. I was tight with Peter Dougherty, a guy who'd been at MTV since the early days, as a producer. He lived on Orchard Street, just below Houston on the Lower East Side. Peter was a cultural sponge. He had a straitlaced vibe on the surface, but underneath he was deep into all the illest, most cutting-edge music, from punk to rap, the same way Glenn O'Brien had always been.

I remember the first time I went over to Peter's place. It was shockingly neat and orderly, especially compared to my usual paint-splattered digs. Lined up on his shelves were rows and rows of clear plastic bins packed with cassette cases, each one perfectly labeled. I was like, "Yo, Peter, what's up with all this?" He told me he went to gigs with a small, high-end recorder and made his own bootlegs. The dude had built a private archive the size of the Library of Congress.

One of my first nights out with Peter, he took me to Madison Square Garden to see Judas Priest. As an MTV producer, he had his pick of the best concerts in town. I had never been to a heavy-metal show before, and I was like, *What the hell is going on here?* It was sold out, and the place was buzzing with this wild, almost scary energy—crazy white dudes from Queens, Brooklyn, and Long Island, all with long frizzy hair or mullets. This wasn't a punk or New Wave crowd. It was something else entirely.

We were one section up, with a perfect view of the stage. Above us, in the nosebleeds, guys were tossing M-80s and cherry bombs like it was a battle royale meets the Fourth of July. These things were exploding in the air all night: *KABOOM!* Total madness.

When the set ended, Peter turned to me and said, "Fred, let's get out of here." I was mesmerized by it all and asked, "Why? They're about to come back for the encore!" Peter said, "Yeah, I know, but we need to get out. I think some serious shit is about to go down." So we split. The next day's headlines were all about the riot that broke out during the encore, inflicting a quarter of a million dollars' worth of damage. Judas Priest was banned from the Garden for life.

I had moved back downtown to Ludlow Street with Kat, into an apartment just around the corner from Peter's place. It was conveniently close to Katz's Deli and Russ & Daughters, which we hit up on Sundays for bagels, whitefish, lox—all the stuff I'd loved growing up, thanks to my moms. The three of us would stock up and head back to Peter's apartment or ours to hang out.

Peter often talked about how he wished there were more rap videos on MTV. Much as I appreciated Peter and his particular genius, I didn't think very highly of the channel. The few times I actually watched MTV—because, to be real, hardly anyone I knew had cable, myself included—I'd find myself sitting there waiting and waiting for something cool to come on. Eventually I'd be like, "I'm sick of this lame-ass VJ. Who is this cornball motherfucker anyway? Play some shit I wanna see!"

In its early days, MTV was notorious for underprogramming Black artists—or just not programming them at all, at least until Michael Jackson and Prince became too massive to ignore. MTV was basically copying the race-based structure of American radio. What was considered pop, or just popular—that meant "white." That's why you had sly marketing terms like "urban contemporary": coded ways to signal so-called Black programming without saying Black.

American radio in the '80s was segregated. I don't think the gatekeepers saw themselves as being overtly racist—they were just reproducing what they considered the commercial norm. But that's pretty much a dictionary definition of structural racism. MTV, in its early form, was practicing a form of television apartheid. I was far from the only one bothered by it. Rick James went hard at them and allegedly threatened to sue. David Bowie famously ripped into Mark Goodman, one of the original VJs, during an MTV interview, pressing him on why Black artists weren't being played.

Wild Style had boosted the visibility of hip-hop culture, but the music itself was still a ways from being a commercial juggernaut. Critics questioned whether rap even counted as music. Within the Black community, plenty of folks wanted to distance themselves from it. BET wasn't supporting rap, and Black radio wasn't doing much for it either. Despite spinning "Rapture," Frankie Crocker, my WBLS hero, wasn't into rap at all. Like a lot of older Black folks at the time, Frankie was concerned with "movin' on up," like George and Weezy on *The Jeffersons*. He saw rap as movin' on down—back to the streets, back to being broke in the ghetto, standing around holding your dick, with all that rough-edged attitude and anger.

I remember an interview Frankie did with James Brown on WBLS. James kept trying to get Frankie to acknowledge rap—no doubt because Frankie himself had helped popularize the word: "They call me candy 'cause my rap is so sweet." But Frankie kept sidestepping. Here was the Godfather of Soul, practically handing Frankie a golden opportunity to claim a little credit for being a spark for this new phenomenon, and Frankie was like, "Uh, no thanks." (Don Cornelius, from *Soul Train*, wasn't feeling it either; he stepped away from the show once rap started changing the musical landscape.)

The irony was hard to miss. It was the Black radio jocks like Frankie—guys who talked slick, rhymed their intros, and always played the hottest music—who were the extremely influential voices, the original disc jockeys who directly inspired early mobile disco, then the hip-hop DJs and, by extension, the first MCs. To my mind, it wasn't so much the Last Poets, the Watts Prophets, or even Gil Scott-

EVERYBODY'S FLY

Heron who gave direct inspiration—great as those artists were—as it was the Frankie Crockers of the world who set the template via broadcasting.

So rap radio was practically nonexistent. A lot of music-industry types—gatekeepers and execs—were still convinced rap was a novelty, a passing fad, some fringe genre that wasn't going anywhere. It was cool that Peter was thinking about a place for rap on MTV, but I was like, *Good luck with that.*

15

I met Gene Kelly!
I hung out with him!

In September 1985, Jean and Andy's joint show opened at Tony Shafrazi's gallery in SoHo. It was meant to be the big payoff for their collaboration—a showcase of the work they had made together over the previous year. There was a ton of excitement around it. Their art friendship had captured the city's imagination: The new kid on the block teaming up with the most famous artist in the world. Posters for the show, styled like a boxing match promo, were wheat-pasted all over town.

Peter Dougherty had been producing short artist profiles called "Art Breaks" at MTV and asked if I could get Jean to do one. I happily set it up. Peter also did one with Andy. It was hard to imagine more hype for one gallery show.

Sure enough, the opening was a mob scene. That was true of a lot of SoHo openings in the '80s, but this one had different energy—more diverse, more electric. You had art people, graff people, Factory people, all packed in together. But the show itself was almost universally panned in the press. *The New York Times* said Jean had become nothing but an "art world mascot."

It was just a lot of hate is what it was. So much of the commentary zeroed in on Jean's relationship with Andy—like, *Oh, Warhol found some homeless Black guy and made a few paintings with him.* Total disparagement. Never mind that Jean and Andy had been hanging out for a few years, building a real friendship and genuine collaboration. Andy was like a big brother to Jean; I could feel that vibe every time the three of us were together.

Keith once wrote about their dynamic: "Jean had the nerve to do anything he felt like, anywhere he felt like, and Andy loved to watch." For Andy, being around Jean reconnected him to what was happening on the street. It even got him painting again, putting his brush to canvas after a long hiatus of mostly silk-screening portraits. But after the show and the hateful critical backlash, Jean started to back off from Andy. That wave of hostility, the mean-spirited pile on, really shook him to the core.

A couple of weeks later, I had an opening of my own at the Holly Solomon gallery, on Fifth Avenue, right across from Tiffany's. It was a major vibe shift from the Fun Gallery days. I was now showing at the same gallery that hosted Nam June Paik, William Wegman, and Robert Mapplethorpe. I loved that Holly, who called herself the "Pop princess," had been painted by both Lichtenstein and Warhol. She was one of the original pioneers of the SoHo gallery scene back in the '70s, before moving her space uptown. (She would eventually return downtown.)

For this show, I was pushing myself, advancing my visual vocabulary with more fantastical figurative imagery. I brought some acrylic and enamel brushwork into the mix while keeping the hand and attitude of graffiti in full effect. For inspiration, I'd been spending long, delightful stretches at the Strand Bookstore, poring over art books and discovering artists I had previously overlooked. The work of William Blake, the visionary English Romantic poet and painter, hit my radar hard. I dug his poetry and the way he connected his rhymes to his imagery—it was totally enlightening to me.

So the pieces I brought to Holly Solomon leaned in a Blakean direction. My favorite was a painting of a flamenco dancer, inspired by that night in Seville during the film festival. Another piece—six feet wide by six high—was called *Wall Painting for a House in New York*. It showed a surreal creature that looked like a mash-up of a deer and a duck, set against a shimmering gold ground. That one ended up in the collection of the Albright-Knox museum in Buffalo. After the opening, a bunch of us headed back downtown to Fourteenth Street and partied our asses off in the Mike Todd VIP room of the Palladium. It felt big-time.

The moment had arrived: I was being swept up into the go-go '80s art world. In addition to Holly, I'd also hooked up with one of the biggest galleries in Los Angeles, the Flow Ace Gallery. They featured me in Kings of Spray, a graffiti-inspired group show, at the end of 1985. Jean had been going out to LA a lot and had a show around that time at Larry Gagosian's gallery. I asked him about LA to get the lay of land—like, "Yo, did you meet any movie stars out there?"

"I met Gene Kelly! I hung out with him!"

"Ain't no way!"

"Yeah, I met his son, Tim, and I was at their house in Beverly Hills. He's actually bald!"

Now it was my turn to get a taste of that scene. Gagosian had put Jean up at L'Ermitage, a luxury hotel in Beverly Hills, and the Ace offered to put me up at the Mondrian on the Sunset Strip for a few months while I worked on a solo show scheduled for the spring.

The owner of the Ace, Doug Chrismas, was a piece of work. He was a pioneer in the LA art scene, no doubt—but if I had to describe him, the vibes I felt were refined thug. I later learned he had a reputation for screwing people over. During a brief trip back to New York before returning to LA, I had dinner at Odeon with Jean and Andy.

Andy asked, "Uh, Fab, what are you working on now?"

I told him I was putting together a solo show at the Ace. A cloud passed over Andy's face.

"Oh, Doug Chrismas," he said. "I've worked with him. But watch out. Be careful."

Doug had serious tough-guy energy—but I grew up around tough, and I could rock pretty well with that. He liked my work and recognized that I was from the hood and could handle myself. I also had a pretty good radar for detecting treacherous energy when it was in the vicinity. So it was all good. I felt like I was doing a decent job of keeping Doug in check, and we were clearly useful to each other.

Still, it was wild to think that the Ace Gallery had so much clout and respect in the art world when the cat behind it was on some gangsta shit. In fact, one weekend during my stay, I was supposed to meet with Doug at the Ace on a Friday afternoon to discuss a commission, but he was a no-show. In fact, nobody saw him all weekend.

Then, on Sunday, I peeped a story in the *Los Angeles Times*: Doug had been arrested for defrauding a Canadian collector out of $1.2 million, having sold the guy's paintings—including a Rauschenberg—to some other people. By Monday, Doug was out, back at the gallery like nothing had happened. We never discussed any of it, but he would later get into tons of legal hot water for allegedly ripping people off.

Just about the only person I knew in LA was Anita Rosenberg, a super-cool aspiring filmmaker who'd gone to NYU with Spike Lee. Anita made a fun short film called *Bachelorette Pad*, starring Patti Astor, that I had a brief cameo in. I gave her a shout when I got to town, and she took me under her wing, chauffeuring me all over the place (like a typical New Yorker, I had no idea how to drive) and showing me what was what.

Through Anita, I met a cat named Matt Dike, who'd worked at Larry Gagosian's gallery. He had also been an assistant to Jean; the two of them had become close buds. Matt found me a studio in South Central and gave me the best possible introduction to the LA scene. He knew everybody and everything cool happening in that town. He also read *The Village Voice* religiously and was totally hip to our downtown NYC scene—he knew all the moves I'd been making—and was basically importing the vibe to the West Coast, where they were putting their own spin on things.

Matt had a club night he put on weekly with John Sidel called Power Tools where he played hip-hop and mixed it with rock, blending everything just right. The folks I met through him were super dope, super open—honestly, probably nicer than our crowd back home. Since Jean had gotten deep with them, when I showed up, Matt was like, "Yo, everybody, this is Fred! He's down with Jean." All the doors opened for me. He even found me an assistant—a young woman on the scene named Laura Jane Bruce—whose main job was driving me around in her VW Rabbit.

Being out on the West Coast was a major refresh—like living in a parallel universe. The LA gangsta rap thing was stoking up, and I met Ice-T, who was just beginning his hip-hop come up, buzzing around, taking notes. He was hip to *Wild Style* and what was going on in New York, and was very aware of who I was. He had been in some of those early Hollywood attempts to jump on the hip-hop bandwagon—*Breakin'*, *Breakin' 2*, *Rappin'*—but I didn't knock it. I could see he was figuring out the game for real. (That's what real players do—play.) Ice-T was doing his due diligence, learning the roots of hip-hop, tossing me questions about the major players.

When he and his beautiful girlfriend, Darlene Ortiz, came to visit me at the Ace Gallery one day, Doug hired her to work there. She would later appear on the cover of Ice-T's first two amazing albums.

I also met the young skateboarder and photographer Glen Friedman, who filled me in on a ton of street-level LA culture and the emerging skateboard scene he was tapped into. He'd taken photos of early pioneering LA skateboarders, a bunch of punk bands, and was deeply into the new rap wave. Glen knew the guys behind Def Jam records—Russell Simmons and Rick Rubin—and he played me two tracks by a new outfit on the label called Public Enemy, songs destined for their debut album *Yo! Bum Rush the Show*, which would come out the following year.

The sound floored me. The lyrics were all about shit I knew so well from growing up in Bed-Stuy. A rush of visuals swarmed my brain—mini movies playing in my head. It was a revelation. I couldn't wait to hear more. I wanted the entire world to hear Public Enemy ASAP.

Every single night in LA was like that—meeting new people in this cool West Coast scene that was just beginning to hit another level. Matt introduced me to his best pal, Mike Ross. The two of them were already scheming on starting a record label to tap into all the flavor bubbling up around them. They kept saying to me, "Yo, Fred, come on! Let's do a record! You were born to rap! We love your flow on 'Change the Beat'!"

But I felt like I'd already done more MCing than I ever imagined I would. So I was like, "Nah, I'm good." My lane was making art and pulling strings behind the scenes. The following year, Matt and Mike launched Delicious Vinyl—the first major California label to dive headfirst into hip-hop.

By the time of my Ace opening, in April, I'd built up a solid body of new work. I'd been experimenting with watercolor, pastel, and crayon, while still working with spray paint, enamel, and acrylics. My father flew out for the opening and stayed with me a few days at the Mondrian. He hadn't been to Los Angeles since the Second World War, when he'd been stationed there for training. During his visit, he tracked down Lester Young's sister, Irma, an incredible sax player and one of jazz's unsung female heroes.

As for the show itself, I was ecstatic that the *Los Angeles Times* gave it a positive review, noting all the elements I'd been trying to juggle: television, superheroes, sci-fi, psychedelia, and Pop Art, all with a jagged graffiti edge. The writer nailed it: "His pictures are brightly colored and collectible, but they're also about as friendly as a clenched fist."

During the opening, my father and I stepped out onto Melrose Avenue for a smoke of some primo Cali bud I had. Both of us felt a deep sense of how far we'd come from Hancock Street. He started reflecting on everything that had happened in my life—the journey from *Wild Style* to the records and tours to this very gallery show. Then he said something that has stuck with me ever since: "Frederick, you sublimate your ego."

I had never heard the phrase used that way before. He explained that I use creativity and connection to redirect my desires—to transform my energy into something positive, something that allowed me to move through a world that might have been once closed off to people like me.

It's an observation that continues to resonate. For whatever reason, I have always had an instinctive connection with creative people and scenes. I've been lucky to find community—birds of a feather—wherever I go and to bring out creativity in others while drawing it out of myself. Whether through art, film, or music, I have always tried to catalyze myself and others to new creations and new modes of expression.

I had never thought about it so literally before, but that night in LA, my dad was laying it on me. And I could sense his pride—not just in what I'd done, but in how I'd done it. I'd created my own playbook, followed my own path, and made a life rooted in creativity and connection. That meant something to him—and it meant everything to me.

After the opening, we went to a big dinner hosted by Doug at a restaurant he owned called Charmer's Market in Santa Monica. Then my dad went back to the Mondrian to crash out, while a bunch of us hit up a Power Tools party in my honor.

Soon enough, I was back on Ludlow Street. I'd been away from New York so long that Kat and I had frayed beyond repair. She'd moved out. I was riding solo again.

I got back to NYC around the time the epic *Raising Hell*, by Run-DMC, came out. It felt like a definite turning point in the hip-hop story. That album had fierce beats, some of them lifted from rock records instead of the usual funk, soul, and disco.

That shift was part of a growing trend. LL Cool J's debut, *Radio*, had come out a little earlier, and I remember playing it for Max Roach to see what he thought. He was like, "It sounds real militant." I hadn't expected that. To me, LL wasn't political—just a fly, loud, and lyrical rap star with a hard flow over dope beats. But Max heard something deeper. The militancy wasn't in the lyrics—it was in the drums, where his ears naturally went.

Raising Hell took things to the next level: "It's Tricky," "You Be Illin'," "My Adidas," and of course "Walk This Way" with Aerosmith—an instant pop-culture bonfire. Hit after hit from one hip-hop album, packed with innovation and attitude. Rap was clearly heading to new places. Charlie and I talked about it all the time. What we'd captured in *Wild Style*—that first wave of hip-hop that was funky, funny, and homegrown—was already becoming "old school." A new school was rising.

Raising Hell was the summer of '86 soundtrack. Not just for hip people in New York and LA, but for kids out in the suburbs too, from South Orange to Orange County. What I had been predicting for years—rap's expanding audience, growing influence, commercial success—was happening. The Beastie Boys and Public Enemy were just about to blow up. A tsunami was coming. The world wasn't going to be able to ignore this much longer.

There was something darker that was proving impossible to ignore that year: AIDS. When Rock Hudson died, the disease hit the front page. But closer to home, it hit even harder. Nicolas Moufarrege—a brilliant artist and critic, and a friend of the Fun Gallery—was one of the first in our circle to succumb.

In early September, I went to a fundraising party at the Pyramid for Martin Burgoyne, an artist and one of Madonna's dancers, who had been diagnosed. Ann Magnuson and John Sex performed. Around the same time, Barney's New York hosted an AIDS benefit and auction, where a bunch of us artists customized Levi's jackets to raise money for the cause—a cause that was suddenly touching more and more lives.

Kate Pierson of the B-52s wore a jacket I painted. I wore one Julian Schnabel made. Keith designed a jacket that was worn by Iman. And Madonna wore the one created by her dear friend Martin. Less than three weeks later, he was gone.

Even in the midst of all that darkness, there were sparks of light. One came from Spike Lee, the young filmmaker I first met when we were gearing up to release *Wild Style*. Like me, Spike had grown up in Brooklyn and gone to Dewey. He asked me to make a cameo in his feature debut, *She's Gotta Have It*, a sexy, black-and-white comedy set in Fort Greene.

The movie was a sensation when it came out. Jean and Andy came with me to the premiere; the three of us were photographed standing in a row with Spike. I ended up with one of the film's most memorable lines: "Look baby, let's go to my house right now, let's do the wild thing!"

Matt Dike and Mike Ross were obsessed with that line and wanted to turn it into a song. They were like, "Dude! Come on, let's do this! You had the coolest line in Spike's movie!" I loved those guys, but I told them again—my MC days were behind me.

Still, they ran with it. Matt and Mike eventually brought the concept to a young rapper from LA they'd signed. So my line from *She's Gotta Have It* ended up inspiring what became the breakthrough single for their Delicious Vinyl label: Tone Loc's "Wild Thing," which went to number one.

February 22, 1987, is a day I will never forget. Andy went in for a routine gallbladder operation and didn't make it out alive. He was only fifty-eight. Everybody I knew was devastated. It felt like a presidential assassination—so unexpected, so shockingly sad, so horrible.

There was a joint off Canal near West Broadway in Tribeca called Madam Rosa, where a lot of us hung out. I met up with Jean there after the news of Andy's death broke. He was wearing black slacks and a white shirt with a black armband and crying uncontrollably as he drifted around the room. If anybody tried to approach him, he'd brush them off: "Leave me the fuck alone. Get away from me." His grief was intense; he had tears down his face and a giant chip on his shoulder. I knew not to say anything to him, so I just went up, put an arm around him, and walked him outside. What could anyone say, really? Andy Warhol was gone.

I've always felt that Jean's grief was made sharper by the fact that he'd distanced himself from Andy over the previous year—there was some guilt and regret in the mix. But that friendship still meant a lot to him, even if it had been in a kind of remission. Andy gave Jean a sense of grounding, and some protection, at a time when the heat on Jean—both the acclaim and the massive backlash—was intense. It was savage the way critics like Hilton Kramer and Robert Hughes went after Jean—so dismissive and so racist. The bigger Jean got, the worse the vitriol became.

There was a general backlash building against the art stars of the '80s, for sure. But nobody went at Julian Schnabel or David Salle with the same level of hate. It was like, *How could some Black guy in his twenties accomplish all this without going to RISD?* The hating-ass motherfucking critics couldn't wrap their heads around the idea that somebody this sharp, this original, this sophisticated had come from the hood and was essentially a self-taught prodigy. And so you got all of this bullshit about Jean being a "primitivist."

Yes, it bothered him; this I know. It also fueled the edgier side of his competitiveness. He had a thing about Julian Schnabel—it was like, *I'm gonna go at this guy and put him in his place.*

Julian was the biggest kid in the game among the hot young painters during the height of the '80s NYC art boom. I personally had no beef with him—he was always cool with me and even bought a couple of my paintings. But Jean and Julian developed a rivalry. I'm sure Julian disregarded it at first, but as Jean kept rising, it became a real thing. Suddenly they were neck and neck—and then, at a certain point, Jean was probably passing him. It wasn't a horse race. Jean just wanted his spot.

This was back when SoHo felt like an extension of Wall Street—high stakes, high energy, and high emotion. The vibe among the artists was as intense as the money swirling around them. Rene Ricard once told me that when Julian left Mary Boone to join the Pace Gallery, he did so with the stipulation that Pace never sign Jean.

So it's ironic that Julian, of all people, later ended up telling Jean's story on film, directing *Basquiat*. That movie did a ton to turn Jean into a full-on cult figure, thanks to a heavy dose of mythmaking and creative license that went way beyond the actual artist and human being I knew. Still, Jeffrey Wright's performance was next level. It wasn't just acting—it felt like channeling. He was spookily spot on.

The period around Andy's death was a time of questioning for me. I'd been making moves with big galleries, and yet I somehow felt... dissatisfied. I loved making art—but maybe I didn't love the art world. I missed the camaraderie and craziness of the Fun Gallery days. By the summer of 1987, *The New York Times* was running stories about the decline of the East Village scene, as galleries either shut down or moved to SoHo. Of all the original East Village galleries that sprang up in the wake of the Fun Gallery, only one remained: Gracie Mansion, on Avenue A.

I was proud to have been the motivator and instigator in pushing graffiti-based art into the global art world. By the late '80s, the city's relentless war on subway graffiti had made galleries—and wall murals—the only viable alternative. A few of us had made real moves and done well, transforming the gallery scene: not just Jean and Keith, but Futura, Rammellzee, Crash, Daze, Lee, A-1, Koor—and me.

Still, I was restless, a little bored. I wanted something more than just me and a blank canvas. More than a couple of group shows and a solo show a year here and there. I loved the work, but I wanted to reach a wider audience. I had always envisioned hip-hop culture filtering out into the whole culture. Gallery shows were part of the mix, no doubt—but they weren't the only way to make shit happen.

Maybe I needed to make another record. Or maybe not.

For the first time, I wasn't sure what the next move should be.

Peter Dougherty was still talking about a rap show for MTV.

"Listen, Fab," he said. "I've been in MTV's ear about this thing for a while now. Run-DMC, LL Cool J, Whodini—they're blowing up. I think they might finally be ready to try something."

I was like, "Yeah, cool, whatever."

But Peter wouldn't let it drop.

"I've been explaining to them who you are—the Blondie connection, the Clash, the graffiti thing, *Wild Style*. I've been pitching you as the host."

If there was ever a guy who could talk people into things, it was Peter. I still had a certain attitude about MTV, though, based on how they had handled Black artists up to that point. And my television experience was pretty much limited to *TV Party*. Peter was like, "Yeah, but you were great in *Wild Style*!"

Sure, but that was me playing Phade—a character. I wasn't convinced I could pull off being an on-screen Frankie Crocker. That was a high bar. And I didn't love the idea of being stuck on camera for hours in a studio with some goofy bullshit happening on a green-screen background. That whole VJ thing felt corny to me.

What I really wanted was to explore directing—getting *behind* the camera. I'd been thinking seriously about figuring out how to harness my interest in film, my connection to hip-hop, and my visual art. Making *Wild Style* had been on-the-job film school for me.

Public Enemy had just dropped their first album, *Yo! Bum Rush the Show*—the one Glen had given me a taste of back in LA—and I lost my mind when I heard the entire thing. It sounded even better now—the message and attitude felt like a riot about to break out. It was Huey P. Newton and Bobby Seale, pure Black Panther spirit set to hard beats. I thought, *I can put something together that'd be dope for this group.* So I wrote video concepts for at least half the album.

By then, Public Enemy were at Greene Street Recording, in SoHo, working on their next record, *It Takes a Nation of Millions to Hold Us Back*—and what I was hearing was astonishing. I'd be hanging out at the studio, campaigning to get them to let me do a video or two.

Chuck D, Flav, and their producer Hank Shocklee of the Bomb Squad all knew who I was—they'd seen *Wild Style* and loved it. I already knew Russell Simmons and Rick Rubin—the Def Jam guys. We were cool. Russell had been part of the downtown scene for a few years and was now making big moves, running Rush Artist Management, which handled most of the top rap acts at the time. One of his smartest plays was teaming up with Rick. Russell understood that this kid had a unique feel for how to make rap records with street-level grit and intensity, and I was totally aligned with that vision.

Russell and Rick were trying to push the music forward, and it was fascinating to see Lyor Cohen step in and watch Def Jam become *Def Jam*. I was in their ear, pitching my ideas for Public Enemy: *Yo, I know I can do this.* They were into it—but they were like, "You gotta get Chuck to understand."

It turns out Chuck understood all too well. Back then, a low-budget video might cost about $30,000 to make. Chuck was like, "Yo, Fred, this is great, but we spent thirty thousand dollars to make the whole first album!" How could they justify spending that kind of money on a video when there weren't even any major outlets that would show it?

MTV sure wasn't going to add Public Enemy to the playlist. The only option, really, was Ralph McDaniels's *Video Music Box* on Channel 31 in New York. Ralph had started featuring rap—*Video Music Box* was dope and ruled NYC but was local. There was still no national outlet for hip-hop videos. (I later learned that Ralph had also been pushing MTV to develop a hip-hop show.)

The opportunity to direct a hip-hop video finally came to me in the spring via KRS-One, an intense young rapper from the Bronx who fronted Boogie Down Productions. He had made a name for himself with "The Bridge Is Over," dissing MC Shan. Now he was back with a new track, "My Philosophy": *"Fresh for '88, you suckers... suckers... suckers!"* It was an incredible song—KRS was rapping with articulate, conscious intensity, pushing the genre forward.

Boogie Down's label, Jive Records, didn't seem to mind spending money on a video, thanks to a visionary VP named Ann Carli. When I got the gig, I called up Peter Dougherty—he had directed a couple of Beastie Boys videos—for advice. "Yo, Peter, how do I do this? What kind of crew do I need?" He broke it all down.

I knew there was no way in hell MTV was going to play the "My Philosophy" video, so I made it as Black as I thought it needed to be. I put in images of Malcolm X and Louis Farrakhan. There was no point in trying to kowtow to MTV. *Because it ain't about them anyway.*

Peter was my guy, but the network he worked for was not addressing the totality of what was going on in the world. So I was like, *MTV? Fuck them.*

I was pleased with how the "My Philosophy" video turned out. Making it was a creative revelation, a breakthrough. It was the new outlet I had been looking for: working with a team, in a different medium, flexing a new set of muscles. The response was strong. I got loads of praise, especially for the moment early in the clip when the music stops and KRS-One steps out of a Jeep, going a cappella for a few bars: *"I just produce, create, innovate on a higher level / I'll be back but for now just sekkle..."*

I showed the finished cut to Peter, who—thankfully—loved it. He was like, "Fred, MTV is close to doing this thing, and I'm still telling them you should be the host."

I was flattered, but I was still like, "Me?"

Peter said that he had been shaking the trees at the network with another producer, Ted Demme—a young, energetic hip-hop head from Long Island who happened to be the nephew of Jonathan Demme, the genius director who'd made the Talking Heads concert film *Stop Making Sense*. A few years later, Jonathan would direct *Silence of the Lambs* and win an Oscar.

Peter and Ted were envisioning a hip-hop version of *120 Minutes* or *Headbangers Ball*. MTV Europe had already launched an in-studio rap show called *Yo!*, hosted by my friend Sophie Bramly, a French photographer and NYC-scene fixture. Since rap was born in New York City, Peter said that we needed our own show, and that I was the guy to do it. He floated the idea of shooting a screen test to show the execs at MTV. I was still hesitant, like, *Yeah, sure, whatever*. He asked how I'd want to do it.

That gave me an opening—not only to shape the test but to lay out a vision for the show itself, if it ever came to pass. I told Peter that I didn't want to be stuck in a studio like every other VJ. I wanted to be *outside*, on the street—in the field, if you will—getting into the environments where hip-hop came from. Bronx, Harlem, Queens, Compton, Philly—wherever this new energy was sparking.

From what I'd seen in LA, hip-hop was now coast-to-coast. The vibe didn't live in a green screen; it lived out there on the pavement. The visual artist in me wanted to shoot in natural light, with interesting camera angles—visual storytelling that captured the unpredictability and rawness I loved in *TV Party*. No overproduced gloss. I wanted spontaneity. And above all, I wanted to do anything I could to help the artists feel comfortable. For many of them, this would be their first time on TV. These guys put up a lot of front when rapping, but I knew they were vulnerable, coming up the way they did, pushing through. I wanted to give them their best shot. I wanted to introduce them to the world—to share the living culture I'd helped codify in *Wild Style* and show how these new voices were living, creating, and innovating.

Peter and Ted went to bat for the concept, and MTV agreed to a screen test. That summer, we set up on the Manhattan side of the Williamsburg Bridge. It was my kind of setting. I riffed, introducing a Run-DMC video, playing it loose. The skyline of Lower Manhattan was behind us like one of Martha Cooper's graffiti photographs—pure downtown energy, total NYC atmosphere.

Through Don Letts, I had gotten tight with Chris Blackwell, the visionary behind Island Records. Chris had produced a film about the go-go funk scene in D.C. called *Good to Go*, starring Art Garfunkel, and he brought on Don to direct. Don cast me in it. But right before shooting started, members of the crew turned on Don for reasons I still don't fully understand and convinced Chris to hand the reins over to the screenwriter, Blaine Novak. From there, the project went way south—it turned into a cheesy exploitation flick, much to Chris's (and everyone's) lasting regret.

Even so, I'd still get the occasional invitation to Chris's elegant Upper West Side prewar apartment, near the Museum of Natural History. Mary Vinson—his partner at the time, and later his wife—would broil some steaks, we'd spark some serious weed, and we'd talk music deep into the night. Chris was the guy who'd signed Bob Marley, Jimmy Cliff, Grace Jones, U2—an infinite variety of dope music across the spectrum. He was a walking music encyclopedia, a true record man.

Chris was also all in on rap. He'd seen *Wild Style* and got it. The highest compliment from him was that it reminded him of *The Harder They Come*. He understood the movement and didn't hesitate to sign Eric B. & Rakim to Island. In the apartment, he had this giant drop-down screen—nine feet wide—for showing the hottest new music videos. It was basically stepping into a private screening room curated by the best ears in the business.

One night, not long after Peter and I shot the screen test, I was hanging out at Chris's place when he said, "Listen, Fred, I'm hearing from the top brass at MTV that you're on the short list to host that rap show."

I was like, "What's a short list?"

16

Let his soul run wild

August 1988: New York was heat-wave city. The tar was melting in the streets. It was like a sauna, and people were sick of it. It felt like the edge of something.

Peter and Ted cobbled together a pilot episode of the MTV hip-hop show by chucking together various videos and clips. Peter gave me the heads-up: "Be sure to tune in! We're going to play the 'My Philosophy' video." There was no way that was actually going to happen. But I went across Ludlow to my pal Bobby G's place; he was a Colab artist and actually had cable. We tuned in and, sure enough, on that muggy August 6, there it was—"My Philosophy" on MTV! I was stunned. It was the final video they played. *Wow.* By the time I grabbed the phone to call Peter, the deal was basically done. I was set to host *Yo! MTV Raps*, the first coast-to-coast hip-hop TV show, slated to go into production in a few weeks. *By any means necessary.*

It was sticky that Saturday night—one of those NYC summer nights when you'd wipe yourself down with a cold rag, open all the windows, and set up a fan to blow the hot air around. Hardly anyone I knew had AC. I certainly didn't have it in my fourth-floor apartment on Ludlow Street. Between the humidity and my head buzzing about MTV, I was lying in bed in a semiconscious daze, listening to a strange rumble outside that wouldn't stop. By about one thirty in the morning, I realized it had to be a helicopter, circling in the sky very close to home. It had to have been going for at least an hour. The phone rang. It was my buddy B Dub—Brian David Williams—a Cali surfer dude and DJ who lived nearby. He was also a great photographer and had been Jean's assistant for a bit.

"Fred! Dude! You hear that helicopter?"

"Yeah, man. I've been hearing it for hours! What the hell is going on?"

"I hear some wild shit is happening on Avenue A—like a riot near the park, tons of cops in helmets and shit. Let's go check it out."

"I'll meet you at Second and A in twenty minutes."

Next thing we knew, B Dub and I were in the middle of the Tompkins Square Riot.

A big, simmering showdown had come to a head between the punks, the squatters, housing rights activists, and the homeless on one side and the police on the other. The city had been clamping down on Tompkins Square due to noise complaints, enforcing a new 1:00 a.m. curfew in the weeks leading up to that Saturday night—when everything finally exploded like a tinderbox.

The Tompkins Square Riot was the most horrific thing I have ever witnessed. It looked like footage from the civil rights movement in the sixties—protesters being brutally beaten down. But what was truly shocking to me was who the victims were. This time it wasn't Black folks. It was *white* downtown working-class New Wave and punk-rock kids getting their heads busted open. They were the ones being mauled by the cops.

It was plain ugly. Bystanders who had nothing to do with anything were getting beaten to a pulp. Rudolf Piper, one of the owners of Danceteria, lived nearby. He wasn't protesting, but the cops did a number on him anyway—blood was streaming down his face.

There were charges and countercharges, a line of mounted police stretching across Avenue A, and more than four hundred cops pouring in on foot. Protesters started chucking rocks and bottles in retaliation. A crowd got hold of a police barricade on Avenue B and rammed it through the glass doors of the Christodora—the co-op that had become a target of anti-gentrification rage.

Some cops were seen covering their badges so they couldn't be identified. They seemed to enjoy it, like a rabid mob.

The poet Allen Ginsberg—whom you'd see sometimes at the Odessa diner on Avenue A—stood and watched the madness unfold. One of his houseguests was clubbed into submission.

The cops were chasing random people down the street and beating the shit out of them. B Dub and I witnessed this savagery for hours and were lucky to escape unscathed, at least physically.

It was soon determined—in part thanks to footage taken by a local videographer named Clayton Patterson—that the Tompkins Square Riot had been a police riot. The cops had overreacted and lost control. It was an orgy of violence, a freakin' war zone.

To me, it marked the end of the East Village—at least as my friends and I had known it. The developers were pouring in, rents were shooting through the roof, and that hip, cool world that had been our home turf and playground was turning into one of the highest-rent districts in Manhattan. Soon the party started migrating to Williamsburg, Bushwick, and other, more affordable corners of Brooklyn—my old borough. People were even saying you could find cheaper apartments on the Upper East Side than in the East Village. Unheard of.

By the following Friday, August 12, the situation around Tompkins

Square had simmered down, but the city was still sweltering. NYC had endured forty straight days of suffocating heat and humidity. You felt like you were losing your mind.

I believe it was Michael Holman who called to tell me the news that day around noon. When I heard it, I practically blacked out.

Jean had overdosed. He was dead.

Glenn said that Jean used heroin and coke as replacements for his friends.

I have to admit, during the months leading up to his death, I hadn't seen Jean much except in passing a couple of times on his small fold-up bike. We chatted briefly and kept it moving. He was on his frequency and I was on mine.

Of course I knew he'd been trying to manage his drug habit—disappearing to Hawaii to get treatment and get healthy. That happened a few times. But Jean would always come back home and get that urge again. That psychological pull. I had other friends who'd done Twelve-Step programs, gone to Betty Ford. I knew how rough it was to get well. Some made it through. Jean didn't. He had gone too far down that road and didn't come back.

In a way, I felt like he'd never been the same since Andy's death.

I learned that Jean had been with our friend Kevin Bray, an up-and-coming filmmaker, earlier the night he OD'd. They were hanging out at M.K., the swanky new club on Madison Square that Eric Goode and Serge Becker had opened. When I called Kevin that day, as the word started to seep out, he sounded severely shaken.

He said, "Jean had promised me, man. He said he was gonna stop using that shit."

But Jean—who'd gotten back from another round of rehab in Hawaii only ten days earlier—was clearly high. They went back to Jean's place on Great Jones Street to hang out, but he just sat in a chair, far away, nodding.

Kevin was like, "Man, look at you! You promised me you were fucking gonna stop."

Jean, deep in a doped-out stupor, said, "Man, I don't owe you anything. I don't owe you anything."

Kevin grabbed an oil stick and wrote on a large piece of drawing paper: *I don't want to sit around here and watch you die. Yes, you do owe me something.*

Jean was nodding, off in another world.

Kevin read the note to Jean, left it there, and took off. They had plans to go see Run-DMC at the Nassau Coliseum the following night.

The next morning, Kevin called to check in. One of Jean's assistants picked up. She went to find him—and discovered his body.

The word went out fast, rippling in every direction. I had a hard time wrapping my head around the fact that Jean was gone. Many moments we shared were racing through my mind, and I felt Kevin's pain—we all did.

When I think of Jean now, I'm just so proud of the mission—short as it turned out to be. It was bigger than anybody could have foreseen. Yet Jean was so confident, so assured that what he wanted to make happen *would* happen: He'd be a great artist. He'd be remembered. He would transcend his time and speak for all time.

I'm sure, like me, he would have continued exploring different media beyond painting—music, film, photography, god knows what. All the things we talked about doing. *By any means necessary.*

In his brief twenty-seven years, he crushed it. He took it to the highest peak and burned bright—loud and proud.

Tributes poured in from all directions, both from the wider world and within our little world of artists. Keith did one of the best: *A Pile of Crowns for Jean-Michel Basquiat.*

Jean's death also triggered some dark shit. Rammellzee, whom I had originally brought into the mix and introduced to Jean (who, by the way, dug him a lot), said to me on a call while I was grieving, "Well, now that he's gone, I can get the prices that I should be getting for my work!"

I was stunned, couldn't believe what I was hearing. I yelled at him, "Shut the fuck up, you bitch-ass motherfucker—I'm coming to bust yo ass!" I hung up on him, seething.

I loved Ramm, but somewhere along the way his process, his whole worldview, got twisted. He became such a disappointment, spewing all kinds of wacked-out mumbo-jumbo pseudoscience and dragging Jean in interviews—just full of hate and disrespect. Schizophrenia? Drinking? The Dunning-Kruger effect? I'm no shrink, but something wasn't right. Mental illness had to be part of it. That was the last time I ever spoke to him.

Jean's memorial was held that fall at St. Peter's Church, on the corner of Lexington and Fifty-Fourth. Three hundred people turned up.

Keith, Glenn, and I spoke, along with others—Michael Holman and his bandmates in Gray. Suzanne Mallouk read A. R. Penck's "Poem for Basquiat." I chose to read the poem "Genius Child" by Langston Hughes, but I changed the last line from "Kill him—and let his soul run wild" to "Free him—let his soul run wild."

When I sat back down in the pew, Dennis Hopper, seated next to me, placed his hand on my shoulder.

Yo! *MTV Raps* turned into a giant boom box for hip-hop. At last, we were being *heard*.

For my on-air persona, I knew exactly where to look for inspiration: I channeled Phade, my character from *Wild Style*. Once upon a time, Charlie Ahearn had to talk me into playing the role. Now, Phade was reborn as the on-air Fab 5 Freddy. It was still me—but with a little more jive, a little more hustle, and little more... *Yo! Yo! Yo!*

The creation of the on-air Fab character wasn't something I overthought, because it all happened on the fly. I'd always just seen myself as myself. And honestly, the show wasn't even on the radar for most of the people I was hanging with. As I've mentioned, hardly any of them had cable. When the show officially aired, I watched the first episodes at my friend Dan Loeb's place near Madison Square Park; he managed Chris Blackwell's investments, and through Chris we became buddies.

But for the most part, there I was, this artist guy, doing a big thing on national television... that no one in my world could even see. It was like that tree falling in the forest: If nobody hears it, did it really happen? On some level, none of it was quite real. At least, not at first.

On another level, I wanted to make damn sure it all *felt* real. The audience, as I saw it, was the same as *Wild Style*'s: our downtown creative friends—that Fabulous 500—along with the homies in the hood who were down with hip-hop culture, down with the flavor. We wanted *Yo! MTV Raps* to be the real deal for them. Because most of the time, when people like us showed up on TV or in the movies, it was all wrong. It was never as right as it should have been.

Again, *The Harder They Come* and *Black Orpheus* were our guiding lights. They got it right. They got it real.

A big part of what made my show work—and feel real—was that Peter and Ted let me to do my thing as a roving host. (They also made sure I had approval over any new artists or videos before they aired.)

On *Yo! MTV Raps*, viewers got to see artists explain their creativity in the environments they came from. I remember standing with N.W.A at the "Welcome to Compton" sign in LA, introducing them to the rest of the country. Or being with Shabba Ranks in the ghettos of

Jamaica. Or visiting the Geto Boys in Houston's Fifth Ward. Or chilling with East Orange's own Queen Latifah, just as she was blowing up as a strong, positive female voice in hip-hop. That was seriously dope. I'd helped connect Latifah with Tommy Boy Records and directed her first two videos, including "Ladies First."

One week I might be with the Bomb Squad at their Strong Island studio, breaking down how they put together Public Enemy's sound. The next, I'd be with Gang Starr at D&D Studios. One time we shot a show with Das EFX, this cool group with a wild, sewer-level underground style of rhyming. We were like, "Yo, how do we capture *this* energy?" Our answer: Interview them inside the Metro-North tunnel beneath the Upper East Side. It gave me serious flashbacks to my graff days.

Basically, Peter, Ted, and I were down to try anything that would bring people closer to the worlds these incredible young artists came from.

Yo! MTV Raps blew up straight out of the gate, quickly becoming one of the network's top programs. It doubled the normal ratings in its weekly slot—so much so that MTV thought something had gone haywire with the Nielsen system. But it wasn't a glitch. The show was pulling hip-hop into every cable-ready household in America and pushing it out to the world.

Yo! arrived before *The Arsenio Hall Show*, before *In Living Color*, before the wave of Black-directed movies in the '90s. It represented a major—and maybe unprecedented—Black presence in national media. Years later, DJ Jazzy Jeff summed it up perfectly: "That was the time that I could sigh and say, 'I think hip-hop is here to stay.'"

Because the show took off so fast, MTV asked if I'd consider hosting a daily show, in the studio. I thought about it and passed. I didn't want to be overexposed. I figured people might start saying, "That

Fab 5 Freddy guy—again?" So I told Peter and Ted, "Nah, I'll stick with the original weekend plan."

I liked being out in the world—traveling from city to city, meeting artists from all over the country. It was mind-blowing to meet these people, the descendants and inheritors of everything I'd seen back in the Bronx, on the Lower East Side, in the parks, and at the Bed-Stuy block parties. And they were building on it, remixing it, making it their own. I got a front-row seat as hip-hop evolved from something of a local NYC dialect into a national language.

So I was more than happy to stick with my weekly roving persona—a "less is more" approach. It just made sense. My video-directing career was taking off, I still wanted to paint, and I already had a legacy and identity in the culture. MTV brought in Ed Lover and Dr. Dre to host the daily in-studio version, and they could not have been a better fit. They had that slapstick, *Abbott and Costello*-style hip-hop clubhouse energy. With all the pieces in place, *Yo! MTV Raps* became a juggernaut.

The first year of *Yo! MTV Raps* was a time of new beginnings. My life shifted overnight. People were stopping me on the street left and right. I had money in the bank. I was on magazine covers. Soon enough I was moving on up to a new high-rise near Times Square—an actual doorman building. I'd heard from a reliable source that some Dominican stickup kids around Ludlow Street were plotting to step to me. The old me would've been ready for war. But now, being on MTV, I didn't want to end up in headlines for dishing out—or catching—violence.

It was also a time of endings. In 1989, the East Village art scene we'd pioneered was officially dead. Short-lived as it was, it left an indelible mark on art history. That spring, the MTA announced that the last graffitied subway car had been retired. The entire fleet had been replaced with new, graffiti-resistant cars that could be quickly and easily buffed. For the graff world, it was a major "Oh well, time's up" moment. There would always be graffiti, but nothing like those whole-car pieces that made every ride through the city a burst of color and surprise.

By then, Keith Haring was so in demand as an art star, and I was so wrapped up with MTV, that we didn't see each other much anymore, not like we used to. Still, I knew Keith was delighted about *Yo! MTV Raps*. (I know Jean would have been too.) That summer, Keith called up and said, "Come by the studio. I want to talk to you." I was like, "Sure, Keith. I'll be there." So I went over to 676 Broadway, and he laid it all out in a way that took my breath away. He'd been diagnosed HIV positive and had AIDS. Just hearing him say it... He was calm, confident, focused—as he always was. "Fred," he said, "I'm going public with this. It's coming out soon in *Rolling Stone*. I wanted you to hear it from me." At the time, very few people were going public like that. I thought what Keith was doing was the most heroic, selfless thing. I was overwhelmed.

Several weeks later, Keith called again. "Listen, Fred, I have some things for you."

By then, Keith had gone very public about having AIDS. He was marching with ACT UP, joining picket lines, putting himself out there. He didn't need to explain why he was giving me things—I knew he was preparing for his departure.

When I went over to his place, he handed me a few drawings that took me right back to earlier times. Keith always loved having people over. He'd pull out some paper and crayons and say, "Hey, let's all draw." You'd end up down on the floor like a little kid. One time it was me, Keith, Jean, and Kenny Scharf. We all started sketching. Jean drew these strange little portraits of me with a metallic gold marker. When we finished, we just left the drawings at Keith's—no big deal. But Keith had kept them all this time. Now he was handing them over to me.

He also gave me a Polaroid he'd taken of Andy Warhol and me in front of the *LIFE IS FRESH, CRACK IS WACK* mural he'd painted way east on Houston Street, in the P.S. 97 schoolyard. (Lee was Keith's huge inspiration when it came to outdoor wall murals.)

Keith knew his time was short. He told me he was leaving something else for me in his will: an orange Day-Glo portrait he'd done of me in 1981. To be in the midst of your young life and thinking in those terms... It made my mind reel, like *Oh no, Keith*. He'd always wanted to have kids. There was still so much he wanted to do.

Keith died on February 16, 1990. There was a huge memorial at St. John the Divine in May, on what would have been his thirty-second birthday. Once again, I found myself paying tribute to a friend who left us too soon.

If it had only been a couple of years later, Keith—like so many taken by the AIDS epidemic—would have had access to the same cocktail of medications that's kept Magic Johnson and thousands of others alive. I think about it often, that my buddy might still be here.

I'm the king of synthesis."

That was me, quoted in *The New Yorker* in 1991. *Yo! MTV Raps* wasn't even three years old, and hip-hop was everywhere.

Tom Freston, the CEO of MTV, read the story—written by Susan Orlean, one of the magazine's best writers—and he was like, "Man! Fab! Wow!" He already thought I'd been doing a solid job on the show. But seeing my face and reading about me in the exalted pages of *The New Yorker*—that impressed the hell out of him. I think our relationship changed in that moment. Ever since, Tom has been a good friend, like a cool big brother to me.

That same year, I produced *New Jack City* and even had a role in it. Naughty by Nature had their massive hit "O.P.P."—and like every major rap act, they were featured on *Yo!*, the show that was beaming hip-hop around the world.

I was directing more music videos, for Gang Starr, Queen Latifah, Shabba Ranks, Nas, Snoop Dogg. The 1990s were fully in effect. It was a new era—the decade when hip-hop came into its own, on its way to becoming not just the most commercially successful music genre in the world, but a full-blown cultural force. That was exactly what I'd been dreaming of since the days of *TV Party* and *Wild Style*, though even I couldn't have imagined how far it would go.

The mainstreaming of hip-hop, in my opinion, began with *Yo! MTV Raps*, alongside the music getting better and better. It also was an explosive era for visuals: thousands of music videos, with the artists loud, proud, and in your face. That was when a breakout rapper went from selling gold records with zero promotion to going multi-platinum overnight. Radio had finally opened up. It all happened fast—starting in the big cities, then picking up the tempo as it filtered out to the rest of the country.

The sheer scale of it took a minute to register. Maybe I was too close to it all. But I'll never forget the moment it hit me: Early on in the *Yo!* days, we flew out to California to shoot an episode. At one point we stopped the car to make a quick pit stop, and a group of young white kids came running right over to me: "Oh my God! It's you! Hey, Freddy! Can we have your autograph?" Until then, I'd mostly gotten that kind of reception from dialed-in Black kids. But now it was happening everywhere. It struck me the same way those German breakdancers had struck me years before: This rap thing has the power to bust down all kinds of barriers.

And then there was MC Hammer blowing up to epic proportions. And at the other end of the spectrum, N.W.A—on a real counterculture rebel tip—shattering every limit for how big a group like that could get in America. The stuff I loved was no longer underground.

I had some bittersweet feelings about that, to be honest. But at least in the early 1990s, that underground edge was still there in the hip-hop world.

That moment on the road in California was also a sharp reminder of just how powerful—and pervasive—the medium of television can be. Getting hit with all those "Oh my god, that's him" reactions was, and sometimes still is, weird and humbling. I never really got used to it. I was grateful for the grounding I got from Chris and Debbie—how to stay cool and down-to-earth in the face of celebrity. The punk rockers I hung out with offered their own version of that lesson: Always do your own thing. Stand apart, even when the spotlight's on you.

And it helped, big time, that Max Roach was basically family. He was always the coolest—major large, yet totally himself. The jazz guys who were my first influence, from my dad and his friends to legends like Monk and Miles, they always kept it real. That's exactly where I wanted to stay, no matter how crazy things got.

King of synthesis.

That was me just following my curiosity wherever it led. I was trying to help spark a cultural revolution—and clear a path for myself and others to create in. I wanted to open doors for people coming from where I was coming from. Trying to make connections. Trying to disrupt—bounce it, flip it, shake it up. Trying to get shit done. Trying to make a mark.

I was inspired by European art movements. By young heads in NYC making new sounds with turntables and a new kind of poetry. By the aerosol daredevilry of Lee Quiñones. By all the downtown creatives, the New Wavers and punks. I was chasing the outlines of a movement in my own time—and trying to share it with the world: hip-hop culture, *our* culture, a global culture rooted in the Black American experience that keeps transcending all boundaries.

There were backlashes along the way, to be sure. I remember a vicious piece in *Newsweek* that went after rap in the most disgusting way. The *Los Angeles Times* called me up for comment, and I gladly told them, "Whenever you have something like rap, that's so black, it's gonna cause a commotion with white people. But you can't take rap's images so straight—it's not violent. It's pure theater."

Our American cultural history is soaked in violence—often glorified in our most popular Hollywood films, made by some of our most celebrated filmmakers. But the moment those recorded voices belong to people of color, rapping over a hard beat? That's when the outrage kicks in. It drives the naysayers mad.

By then, I was used to misunderstandings, to barriers thrown up in front of me. I'd been in enough of those rooms to know how to read the resistance—and how to rewrite the script. I was constantly being challenged by self-appointed cultural gatekeepers. Finding ways around their ignorance was like playing chess: I always had to think three moves ahead. Checkmate!

Graffiti was like that too: A graffiti writer learns how to be stealthy and smart—how to get your name wherever you feel it needs to be, and then vanish when the moment calls for it. That mentality never left me. I knew that my moves needed to be wise as well as relentless. I was clear on the mission: to engage with the culture of my time, to be a champion of new modes of expression, to make art the centerpiece of life. And nothing was going to stop me. Not ignorance.

Not closed doors. And definitely not racism—subtle or blatant. It was always rearing its head. Still is.

By the early 1990s, critics were declaring that graffiti had had its moment in the galleries and the art world had moved on. But then something unexpected happened. Street art began to rise out of the moves we made. It became a thing—and stayed a thing into the next century. Call it what you will: neo-graffiti, post-graffiti, guerrilla art... artists like Shepard Fairey, with his Obama *Hope* posters, and Banksy, a massive global star, were operating with tactics straight out the graff playbook. Stealth, surprise, impact. You could see it everywhere: street-art festivals, mural projects, museum shows, and pop-up installations in cities all over the world.

In time, hip-hop, once a fringe culture, became *the* culture. I don't need to tell anyone that it's proven capable of endless reinvention, elasticity, and innovation. If the music, after so many decades, can sometimes seem kind of staid or overly commercial, a little too slick or formulaic, there is still no end of surprises that shake up the game—some new track, a viral beef, a burst of raw energy that makes everyone snap their heads around like that Nas lyric, "*They shootin', ah, made you look.*"

It could come in the form of Drake and Kendrick Lamar taking the classic rap battle tradition to unheard-of levels—real gladiator shit. Their diss tracks hit every nook and cranny of social media, with billions of ears hanging on to every word. In *Wild Style*, it was the Cold Crush Brothers and the Fantastic Freaks squaring off on an asphalt basketball court in the Bronx. Drake and Kendrick are massive, hip-hop-based pop stars who go toe-to-toe with Super Bowl-level theatrics. But it's still hip-hop, still rooted in the same spirit.

It could come in the form of Lin-Manuel Miranda setting Broadway—and the entire planet—on fire with *Hamilton*, a hip-hop musical with race-blind casting that became one of the biggest pop-culture phenomena of my lifetime. With *Hamilton*, hip-hop reshaped the very language of musical theater.

It goes on and on. As an American musical export, hip-hop can proudly take its place alongside jazz and rock 'n' roll: It has changed the world forever. In every country with access to technology, the sights and sounds of hip-hop have left their mark. In some places, it's practically the *only* platform of expression available. A rap recorded on a phone and uploaded to YouTube—in developing countries, from Africa to Asia—can sway a national election.

Here at home, the impact is just as deep. When Barack Obama was first running for president, a reporter asked him about attacks from the Clinton campaign. His response? Coolly brushing the dust off his shoulder—just like Jay-Z had done in "Dirt off Your Shoulder." That was hip-hop *culture* in full effect. Everyone got the reference. It was fluent and instinctive, a shared cultural language. And I believe that moment helped him get elected—not once, but twice—as the first Black president of the United States.

When I think back to my younger self, riding the subways and looking for the next frontier, that still blows my mind.

I hosted *Yo! MTV Raps* until it went off the air in the summer of 1995: hundreds of interviews, an avalanche of new artists. I developed friendships with many of them—Snoop to Tupac, Ice Cube to Ice-T. When Nas came on the show, he told me that when he was ten years old, his dad had taken him to see *Wild Style*, and it changed his life. I'd soon be directing the video for "One Love," a song produced by my good friend Q-Tip from Nas's now-classic debut album, *Illmatic*.

ANY MEANS NECESSARY

My years as the face of *Yo! MTV Raps* ensured that I would not just be associated with old-school rap. I'd also be linked with hip-hop's golden era, when millions of people heard the foundational pillars of the genre for the very first time. Grandmaster Flash had once called me the "town crier." Thanks to MTV, I became hip-hop's town crier on a scale I never could have imagined. And now that hip-hop was here to stay, there would be many more town criers to come, all over the world.

These days, the town criers are likely to be influencers on social media. There seem to be a billion-plus people with their own channels—and growing—each doing some version of what I once did on *Yo! MTV Raps*, and then some. I'm watching as people around the world figure out how to communicate with one other at near-light speed, everything accelerating so fast from where we were at the beginning of hip-hop.

Just look at YouTube: the world's biggest streamer, where people run their own monetized channels. With a smartphone and a few inexpensive apps, practically anyone can create slick, professional-looking content now. As the AI avalanche permeates every aspect of our digital lives, more and more people—especially those on the cultural margins—will be making well-produced, nonstop media. "The medium is the message," as Marshall McLuhan famously said. That has only become more true as we find ourselves living with a cascade of brand-new mediums that are not just changing but, in many ways, dominating our lives.

I think we should all be listening to the red alerts from Jaron Lanier, the VR pioneer and godfather, who's been warning about the dangers of technology-driven manipulation, the digital echo chamber, the algorithmic traps. That's where we are. And it's only going to be *more, more, more* as we rage into the future.

Oh wait—scratch that. The future is *now*. We're already living in *The Jetsons*. Here we go!

It does feel sci-fi out there these days. It's thrilling—but it can also get dark. George Orwell's *1984*, with its doublespeak and thought police; Ray Bradbury's *Fahrenheit 451*, named for the temperature at which books burn—those books I read as a kid are starting to feel uncomfortably prescient. And then there's Octavia Butler. In 1993, she published *Parable of the Talents*, a great novel in which a presidential candidate's slogan is "Make America Great Again" and virtual-reality headsets are all the rage. (Also, slavery has been reinstituted.) She saw it all coming.

And though he wasn't a sci-fi writer, Andy Warhol might have been the most prophetic of them all. Those famous fifteen minutes he talked about, as many of us have noticed, are now looking more like fifteen seconds.

I find that to be one of the biggest differences between now and then: The internet has made everything instant, right at your fingertips. It's amazing—but it's also kind of *poof,* and it's gone. *Next!* (By the way, go online and check out 1994 me on *Yo!* explaining this crazy new thing called "email" to my TV audience and the population at large.)

Back in the analog days of old-school media, things had to really sink in. You'd find a handful of cool magazines on a newsstand—sometimes hyperlocal to a certain city—or make your way to Bleecker Bob's to grab the latest vinyl, maybe get a recommendation straight from Bob himself. You'd cop a mixtape from a friend or buy one at a Bronx rap party. If you wanted to learn about graffiti culture, you tracked down a copy of Martha and Henry's *Subway Art*.

It all took a little more effort, more intention. Boots on the ground. Word of mouth. You stuck your neck out a little. You were joining a scene, you know? *IRL*.

ANY MEANS NECESSARY

And while I have always embraced new technology—I've been waiting for AI since HAL 9000—I'll admit that the old way made things *stick*. It helped culture take root. In retrospect, it was a pretty damn effective way of planting seeds and watching a whole movement sprout.

In September 1998, I got a call to come uptown to Harlem for a photo shoot. The idea was to do a hip-hop version of *A Great Day in Harlem*, the renowned Art Kane group portrait my dad and his jazz pals revered. This new version would be shot for the cover of *XXL* magazine—and the photographer was none other than the legendary Gordon Parks, whose movie *Shaft* had made such a huge impression on me when I was a kid.

When I showed up on 126th Street at Lenox Avenue in Harlem for the shoot, the vibe was like a block party. I was glad to see so many friends and familiar faces—innovators and giants in hip-hop culture. Grandmaster Flash, Debbie Harry, Chris Stein, Kool Herc, De La Soul, Ice Cube, Rakim, Melle Mel, A Tribe Called Quest, Fat Joe, and Slick Rick, who I'm standing right behind in Gordon's photo.

It was everybody from every era, gathered at the original location of that iconic 1958 jazz photo—177 members of the extended hip-hop family, taking our place in the lineage.

And there was the maestro himself, Gordon Parks, in his eighties, trying to wrangle all of us into position. I went over to introduce myself and humbly bowed while shaking his hand. He told me he had learned a lot watching *Yo! MTV Raps*. Then he smiled and went back to his camera.

I stood there a moment, goose bumps rising, taking it all in—knowing *this* was one of those once-in-a-lifetime things. To be surrounded by so many peers, captured by one of my all-time heroes. I remembered telling Jean that someday I'd pose for Gordon Parks. Now, here I was, not just in front of his lens but part of something bigger.

The resulting image—*A Great Day in Hip-Hop*—has become part of hip-hop history and lore. It's an honor to be a part of that history and lore, having been given a platform to speak hip-hop's language to the world. *By any means necessary.*

Back on Hancock Street, my folks didn't even have cable for much of the *Yo! MTV Raps* run. So every week I'd send VHS tapes out there so they could see what I was up to.

It was like, *Yo, Mom and Dad! We did it, can you believe it? I'm on TV, for real!*

Afterword

Right after *Yo! MTV Raps* ended, I was blessed with a daughter I named Sparkle, who I had with a beautiful Jamaican woman I was dating named Julie. A few years after that, I moved to the Sugar Hill section of Harlem, not far from where I'd first stepped off the A train back in the '70s, in search of the Uptown Sound. My place is a nineteenth-century limestone townhouse, steeped in history, where W. E. B. Du Bois and Billie Holiday once hung out. It breathes Harlem Renaissance, jazz history.

The first thing you see when you walk through my front door is a painted portrait of Lee Quiñones, my friend and inspiration. Over the fireplace hangs a framed TAKI 183 tag. There's Keith's photo of me and Andy Warhol. There's Bobby Grossman's shot of me at the Times Square Show. There are framed portraits of Biggie Smalls from his last photo shoot, wearing the famous King of New York crown. Like Jean and Keith, he was a generational talent who left us too soon. These artifacts—and many more—are reminders of the threads that were woven together to make me who I am: the jazz consciousness and Black-centric politics I inherited from my father; the Pop Art aesthetics of Warhol; the raw brilliance of graffiti and street art; the contrarian, DIY spirit of punk and New Wave; and the cultural inventiveness and street-level honesty of hip-hop music.

My life is still about pushing into new territory, just like it was when I was hopping the A train out of Bed-Stuy. These days, I'm busy in my studio, so that means exhibits and gallery shows, along with podcasts, film, and TV projects. I went to Burning Man in 2010 to see for myself what that was all about, and it blew my mind! The creative energy among the fifty thousand plus attendees deep in the Nevada desert reminded me of the creative energy now long gone from the New York downtown scene. I went a few more times, and leadership invited me to sit on the board of directors in 2020. It's been a treat. I founded a cannabis company, B Noble Global, with Ron Samuel and Bernard Noble—a Black man from Louisiana who served seven years of a thirteen-year hard-labor sentence for possessing barely enough weed to roll two joints. I told his story in *Grass Is Greener*, a film I directed for Netflix about the history of cannabis in America. B Noble is now in business on three continents, and we donate a percentage of our US revenue to organizations working to repair the harm done by excessive jail sentences for nonviolent weed charges. It goes on.

"This Black pop-life shit can get hectic sometimes," I told *The New Yorker*. I wouldn't have it any other way.

ACKNOWLEDGMENTS

It took a lifetime—hence a long time—to get to this point, and I'm extremely glad it happened when it did. Getting this all done has been on my mind for the last twenty-five years. Many of my smart and well-read friends and acquaintances have leaned in to tell me, numerous times: "Fab, you've got to put it all down for history's sake. Come on, man, what are you waiting for?!" "You're right," I'd say to them—and their voices, like a gospel choir, have been singing in my mind, reminding me to get this done for decades. Eugene Holley, a brilliant freelance journalist, Black culture expert, and my former Harlem neighbor, is one of these friends. I don't think I ever had a conversation with Eugene where he didn't enthusiastically mention how great a memoir from me would be and ask when I would make it happen.

I've written some essays for various books and publications over the years—four-to-six-thousand-word jobs—and I can definitely get my voice down on the page. But a lifetime, spread over many decades—I'm talking tens of thousands of words, hundreds of pages across more than a dozen chapters—and the way I always multitask, I knew I'd need help.

ACKNOWLEDGMENTS

My memoir journey shifted into high gear during the pandemic, when longtime friend—the brilliant thinker, nightclub and restaurant designer—Serge Becker suggested to me: *It's memoir time*. And I agreed. He said a good place to start was with Luke Janklow, a great literary agent who knows people from the New York scene we know, and he'd totally get who I am and what I've done. He was right about Luke, who I liked, made a deal with—and then the search for a collaborator began. After Zoom interviews with several bright candidates, I still hadn't found the right one.

Enter Mark Rozzo, who showed up to my pad casually dapper in jeans and a cream-colored pair of Wallabee Clarks—old favorites of mine. We chatted for hours, met up a few more times, and the energy felt good. Soon after, he profiled me for the October 2023 issue of *Vanity Fair*—and reading that, I knew he was the one. Shortly after, we rolled up our sleeves and dove in.

Back in the beginning of this century, it was John McGregor, a book-loving friend, who also pleaded with me to get my memoir going. He was very helpful in explaining the process, getting me examples of various book proposals, and setting up a few meetings with prominent editors and publishers—including Ibrahim Ahmad. It's ironic that while working with Luke and Mark, we thankfully got numerous offers once the proposal went out, along with Mark's *Vanity Fair* piece—and it turned out to be Ibrahim and Viking Press I chose to work with.

Some of my friends back then were photographers, many professionals, and others were just in the right place at the right time taking pictures, capturing the moments. I must acknowledge: Bobby Grossman, Nan Goldin, Patrick McMullan, David LaChapelle, Martha Cooper, Henry Chalfant, Ai Weiwei, the Keith Haring Foundation, Gerb, Rainer Hosch, Kate Simon, Sophie Bramly, Maripol, Jane Dickson, Ande Whyland, Chris Stein, Cathleen Campbell, Anita

ACKNOWLEDGMENTS

Rosenberg, Elinor Vernhes, Lina Bertucci, Bob Gruen, Ricky Powell, Debi Mazar, Tony Allen, Carol Jackson, Rene Ricard, James Van Der Zee, Jimmy Morton, and Charlie Ahearn.

Another I must mention: Paul Chandler, like a big brother and part of the village that raised me. Paul's the last surviving member of my dad's crew, now in his early eighties. He was the youngest, and he's still got his finger on the pulse. He's very excited about *Everybody's Fly* becoming a reality.

And to Chris and Debbie, whose support and friendship were unwavering from the beginning.

Lastly, my darling daughter, Sparkle—my greatest creation and biggest inspiration, best friend and sounding board on all things now, cool, and cultural.

IMAGE CREDITS

page ii: Photograph by Charlie Ahearn
page x: *Campbell's Soup* by Fred Brathwaite, 1981 © Henry Chalfant
page 5: *Five*, ca. 1980–1981 © Fred Brathwaite
pages 6–7: Photograph © Martha Cooper
pages 88–89: Photograph © Martha Cooper
pages 216–17: Photograph © Martha Cooper

Insert page 1: (*clockwise from top left*): Photograph by James Van Der Zee. Courtesy of Fred Brathwaite; Courtesy of Fred Brathwaite; Courtesy of Fred Brathwaite; Courtesy of Fred Brathwaite; Photograph by Jimmy Morton. Courtesy of Fred Brathwaite; Photograph by Jimmy Morton. Courtesy of Fred Brathwaite; Courtesy of Fred Brathwaite

Insert page 2 (*clockwise from top left*): Courtesy of Fred Brathwaite; Photograph by Tony Allen. Courtesy of Fred Brathwaite; Photograph © Bobby Grossman; Photograph © Bobby Grossman; Photograph by Anita Rosenberg; Photograph by Carol Jackson. Courtesy of Fred Brathwaite; Photograph by Carol Jackson. Courtesy of Fred Brathwaite.

Insert page 3 (*clockwise from top*): Photograph by Charlie Ahearn; Photograph by Maripol. Copyright © New York Beat Films LLC.; Photograph © Elinor Vernhes; Photograph by Lina Bertucci; Photograph © Elinor Vernhes

Insert page 4: (*clockwise from top*): Photograph by Rene Ricard, 1981. Courtesy of Jane Dickson; Photograph by Jane Dickson, 1981; Photograph © Bob Gruen/www.bobgruen.com; Photograph © Bob Gruen/www.bobgruen.com; Photograph by Jane Dickson, 1981

IMAGE CREDITS

Insert page 5 (*clockwise from top right*): Photograph by Chris Stein; Photograph by Chris Stein; Photograph by Chris Stein; Photograph by Ricky Powell; Photograph by Charlie Ahearn; Photograph by Charlie Ahearn; Photograph by Charlie Ahearn; Photograph by Chris Stein

Insert page 6 (*clockwise from top*): Photograph by Chris Stein; Photograph by Charlie Ahearn; Photograph © Nan Goldin; Photograph © Nan Goldin; Photograph © Nan Goldin; Photograph © Nan Goldin

Insert page 7 (*clockwise from top left*): Photograph by Charlie Ahearn; Photograph © Bobby Grossman; Photograph © Kate Simon; Photograph © Bobby Grossman; Photograph © Bobby Grossman; Photograph © Bobby Grossman; Photograph © Bobby Grossman

Insert page 8: Photograph © Rainer Hosch

Insert page 9 (*clockwise from top left*): Photograph © Martha Cooper; Photograph © Martha Cooper; Photograph © Martha Cooper; Photograph © Martha Cooper; Photograph by Cathleen Campbell. Courtesy of Charlie Ahearn

Insert page 10: (*clockwise from top right*): Photograph © Cathleen Campbell; Photograph © Cathleen Campbell; Photograph © Cathleen Campbell; Photograph by Ande Whyland; Photograph © Martha Cooper; Photograph © Cathleen Campbell

Insert page 11 (*clockwise from top left*): Photograph © Patrick McMullan; Photograph © Patrick McMullan; Photograph by Charlie Ahearn; Courtesy of the Keith Haring Foundation Archive; Photograph by Charlie Ahearn

Insert page 12 (*clockwise from top left*): Courtesy of Fred Brathwaite; Courtesy of the Keith Haring Foundation Archive; Archive of Debi Mazar; Photograph © Sophie Bramly; Photograph by Fred Brathwaite; Photograph by Fred Brathwaite; Photograph © Sophie Bramly

Insert page 13 (*clockwise from top left*): Photograph © Sophie Bramly; Photograph by Fred Brathwaite; *Fab 5 Freddy* by David LaChapelle, 1985, New York © David LaChapelle; Photograph by Fred Brathwaite; Courtesy of Fred Brathwaite; Photograph © Martha Cooper

Insert page 14: All photographs on this page by Fred Brathwaite

Insert page 15: (*clockwise from top right*): Photograph by Fred Brathwaite; Photograph © Bobby Grossman; Courtesy of Ai Weiwei Studio; Photograph by Fred Brathwaite

Insert page 16 (*clockwise from top left*): Portrait of Fred Brathwaite, 1981, Gouache, ink, and stickers on paper © The Keith Haring Foundation; Photograph by Jane Dickson; Jeff Kravitz/Getty; Photograph © Martha Cooper; Al Pereira/Getty